# Representing Red and Blue

**Series in Political Psychology**



*Image Bite Politics: News and the Visual Framing of Elections*
Maria E. Grabe and Erik P. Bucy

*Social and Psychological Bases of Ideology and System Justification*
John T. Jost, Aaron C. Kay, and Hulda Thorisdottir

*The Political Psychology of Democratic Citizenship*
Eugene Borgida, Christopher Federico, and John Sullivan

*On Behalf of Others: The Psychology of Care in a Global World*
Sarah Scuzzarello, Catarina Kinnvall, and Kristen Renwick Monroe

*The Obamas and a (Post) Racial America?*
Gregory S. Parks and Matthew W. Hughey

*Ideology, Psychology, and Law*
Jon Hanson

*The Impacts of Lasting Occupation: Lessons from Israeli Society*
Daniel Bar-Tal and Izhak Schnell

*Representing Red and Blue: How the Culture Wars Change the Way Citizens Speak and Politicians Listen*
David C. Barker and Christopher Jan Carman

# Representing Red and Blue

## How the Culture Wars Change the Way Citizens Speak and Politicians Listen

David C. Barker and Christopher Jan Carman

OXFORD
UNIVERSITY PRESS

**OXFORD**
UNIVERSITY PRESS

Oxford University Press is a department of the University of Oxford. It furthers the University's objective of excellence in research, scholarship, and education by publishing worldwide.

Oxford New York
Auckland Cape Town Dar es Salaam Hong Kong Karachi
Kuala Lumpur Madrid Melbourne Mexico City Nairobi
New Delhi Shanghai Taipei Toronto

With offices in
Argentina Austria Brazil Chile Czech Republic France Greece
Guatemala Hungary Italy Japan Poland Portugal Singapore
South Korea Switzerland Thailand Turkey Ukraine Vietnam



Published in the United States of America by
Oxford University Press
198 Madison Avenue, New York, NY 10016



---

Library of Congress Cataloging-in-Publication Data
Barker, David C. (David Christopher), 1969-
Representing red and blue : how the culture wars change the way citizens speak and politicians listen / David C. Barker and Christopher Jan Carman.
p. cm. — (Series in political psychology)
Includes bibliographical references and index.
ISBN 978–0–19–979656–4 (hardback : alk. paper)
1. Party affiliation—United States. 2. Voting—United States.
3. Social choice—United States. 4. Political socialization—United States.
5. Politics and culture—United States. 6. Constituent power—United States.
7. Representative government and representation—United States.
I. Carman, Christopher J. II. Title.
JK2271.B36 2012
306.20973—dc23 2012007393

---

9 8 7 6 5 4 3 2
Printed in the United States of America
on acid-free paper

*To Meg, Matt, and Dorothy (Mom), with all my love...*

*DCB*

*To Ronda, Mason, and Izzie (dog), with all my love....*

*CJC*

# Contents

# Preface

This book has been a long time coming. When we fielded our first pilot survey for the project, we lived on the same continent, our hairlines were fully intact, everyone "knew" Hillary Clinton was going to be the next president of the United States and no one outside of Illinois had ever heard of Barack Obama.

But really, the book began germinating many years before that, in a graduate seminar taught by Bob Erikson at the University of Houston. It was there that we began to think and argue about what the proper role of an elected representative really ought to be (eager graduate students that we were). During the 16 years that followed, while navigating our share of hiking trails and perhaps more than our share of barstools, we found a few other subjects to debate as well (stripes vs. solids, *Anchor Man* vs. *Talladega Nights*, and Giordano's vs. Gino's East come to mind), but sooner or later our attention always turned back to the political events of the day—and not infrequently to the subjects discussed in this book.

The next 65,000 words are a byproduct of those many spirited conversations. Chris first had to convince David that most citizens have instinctive and discernible preferences about the way they want their elected officials to represent them—that some citizens prefer leaders who pander to public opinion, while other citizens prefer leaders who shirk it—and that those preferences influence the actual governing habits of elected officials. Some time later, David had to invest even more time making the case that the Red/Blue Culture Wars in fact underlie those dynamics—specifically, that over the past generation, by championing and rewarding "principled leadership," the Christian Right has prompted many Republican politicians to turn a deaf ear to constituents' policy demands. Eventually, we came to see eye to eye on just about everything (except the title, but that is a longer story). We hope that those exercises in persuasion eventually produced a narrative that at least some readers will find compelling.

The data, of course, helped each of us argue our cases. It was with queasy stomachs, though, that we would analyze each new year of mass survey responses and congressional roll-call votes. In our careers, we have been struck by how often those pesky human subjects fail to behave as they "should," according to some seemingly brilliant theory that we think we have concocted. In light of those experiences, we would wonder whether "last year's findings" had been artifacts or the byproduct of an anomalous period in time. After all, our theory was constructed, little by little, with Culture War flashpoints serving as backdrop: the "two-for-one" Clinton presidency, the Gingrich rise and fall, the Lewinsky scandal and impeachment overreach, the Bush versus Gore electoral college mess, George W. Bush's outspoken Christian traditionalism, same-sex marriage controversies in state after state, and so on—all fueled by increasingly popular partisan media sources that seemed to amplify the cacophony. Indeed, it was during precisely this stretch in time that the terms "Red America" and "Blue America" emerged and became ensconced in the American lexicon.

What if all of that were to cool down, we wondered, once Clinton and Bush faded from public memory? What if Barack Obama was right when he told the audience at the 2004 Democratic National Convention that "we are not a collection of Red States and Blue States, but the United States…"? Might voters, once different issues and a different kind of leader emerged, stop wielding their Sunday-morning habits as cudgels and return instead to the norm of a collective "civil religion" that had characterized most public discourse for the previous three generations? If so, then the story we were crafting with this research might have fallen apart before we had even had the chance to open Microsoft Word.

The answer to these questions turned out to be a decisive "No." It is clear that the Republicans have cemented their hold on white Christian traditionalists as a constituency, just as seculars and progressive Christians continue to migrate unabated to the Democrats. And as we see it, the past few years have seen public debates over religious questions become, if anything, more pronounced. For example, the controversial comments made by Obama's former pastor, Reverend Jeremiah Wright, might have hurt the candidate more if so many Americans hadn't already been convinced that he is a Kenyan-born Muslim. Moreover, just as Fox News annually bemoans the liberal "War on Christmas," progressive authors and commentators continually decry a Republican "War on Science." And when it comes to outspoken Christian traditionalism in the public sphere, recent Republican presidential hopefuls Huckabee, Palin, Bachman, and Santorum make George W. Bush look like an Episcopalian by comparison. Meanwhile, on the *New York Times* bestseller list, the smug-atheist manifesto has practically become a literary category unto its own (e.g., Dawkins, Harris, Hitchens, Maher).

So it is clear to us that, as of this writing, the Culture Wars have not cooled and the role of religion in American politics has not waned. But that isn't exactly big news. What is more relevant is the staying power of our claim that in Blue America, politicians tend to listen more intently to public opinion than they do in Red America, because that is the way each respective constituency likes it. It was easy for us to see a pattern when Bush and Clinton were serving as primary reference points. After all, Bush won points with his base by routinely bragging throughout his presidency about "standing on principle" (especially when it came to the increasingly unpopular Iraq war), which was a deliberate dig at Clinton, who had habitually consulted polling data to determine everything from his position on welfare reform to his vacation whereabouts (Yellowstone was deemed much more "American" than Martha's Vineyard). These observations helped to spark our theory in the first place.

And as time went on, former Democratic presidential nominees Gore and Kerry didn't hurt our case either. In 2000, Gore's poll-driven personality makeovers were so quick and pronounced they might have made Philip Seymour Hoffman envious. And Kerry, of course, was the guy who famously "voted for it (the Iraq War) before he voted against it."

But maybe what we had taken as evidence of a Red/Blue pattern toward one style of representation or another was really just idiosyncratic to the Clinton–Bush years. Maybe Blue America doesn't *necessarily* embrace policy pandering after all, we wondered. And maybe Red America doesn't instinctively reject it. Could the age of Obama reverse the trend?

As of this writing (in February 2012), it would not appear so. Can there be any doubt, from 2008 to 2012, which party's members were more inclined to bargain, compromise, moderate, and mollify the other side in order to appeal to the median voter? Whether the issue was the federal stimulus package, or health care reform, or taxes, or shutting down the government, or raising the debt ceiling, or collective bargaining rights, or reforming Medicare, or closing the Guantanamo Bay detention center, or whether religiously affiliated hospitals would be required to deny/provide coverage for contraception in their insurance plans, it was the Obama administration and the Democrats in Congress that regularly moved ever-closer to the ideological Center, while the GOP folded their arms on the Right and stayed put—even as congressional approval rates fell to historic lows (and disproportionately for Republican legislators). All of this makes sense in light of a CBS poll taken on September 16, 2011, that revealed Republican voters to be seven times more likely than Democrats to say that politicians "should stick to their positions, even if it means not getting as much done" (http://www.cbsnews.com/stories/2011/09/16/politics/main20107599.shtml).

Perhaps the most compelling anecdotal evidence in support of our argument can be observed by taking a casual glance at the 2012 GOP nomination contest, and by comparing it to past Democratic contests. Recall the reputations for compulsive pandering that Clinton, Gore, Kerry all garnered. And recall how the Right hated them for it. But when it came to the Democratic faithful, the candidates' eagerness to please may have induced some head shaking at times but it didn't keep voters from supporting those guys at the ballot box; Clinton, Gore, and Kerry all won their party's nomination rather easily, after all.

By contrast, in 2012, establishment frontrunner Mitt Romney's reputation (fair or not) as a popularity-chasing opportunist who lacks core convictions has led the conservative base to desperately search for almost any alternative who will be willing to thumb his or her nose at the median voter. One Christian-Right darling after another—no matter how unpalatable to the general electorate—has gotten his or her chance to seize the nomination from Romney: Michelle Bachman, Rick Perry, Herman Cain, Newt Gingrich, Rick Santorum. Even Ron Paul has a lot of admirers for his apparent consistency. Romney may get the GOP nomination yet, but if he does it will be over the objection of a traditionalistic base that divided its support between other, more "trustee-oriented" candidates.

So, when it comes to acknowledgments, we suppose we should start by thanking Messrs. Clinton, Bush, Gore, Kerry, Obama, Romney, and Santorum (et al.) for making our argument easier than it otherwise might have been.

Second, we want to recognize all the people at Oxford University Press—especially John Jost, the editor of this series; Abby Gross, our publishing editor; and Joanna Ng, her editorial assistant—for a careful, expedient, supportive, and thoroughly professional publishing experience.

Third, we thank Steve Ansolabehere for organizing the Cooperative Congressional Election Studies, without which our data collection would have likely been cost-prohibitive, and the folks at YouGov/Polimetrix (especially Samantha Luks [whose life we made much more difficult than it needed to be on a few occasions]), for managing our data collections.

Fourth, we offer our gratitude to our home institutions, the University of Pittsburgh and the University of Strathclyde, for supporting our research (including grants from the Central Development Research fund and Richard D. and Mary Jane Edwards Endowed Publication Fund at Pitt and the John Anderson Research Lectureship funds at Strathclyde)...and for hiring us in the first place.

Fifth, we want to acknowledge our instructors, advisors, and mentors at the University of Houston from 1994 to 1999, who taught us how to be political scientists: Christopher Wlezien, Kathleen Knight, Robert Erikson, Mark Franklin, Robert Lineberry, Kent Tedin, Dick Murray, Rick Matland, Ray Duch, Jim Gibson, Greg Weiher, and Ross Lence. David would also like to honor the memory of Ann Miller, the outstanding English professor at Baylor who really encouraged me to write, whose example inspired me to pursue academia in the first place, and who remains my role model when it comes to teaching.

Sixth, we are greatly indebted to the many people who have offered their thoughts and/or encouragement on this project over the years. The biggest thanks go to Jamie Druckman, who offered so many helpful comments, on multiple occasions, that we feel like he should practically have a co-authorship. Nearly as helpful was David Leege. Others whose help and/or support was invaluable include Marc Hetherington, Robert Shapiro, Morgan Marietta, Paul Djupe, Brian Calfano, Keith Gaddie, David Dohorty, LJ Zigerell, Christopher Wlezien (also for sharing data!), Kathleen Knight, Gary Jacobson, Shanna Pearson Merkowitz and John McTague (also for sharing data), David Sears, Jim Guth, Shaun Bowler, Ken Wald, Richard Wood, John Hibbing, Jeff Cohen, Walt Stone, Steve Ansolabehere, Michael Goodhart, Jon Hurwitz, George Krause, Jonathan Woon, Kris Kanthak, Steve Finkel, Barry Ames, David Judge, Robert Johns, Val Brkich, Amy Erica Smith, and PadiHallam Joseph (for excellent research assistance!). We also thank the many discussants at the many conferences where we presented papers developing our argument and research (whom we have to admit are too numerous for us to remember at this point. Or maybe it is just that we are getting too old to remember. Either way . . . ).

Personally, David would like to acknowledge my mother, Dorothy Notgrass, for her tireless support and for teaching me, by example, how to work hard, to keep on "keeping on," and to stay kind. Mom, you will always be my role model. I also want to recognize my son, Matthew, for showing me what courage really looks like. You can do anything, Matt, and I am very proud of you. Finally, I want to thank my lovely bride, Meg, for all the daily encouragement, warm companionship, laughter, and sincere love a person could ever ask for (and for patiently helping me find my keys, wallet, phone, eye drops, way to the grocery store, etc.). I am, without a doubt, The Luckiest.

In the same way, Chris would like to thank his family (and gimlets) for all of their love and support over the years. This book was started well after my mother was long gone, but there is no doubt that it would not have begun without the love and encouragement she provided when she was around. And she had the good forethought to leave Josephine, Tom, and Kendel around to take over for her. Mason, my best buddy, has helped to keep me grounded over the years, never ceasing to remind me that it is important to do your own thing (even if others might tell you it is daft). And to Ronda, there is no way I would have completed my contribution to this project without your love, support, encouragement, affirmation, and general putting up with me. Thank you.

CHAPTER 1

# Introduction: Saddling the Drunken Mule

Many progressives slavishly follow polls.

—*George Lakoff,* Thinking Points *(2006)*

So?

—*Vice President Dick Cheney (March 19, 2008), in reference to polls showing that two thirds of Americans then opposed the Iraq War*

How, exactly, do you want your government to represent you? Should the leaders you elect simply do what you tell them, even if it means compromising some of their deeply held beliefs? Or should they doggedly stand on principle, even if it means neglecting some of your demands for change? Of course, how you answer this question may depend (in part) on your policy preferences and whether your political "team" currently holds power. That is, we citizens tend to admire politicians when they respond to the sounds of *our* voices, but we decry "shameless pandering" when they listen too intently to those from the other side of the aisle. So when we read the quotation above by Vice President Cheney, in which he appears to casually dismiss public calls for policy change, our impression of him as either a "principled leader" or an "out-of-touch tyrant" might simply come down to how we felt about the war in Iraq.

In this way, and others, the American voter[1] is not unlike a drunken mule: unfocused and fickle, but also stubborn and ornery. We mules can't be expected

[1] *The American Voter,* by Angus Campbell, Philip Converse, Warren Miller, and Donald Stokes (1960), famously offered evidence that voters in the United States are, for the most part, ill informed and capricious, but also psychologically attached to political parties for reasons that have little to do with rational calculations or issue preferences. While scholars have debated the finer points of these characterizations for decades, the basic conclusions have held up quite well over time (e.g., Jacoby, 2010).

to pay attention to the nuances of policy (let alone to keep up with what our representatives are doing), but that doesn't mean we won't buck if we get spooked. These equine tendencies create a tricky dilemma for lawmakers trying to represent their constituents: if they turn a blind eye to public opinion they may anger the majority, but if they mindlessly obey the majority they may alienate core supporters. It would seem that policy pandering (shameless or not) is quite the delicate art.

But maybe there's a way around this dilemma that lawmakers face. Suppose we voters are not all the same in terms of how we react to policy pandering. Could it be that by dutifully following public opinion, politicians keep some of us pacified with our oat-bags while prompting others of us to rear up? Might those of us in the latter group give off cues that encourage lawmakers to resist the majority's ever-changing policy demands? And might campaigning politicians send signals of their own, letting voters know ahead of time the degree to which they plan to either lead public opinion or follow it?

In this book, we suggest that the answer to these questions is "yes," and that the consequences are profound. Political scientists have spilled plenty of ink trying to understand how democratic representation "works" (for theoretical discussions of the subject, see Pitkin, 1967, and Mansbridge, 2003; for reviews of the empirical research on representation, see Wlezien & Soroka, 2007, and Hurley & Hill, 2010). Unfortunately, we still do not know very much about the *demand* side of the representation equation—who wants representatives to "listen," who wants representatives to "lead," and what difference any of it makes.[2]

Our starting point, then, is the nagging sense that because students of American politics don't really know anything about the style of representation citizens *want*, they cannot possibly know all that much about the style of representation citizens actually *get*. Our goal is to shed some light on these things.

## INSTRUCTED DELEGATES VERSUS TRUSTEES

Of course, in trying to understand how the public prefers to be represented, there are many trails of inquiry down which we could travel. For example, we

[2] However, Hibbing and Theiss-Morse (2001, 2002) have demonstrated that public preferences regarding matters of political *process*, in general, are at least as consequential for democratic politics as are public *policy* preferences. In that way, since preferences regarding representation style are also matters of political process, rather than policy, Hibbing and Theiss-Morse's research lays important groundwork for this project.

could try to explain how the public defines a constituency in the first place (e.g., Should lawmakers focus on representing their local constituents, or do they have a national constituency? Furthermore, do lawmakers have a responsibility to represent *all* constituents, or only those who voted for them?). Or, for another thing, we could try to understand preferences regarding whether representatives should look and sound like a majority of their constituents (i.e., should mostly Italian American constituencies be represented by Italian American lawmakers, Catholic constituencies by Catholic lawmakers, and so on?). And that is just the beginning.

Alas, if we were to try in this one book to understand how people think about all (or even some) of these different aspects of representation, things would get messy, and fast. Thus, in case the point is not already clear, we restrict our inquiry here to the question of why some citizens seem to prefer and reward politicians who follow the public's policy demands, while others seem to favor politicians who rely more on their personal judgment when making policy.

In keeping with longstanding political science vernacular, we label these styles of representation the *instructed delegate* style and the *trustee* style. The instructed delegate style is so named because constituents "instruct" their "delegate" (the representative) as to how he or she should vote on legislation and on what issues should be at the top of the legislative agenda. By contrast, the *trustee*-style moniker stems from the fact that constituents "entrust" the representative to make decisions in their interest.

If we can figure out even part of the answer as to why citizens vary in terms of whether they prefer instructed delegates or trustees, we think we can gain some perspective into why some politicians actually do seem to follow public opinion more often than others do. The eventual punch line to this book is that certain citizens, by encouraging representatives to turn a deaf ear to public opinion, effectively mute the democratic voices of other citizens. In other words, we think we have identified a way that citizens can "quiet" their neighbors—in the political arena, at least.

## WHY THESE TERMS?

The terms "instructed delegate" and "trustee" are far from perfect labels for each of the respective styles of representation on which we will be focusing. For one, readers unfamiliar with the primary scholarship on this subject may find these terms obtuse and not all that intuitive. After all, one cannot just glance at those words, out of context, and have much of an inclination as to what they could mean. The "delegate" term is particularly difficult, because it could be confused with the verb (and homograph) "delegāte," which suggests precisely the opposite of what we are trying to convey. However, in wringing our hands over these terms, all of the potential alternatives seem to suffer from even bigger problems. For example, if we replace "instructed delegate versus trustee" with "poll-based versus principle-based," the normative implication is that those who prefer instructed delegate-style representation somehow lack consciences or principles, which is of course not true. Furthermore, if we use "public opinion-based versus internal judgment-based" it is not clear what exactly "public opinion" is—is it the opinion of the district's constituents, of the country as a whole, of just those in the representative's political party, or what? Of course, we could have adopted Jane Mansbridge's (2003) reformulated terminology of "gyroscopic," "promissory," "anticipatory," and "surrogate," but these concepts incorporate more than the simple dichotomy represented by the "instructed delegate" and "trustee" terms, which would have *really* complicated things (and in our experience, students have a very difficult time understanding some of the Mansbridge terms anyway). On the whole, then, we have decided to hold our noses and stick with the terms that have the broadest and longest-standing tradition of usage within the political science community—so as to maintain continuity if nothing else.[3]

[3] In this book, we are writing to audiences from many different research traditions, including political psychology, legislative studies, religious studies, and American politics more generally. We think we even have a few things to say to the "normative political theory" community. Many of these academic audiences are surely not familiar with the newer terminology that Mansbridge (2003) has suggested. That is yet another reason to follow convention and use the terms of which most political scientists have probably at least heard. In short, we get it—we understand that representation styles are a lot more complicated than the simple delegate versus trustee dichotomy, and we applaud the efforts of Mansbridge and others to provide more precise definitions and distinctions. But the other considerations we have listed provide compelling reasons to stick with the older terms. As they say in "Monty Python and the Holy Grail" (1975): "Look... Camelot!" [repeated twice, as trumpets play a fanfare as the camera cuts briefly to the sight of a majestic castle] "It's only a model." "Shhh!"

## THESE ARE GUT-LEVEL PREFERENCES

Importantly, we do not suspect that people spend much cognitive energy sitting in their back gardens and pondering these matters, Rodin's *Thinker*-style. Furthermore, to the extent that citizens ever do think about such things, we suspect that their preferences are often, in the main, motivated by policy or partisan interests. In other words, as we alluded to in the first paragraph above, when someone knows that her opinion on an issue matches that of the majority, there is a good chance that she prefers the instructed delegate style, because that style would probably give her the policy outcome she wants. On the flip side, when she perceives herself to be part of the minority on an issue but sees her elected representative as a kindred spirit, she has an incentive to prefer the trustee style, because under those conditions the trustee style would increase the odds of getting the policy outcome she wants.

But if that was all there was to the story, this book would not be very interesting, and we could stop writing right now. We argue there is much more to people's representation-style preferences than figuring out which style is most likely to get them what they want—something deeper and more systematic. After all, given widespread public disinterest regarding politics, many citizens may not even know whether theirs is the majority or minority opinion on a given policy matter; nor do citizens really have a much of a clue, much of the time, whether their representatives' policy stances really match their own. Drunken mules, remember?[4]

What citizens may have a sense for, however, is the degree to which they just instinctively like "leaders who lead" (trustees), on the one hand, or "public servants who listen" (instructed delegates), on the other. In other words, without

[4] Some readers may be familiar with the mathematical concept of a "drunkard's walk," which has to do with randomness (for more on this subject and how it may affect all kinds of human behavior, see Mlodinow, 2008). Our reference to a drunken mule does *not* suggest anything about citizens' representation preferences being random. The behavior of a drunken mule may be unfocused, fickle, stubborn, and ornery, but it is not necessarily random. Indeed, a great deal of research we will discuss later (e.g., Erikson, Wright, & McIver, 1993; Soroka & Wlezien, 2010; Stimson, Mackuen, & Erikson, 1995) argues that the public has discernible preferences on all sorts of political matters, which both predict and respond to what the government does. Now, when it comes to preferences regarding representation styles, we suspect that they are mostly instinctive, rather than well-thought-out, but we certainly do not think they are random. That is our point in this book: preferences about representation styles are systematic and predictable to a certain extent, which has meaningful consequences for political governance.

ever really thinking about it at all, a citizen might pick up cues about a potential representative's representation style from the politician's campaign rhetoric. She may then reward the politician with her support when she recognizes a kinship (she may not even know *why* she likes a given politician's style, only that she does). And once the politician is in office, this pattern may continue: overall patterns of approval or disapproval may be shaped, in part, by whether the representative's governing style is consistent with the one constituents find most instinctively palatable. We suspect that enough elected officials get recognized, elected, and rewarded/punished in this way so as to ultimately color representation itself in predictable hues across different American constituencies.

## THE ARGUMENT, IN BRIEF

So if citizens' preferences for one or the other style of representation ultimately affect electoral outcomes and the way politicians actually govern, what exactly are the factors that determine whether citizens prefer instructed delegates or trustees in the first place? Our central claim is that cultural traditionalists—especially, but not exclusively, evangelical Christians—tend to embrace trustee-style representation more readily than do seculars, religious progressives, or civil libertarians. By extension, we contend that as long as religious and other cultural differences continue to color ideological identification, partisanship and vote choices in the United States—with cultural traditionalists trending Republican, and seculars, religious progressives, and civil libertarians migrating Democratic—then preferences regarding styles of representation may also come in distinct partisan shades of "Red" and "Blue."[5]

But *why*? Drawing significantly on James Davison Hunter's (1991) "Culture Wars" thesis (see also Wuthnow, 1989), Marc Hetherington's and Jonathan Weiler's (2009) research on American authoritarianism, Jonathan Haidt's (2012; also Kessebir & Haidt, 2010) work on moral reasoning, and John Jost et al.'s (2003) work on motivated social cognition (to name just three), we suggest that the distinction stems from clashing cultural worldviews between

[5] When we use the terms "Red" and "Blue" in this context, we do not simply use them as synonyms for Republican or Democratic partisanship (though that is obviously what they technically stand for on television networks' electoral maps). We believe that these terms have taken on a more subtle meaning, colloquially, referring more to the cultural distinctions that divide some Americans politically. In other words, a crimson "Red" state or district is not simply one that votes solidly Republican, but rather one that votes solidly Republican for reasons that include a strong religious, racial, or otherwise cultural component.

traditionalists and progressives. When it comes to the so-called Culture Wars, we hear a lot through the media about how "Red Americans" supposedly love barbeque, SUVs, and Hank Williams Jr., whereas "Blue Americans" apparently favor brie, Subarus, and John Coltrane. Really, though, the Culture Wars thesis has much less to do with differences in personal taste than it does with core value priorities—whether one prioritizes equal rights and social tolerance, on the one hand, or religious and cultural traditions, on the other.[6]

To break it down even further, the original Culture Wars thesis supposes that cultural progressives and cultural traditionalists differ with regard to very basic assumptions: Is human nature good or bad? Is morality absolute or contextual? Should authority be hierarchical or egalitarian? Is human progress inevitable or hopeless? Putting it rather provocatively, Hunter summarized by claiming that American political conflict is no longer only about whether the New Deal or even "the Sixties" were good ideas, but also about whether the 18th-century Enlightenment was a good idea.[7]

"Fine," a reader might say, "but how could this kind of cultural conflict explain something as seemingly unrelated as differences in preferences regarding representation styles?" To preview our argument, we suggest that cultural traditionalists tend to instinctively embrace a relatively constricted vision of representative government (much like their conservative forbearer Edmund Burke did), wherein leaders try to act in the interests of the public by not allowing public whims to modulate principled commitments (assuming of course that the leader in question is principled and devout). As such, these traditionalists (as compared to progressives) often feel less comfortable with instructed delegates as representatives, because instructed delegates empower those whims—allowing them to compromise what traditionalists view as certain essential truths.

To elaborate (and, we hope, simplify) this point just a bit more, we suggest that the style of representation one prefers has a lot to do with the particular brand of democracy with which one instinctively feels most at ease. That is, instructed delegate-style representation corresponds to a fairly radical vision of democratic government that emphasizes popular sovereignty—a

---

[6] This is not to suggest that conservative Republicans do not value equal rights or that liberal Democrats reject traditional morality. It is merely to suggest that when these two sets of values come into conflict as they pertain to a particular policy issue, the "New Right" of the past 40 years has been more likely to prioritize cultural traditions than has the "New Left," and vice versa (e.g., Layman and Green, 2006).

[7] For details of the argument, see Hunter (1991). For empirical assessments in support of this view, see Layman (2001), Hetherington and Weiler (2009), and Barker and Tinnick (2006).

participatory "marketplace of ideas" in which the *demos* shape policies on an ongoing basis. By contrast, trustee-style representation corresponds to the much more limited *institutional* model of representative government, in which citizens cede policymaking power to a presumably exceptional few—maintaining the option to "kick the bums out" after some established period of time, of course, but otherwise demanding that representatives merely follow the rule of law and make sure Yellowstone opens on time.[8]

The basic point we are trying to make is that instructed delegate-style representation is simply more radically democratic than is trustee-style representation, so those inclined to support more radical visions of democracy are also more inclined to support instructed delegate-style representation. And cultural traditionalists are among the least inclined to favor radical visions of democracy, so our argument goes, because they are among the least inclined to trust the changing tides of public opinion.[9] There are several underlying reasons why we believe this is so. In Chapter 3, we will delineate and discuss

[8] Importantly, as we will discuss in more detail in Chapter 3, the instructed delegate style could in theory place even greater value on popular sovereignty than does a direct democracy in which citizens make policy directly by voting "yes" or "no" on referenda. That is, in a direct democracy, policy decisions come down to which side can better mobilize supporters to the polls to vote on that policy. Policy then moves in a particular direction regardless of the size of the majority that voted for it—50.05% voting "yes" means the policy is adopted. On the other hand, in a representative democracy with instructed delegate-style representation, representatives may seek to moderate agendas and bills (introducing amendments and the like) based on the *distribution* of majority/minority opinion among their constituents, thereby amplifying minority voices to a somewhat greater extent than is possible in a direct democracy. At this point, we are making a theoretical, not an empirical, point. That is, we are not arguing that representatives necessarily do moderate agendas, bills, etc., so as to reflect minority opinions in their districts. They may or they may not—we don't know. Our point is that they *have the opportunity to do so* in a representative democracy with instructed delegate-style representation, whereas there is no such opportunity for minority voices to be reflected in a strict direct democracy.

[9] However, to the extent that certain negative stereotypes about Blue Americans are accurate (namely that progressives tend to be a bunch of pointy-headed elitists who think they are too good to drink domestic beer or drive domestic cars, etc.), one could certainly imagine our hypothesized relationship going the other way. That is, if cultural traditionalists really do constitute the majority of "real Americans," as former Alaska Governor Sarah Palin would say, then perhaps it is they, not secular progressives, who agitate for more popular sovereignty in society. We do not "buy" this framework, but it provides useful alternate hypotheses to our own, which helps to establish the falsifiability of ours.

all of those reasons in full. For now, though, we will go ahead and briefly outline those reasons, so as to offer a preview of what will come later.

In short, we argue that cultural traditionalists are more suspicious of popular sovereignty—and thus of instructed delegate-style representation—because:

- Traditionalists are more likely to hold absolute and unwavering views when it comes to matters of right and wrong, meaning that they view changes in opinion to accommodate constituent demands (e.g., "flip-flopping") with suspicion.
- Traditionalists tend to respect hierarchical structures of authority, so they feel more comfortable handing over leadership to a trusted elite (which also means that the personal qualities of candidates are sometimes more important to them than the candidates' policy positions).
- Traditionalists question human beings' natural capacity to make moral and reasonable decisions without divine guidance, leading them to worry about the policymaking wisdom of the "worldly" masses.
- Traditionalists doubt the efficacy of secular institutions' (e.g., governments') efforts to improve society, especially in the long term, which again leads them to distrust governmental expansion brought on by non-traditionalistic majorities.

### CULTURE WARS... REALLY?

Given that the preceding argument rests, to some extent, on certain aspects of the Culture Wars thesis, it is important to mention that the thesis has its detractors. Most conspicuously, Fiorina, Abrams, and Pope (2005) demonstrate that the nation is not as polarized on ideological grounds as the Culture War claimants have sometimes asserted. Indeed, when examining differences in issue positions, it appears that "Red America" and "Blue America" really come in different shades of purple, most of the time.[10]

[10] We should point out, though, that even when areas appear moderate in the aggregate, it does not necessarily mean that they are populated with moderate citizens. Many times, a state's "swing" status actually reflects extreme polarization across different demographic groups within that state (perhaps the best example of this is Colorado—think Colorado Springs vs. Boulder). Furthermore, what appears to be moderation in the aggregate is driven largely by the fact that so many citizens are tuned out altogether. Among the subset of Americans who pay close attention to politics, moderation is anything but the norm.

However, much less controversial than this color spectrum is the idea that electoral conflict has been gradually extended over time to reflect cultural values, pitting traditionalists and authoritarians (both Christian and otherwise) on one side against seculars/religious progressives on the other. That is, while partisan cleavages stemming from differences in attitudes toward economic and social welfare issues have certainly not diminished over the past 70 years (indeed, they have become stronger—e.g., Bartels, 2006; Gelman et al., 2008), it is nevertheless undeniable that the bounds of partisan conflict have been *extended* to include several religious and culturally based issues that were immaterial 50 years ago—resulting in a political climate that is more ideologically charged and vitriolic, overall (also see Abramowitz & Saunders, 1998; Bafumi & Shapiro, 2009).[11]

## SO WHAT?

Even if everything we have said so far is accurate, what difference does any of it really make, politics and policy-wise? We suggest that a few important political consequences naturally follow from the dynamics described above. Namely:

- The higher the proportion of cultural traditionalists in a given place at a given time, the greater the likelihood that trustee-style politicians will be elected (and reelected, because traditionalists are less likely on average to expect policy responsiveness to the masses in the first place or to punish legislators who fail to provide it).

And as we briefly mentioned above, we further suggest that this pattern has partisan implications:

- From the time that partisanship and voting behavior became highly predictable according to differences in religious belief and practice, some

[11] For the fullest treatment of the ways that cultural differences—which include not only religious differences but others pertaining to race, militarism, patriotism, and others—have changed the political landscape in America, see Leege and Kellstedt (1993). Our argument about how cultural differences affect preferences regarding representation style acknowledges the non-religious aspects to cultural conflict, and includes some of those factors, but emphasizes the religious-based differences as the *most* salient factors when it comes to explaining representation preferences.

30 years or so ago, Republican voters have been more likely than Democrats to choose candidates whose governing philosophy reflects the independent trustee style of representation.

By extension, if our reasoning is correct:

- Politicians representing more culturally progressive constituencies (who tend to be Democrats) should generally get more political mileage out of mimicking constituents' fluctuations in opinion, whereas those representing more traditionalistic constituencies (usually Republicans) can fare better in their reelection bids by appearing to "lead" constituent opinion. Accordingly, over the past 30 years or so, lawmakers representing culturally progressive constituencies have been more likely to make policy decisions that reflect constituents' (changing) preferences, even if that means sacrificing an ideological standard or "flip-flopping" a position that was taken at an earlier time. In other words, Republicans are more likely to "stick to their guns" in service to what they view as unchanging principles.

Intuitively, then:

- Citizens living in culturally traditionalistic districts (which will more often than not be characterized by Republican majorities and therefore Republican lawmakers) may have less "say" over policy, on average, than do citizens in neighboring districts or states that we would classify as culturally progressive. In other words, just as real estate values and the number of Advanced Placement courses offered at the local high school often come down to "location, location, location," so may your political power.

What is more:

- As Hetherington and Weiler (2009) have also pointed out, the much-ballyhooed polarization in the U.S. Congress observable over the past 20 to 30 years may have been disproportionately one-sided, with Republicans much less inclined to moderate or compromise than Democrats.
- These dynamics should apply not only to legislators but to governors and to the occupants of 1600 Pennsylvania Avenue as well. While we do not fully put this executive-branch–based hypothesis to empirical test in this book, some anecdotal reflections seem to bolster this intuition. For example, while the Clinton administration is routinely portrayed (fondly or not) as the prototype of poll-driven governing (e.g., Luntz, 1994), conservative icons Barry Goldwater and Ronald

Reagan are often remembered for their devotion to principle. Regardless of whether these stereotypes correspond to reality (e.g., Druckman & Jacobs, 2011; Ignatius, 2004), the fact that such impressions are so widespread is in keeping with our expectations and certainly deserves scholarly attention.

## IMPORTANT CAVEATS REGARDING PARTISAN DIFFERENCES

Now, when it comes to these partisan implications of our story, two important caveats should be emphasized. First, based on our theory, there is only one reason why we expect contemporary Republicans to be observably more inclined toward trustee-style representation than are Democrats (on average). That reason stems from the fact that white evangelicals and other traditionalists just so happen to vote Republican by a margin of roughly 3 to 1 these days, and constitute more than half of all votes cast for Republicans (based on national exit polls in 2004 and 2008). Thus, the partisan patterns we expect to observe are merely implications of that tendency—nothing more. After all, there are significant numbers of religiously traditionalistic Democrats, both in the electorate and in Congress (especially within the African American community), and we expect their representation preferences and governing styles (but not their policy preferences) to resemble those of Republican traditionalists. Furthermore, by the same token, there are plenty of secular or religiously nontraditionalistic Republicans who hold *laissez-faire* economic attitudes but otherwise possess an egalitarian and tolerant outlook when it comes to social/cultural matters. As we will elaborate in Chapter 3, we do *not* expect such libertarian Republicans to embrace trustee-style representation any more readily than do secular/religiously progressive Democrats. For the same reasons, we would not expect to observe much of a relationship between Republican party identification and trustee-style preferences prior to 1980 or so, because party identification had not yet become wrapped up in religious and cultural identity.

Second, while our theory is that certain traditionalistic religious predilections (and the psychological predispositions they sometimes reflect) may incline individuals toward trustee-style representation preferences, everything else being equal, it is important to remember that everything else is rarely equal. As we discussed earlier, voters' preferences regarding styles or representation at any given point in time, as reflected in "top of the head" responses to survey questions (Zaller, 1992), should be heavily influenced by individual perceptions of what would be best for them in terms of their policy interests (see Sigelman et al., 1992, for a discussion of using survey questions to assess representation preferences). Indeed, when political opportunity strikes, we expect that traditionalists are just as inclined as progressives to rhetorically champion the cause of popular sovereignty, and to use the instruments of public opinion—including rallies, referenda, and ballot initiatives—to serve their policy interests. So at given points in time, it has not surprised us to observe Tea Partiers rallying around the cause of populism, or to see conservatives using the ballot initiative to ban gay marriage or late-term abortions. The political climate dictated such tactics as a means to their policy ends. Our point, remember, is that traditionalists find popular sovereignty less attractive than do other Americans, *after holding policy interests constant*. We do not expect inclinations toward more or less popular sovereignty to trump instrumental calculations of policy interest. Thus, if Democrats occupy the offices of power but individual Republican citizens believe that the conservative perspective reflects the majority opinion on some issue or set of issues, there is an obvious incentive for those individuals to report a preference for instructed delegate-style representation, in the same way that individual Democrats probably would when the roles are reversed. We do contend, however, that over time, more times than not, the frequency and intensity of popular democratic efforts should be more observable among Democrats, as long as partisanship is predictable according to Culture War dynamics.

## SUMMING UP, SO FAR

In this book we suggest that the politico-cultural fault line pitting cultural traditionalists against cultural progressives may produce more tremors than researchers have previously noticed—extending beyond differences in policy preference and even beyond differences in electoral choice. Indeed, we argue that as the Religious Right and other traditionalistic movements became "movers and shakers" within the Republican Party (and American politics more generally) over the past generation, all that shaking has reshaped the topography of representative governance itself.

All of this may also mean that we, as students of representative governance, need to rethink the way we conceptualize different styles of representation. Distinctions between instructed delegates (a.k.a. "shameless panderers") and trustees (a.k.a. "arrogant shirkers") might not be so simple, once citizen preferences over such things are taken into account. We normally think of pandering as representatives following constituent opinion (especially polls) as it pertains to public policy. But that is not quite right. Pandering is really anything that a politician does solely for the purpose of gaining favor with constituents.[12] Thus, in something of an ironic twist, Republican pandering (in certain traditionalistic districts, at least) might take the form of ignoring constituent policy preferences.

The following section describes our organizational framework for the chapters that follow.

## ROAD MAP

This book proceeds in two parts. The first part analyzes how and why citizens vary in terms of the style of representation they prefer, focusing ultimately on the role that is played by religion and other traditionalistic influences. The second part illustrates how those influences ultimately become manifest in the behavior of elected leaders, resulting in different styles of leadership being practiced across different locations and points in time. The following summaries provide brief overviews of each chapter.

### *Part I. The Demand Side of Political Representation*

The first part of the book gets inside the head of the mass public, to determine whether and why preferences differ with regard to representation styles.

#### Chapter 2: How Do We Want to Be Represented? How Do We Differ?

We lay some important groundwork in this chapter. First, we discuss existing literature as it pertains to the instructed delegate versus trustee question.

---

[12] The term also tends to have something of a pejorative connotation, but it need not. The activity it represents (representatives trying to please constituents) can also be interpreted as the essence of what is supposed to happen in a representative popular democracy. We will elaborate that point much more fully in Chapter 3.

Then we consider how, generally speaking, citizens tend to think about this question. We show that citizens tend to prefer instructed delegates—but not overwhelmingly so. We then examine how the distribution of opinion changes according to (a) the types of issues being considered (e.g., foreign vs. domestic, and "hard" vs. "easy") and (b) the institution doing the representing (the president vs. Congress). We observe that citizens expect more trustee-style representation out of the president than they do of Congress, and slightly more trustee-style representation when the issues in question are cultural rather than economic.

### Chapter 3: Theory: Cultural Warfare and Styles of Representation in the United States

In this chapter, we lay out our argument in a detailed and systematic way. We argue that (a) ordinary people *do* hold ideological predilections regarding the nature of democratic governance; (b) those predilections stem, in part, from different expectations regarding the nature of democratic governance; (c) such differences in democratic worldviews are partially a byproduct of cultural progressivism/traditionalism. That is, in this chapter, we provide the detailed theoretical rationale undergirding the empirical analyses that follow.

### Chapter 4: Mapping the Cultural and Partisan Divide in Representation Preferences

This chapter provides our argument with its central nervous system, empirically speaking; it takes the theory provided in Chapter 3 and applies it to things we can actually observe. In other words, this chapter provides the essential empirical tests necessary to evaluate our theory about the cultural and partisan psychology behind political representation.

## *Part II. The Fine Art of Pandering*

The second part of the book describes the processes through which differences in representation preferences, as derived from differences in religious/cultural traditionalism, ultimately translate into differences between citizens in terms of how much political power they wield.

### Chapter 5: Representation Styles, Candidate Cues, and the Voting Booth

In this chapter, we attempt to begin connecting the dots between the results discussed in Chapter 4 and our ultimate argument that representation itself comes in culturally "Red" or "Blue" shades. The first step is the ballot box, and that is the focus of this chapter. First, we show that in both 2006 and 2008, those who prefer trustee-style representation tended to vote overwhelmingly for Republican candidates at all levels of government. Next, we report evidence from a controlled survey experiment in which respondents were asked to evaluate hypothetical candidates based on their representation style as evidenced rhetorically.

### Chapter 6: Constituent Perceptions of Representation Styles and Democratic Accountability

This chapter explores other ways that trustee-style representation preferences within constituencies could ultimately translate into trustee-style governing styles on the part of elected representatives (and vice versa). Using the same data from previous chapters, we demonstrate that citizens who are represented by Republicans are more likely to say that their representative *is* a trustee, regardless of their own preferences regarding one or the other style. We also explore matters of democratic accountability—does disappointment in a legislator's representation style translate into lower job-approval ratings (and thus job insecurity) for that representative? And is it worse for those representatives who are deemed not responsive enough, as opposed to those who are considered too responsive? Democratic theory answers both of these questions in the affirmative, and so do our empirical tests. However, Christian traditionalists (and Republicans) are much less likely to express disapproval toward a legislator who is perceived as nonresponsive than are secular progressives (and Democrats). This pattern suggests that trustee-style representatives are much less likely to suffer electoral defeat if they represent culturally Red districts than if they represent culturally Blue ones.

### Chapter 7: Red Representation, Blue Representation

If the analyses presented in Chapter 4 acted as our argument's central nervous system, those presented in this chapter give our argument legs. That is, if secular progressives are more inclined to (a) expect instructed delegate-style representation, (b) elect representatives with instructed delegate-style governing styles, and (c) hold them accountable when they fail to deliver, then we should expect elected officials who represent progressive (especially secular) constituencies to respond more consistently to constituent opinion than do those who represent traditionalistic constituencies. Looking directly at roll-call voting behavior on the part of legislators from 1985 to 2010, we provide direct evidence in support of that narrative.

### Chapter 8: Quieting the Stable, Polarizing the Ranch

This chapter summarizes all of our findings, discusses their implications as they pertain to empirical democratic theory, and addresses the many questions left unresolved.

# I

# The Demand Side of Political Representation

American political representation shares some things in common with a pubescent boy going to Supercuts with his mother before the first day of 8th grade. For some people, it's easy. After all, if you know exactly what you want and mom indulges you, then all you have to do is make sure your representative (the one holding the scissors) knows how to follow orders. But maybe you're not so confident. You feel silly even talking about that kind of stuff—and you sure aren't going to stroll in there clutching some picture of a celebrity that you tore out of *People* magazine. If this is you, all you can really do is slide into the chair and place your fate (or at least your popularity at school) into the hands of the expert who is wrapping the cape around your neck. After all, she can hold a comb, a mirror, and a pair of scissors all in one hand—shouldn't that count for something? Besides, she's been grooming two of your classmates (Ricky and Bobby) for over a year now, and some of the girls in your class actually seem to find them appealing. In short, there are good reasons to believe that this stylist has the right values for the job.

The real snag in this operation is your mother. The stylist knows that mom is her primary constituency; after all, she has the power of the purse *and* the ability to mobilize (the minivan). And unfortunately, she has strong opinions—which you do not share—about what makes you look "handsome." Your only hope, it would seem, is that the stylist will stick to her principles and find a way to convince mom that the "high and tight" just isn't in her son's best interest at this point in time. If she can demonstrate that kind of fortitude, she'll not only have your respect; she'll have your vote when she stands for reelection in about 5 weeks. If she caves, though, you'll surely campaign for someone else.

This section (Chapters 2–4) examines mass preferences regarding different styles of representation. How many citizens want the stylist to simply follow mom's directions? How many pray instead that she will stand on principle? And just *who* tends to occupy each group?

CHAPTER 2

# How Do We Want to Be Represented? How Do We Differ?

In this chapter, as groundwork for the chapters that follow, we paint a broad portrait of mass representation preferences. We describe the public opinion data we have collected, considering the distribution of opinion regarding the instructed delegate versus trustee question and its contingencies.

Before we discuss the data, though, we provide a bit of background by reviewing the literature—both classical and modern, both normative and empirical—as it relates to the instructed delegate versus trustee dilemma.

## INSTRUCTED DELEGATES VERSUS TRUSTEES: A FEW OBSERVATIONS FROM CLASSICAL PHILOSOPHY

Arguments about how much policymaking power citizens should have are as old as political philosophy itself. Marking one extreme end of the debate, Thomas Hobbes thought *every* act of the sovereign to be "pre-authorized" by the citizenry, which means that a Leviathan is essentially free to "act for" the polity (1651). Additionally, although John Locke (1689) expressed greater democratic sympathies than did Hobbes, he also considered the proper role of the citizen to be primarily passive—offering or withholding *consent* to the government, but not much else.

At the other end of the spectrum, Jean-Jacques Rousseau (1762) had no use for representatives at all, instead envisioning a system in which citizens have direct power to determine legislative outcomes.[1] And Rousseau's position is not a lonely one; contemporary proponents of "deliberative" and

[1] We should note, however, that Rousseau did not believe the mass public was entitled to or even necessarily capable of bureaucratic administration after policy decisions have been made.

"strong" democracy have put forward similar arguments (e.g., Barber, 1985; Fishkin, 1995).

Of course, the instructed delegate vs. trustee-style dilemma is not nearly so extreme, on either side. Perhaps the most famous spokesman for trustee-style representation was Edmund Burke (whom many consider, not coincidentally in our view, to be the founder of modern Anglo-American conservatism). In his famous admonition to the electors at Bristol, whom he had just been elected to represent, Burke argued that "his unbiased opinion, his mature judgment, his enlightened conscience, he ought not to sacrifice to you, to any man, or to any set of men living.... Your representative owes you, not his industry only, but his judgment; and he betrays, instead of serving you, if he sacrifices it to your opinion" (Burke, 1774/1906).[2]

John Stuart Mill (1861) was conceivably the most prominent advocate for a vigorously empowered yet still *represented* citizenry. Although he did not use the same terminology, he argued that instructed delegate-style representative government was morally preferable (from a utilitarian point of view) not only to non-democratic forms of government but also to direct democratic systems. According to Mill, instructed delegate-style representation could ensure that policymaking reflects *all* constituent voices, while actual "direct" democracy might simply reflect the will of the (potentially tyrannical) numerical majority.

Philosophical debate over instructed delegate versus trustee representation has notably deep roots in the founding of the American republic as well. Like Locke (if not quite like Burke), most Federalists (the architects of the Constitution) believed that the public's influence over legislation should begin and end with the choice of *who* makes decisions for the country. Conversely, like Mill, Anti-Federalists tended to argue that governors should be bound (ethically, and perhaps even legally) to follow the will of the governed, but should also guard against "tyranny of the majority" by explicitly ensuring the protection of minority rights (King, 1997; also see Rosenthal, 1998).

---

[2] Perhaps not all that surprisingly, Burke was removed as a representative of Bristol just six years later, because of his unpopular but presumably conscience-driven support for free trade with Ireland and Catholic emancipation (Burke was himself Irish by birth).

## EXAMPLES FROM EARLY HOUSE DEBATES

Disagreement over the nature of representation was clearly manifested in debates held during the first session of the House of Representatives. For example, during deliberation over what would become the First Amendment to the U.S. Constitution, Thomas Tudor Tucker (SC), an avowed Anti-Federalist, moved to insert the language "to instruct their representatives" into the proposed amendment—which at the time read: "The freedom of speech and of the press, and the right of the people peaceably to assemble and consult for their common good, and to apply to the government for a redress of grievances, shall not be infringed."[3]

A notable "back and forth" ensued. Federalist Thomas Hartley (PA) made the case for trustee-style representation: "The great end of meeting [as a legislature] is to consult for the common good; but can the common good be discerned without the object is reflected and shown in every light [*sic*]. A local or partial view does not necessarily enable any man to comprehend it clearly; this can only result from an inspection into the aggregate. Instructions viewed in this light will be found to embarrass the best and wisest men."

Not to be outdone, Anti-Federalist Elbridge Gerry of Massachusetts (later of "Gerrymander" fame) laid out his support for instructed delegate perspective in provocative fashion, stating:

> Now, though I do not believe that the amendment would bind the representatives to obey the instructions, yet I think the people have a right both to instruct and bind them.... to say that the sovereignty vests in the people, and that they have not a right to instruct and control their representatives, is absurd to the last degree. They [who oppose the instruction clause] must either give up their principle or grant that the people have a right to exercise their sovereignty to control the whole Government, as well as this branch of it.[4]

---

[3] The First Amendment, as ultimately adopted, reads, "Congress shall make no law respecting an establishment of religion, or prohibiting the free exercise thereof; or abridging the freedom of speech, or of the press, or of the right of the people peaceably to assemble, and to petition the Government for a redress of grievances." Thus, the efforts of Anti-Federalists such as Tucker and Gerry obviously failed.

[4] See Kurland and Lerner, 1987, Chapter 13, for a more extended discussion of founding period thought on the topic of political representation.

## FROM HISTORY TO EMPIRICAL EXAMINATION

Without belaboring the point any further, it is unquestionably the case that the instructed delegate versus trustee debate has been central to the historical "democratic conversation" among both philosophers and practitioners of democracy. But this debate has not been restricted to the pens of philosophers or to the mouths of historical figures. To the contrary, the framework has guided a large body of modern scholarship that has sought to assess the relationship between governors and the governed. One stream of research in this tradition considers how elected elites believe they should behave as representatives of their constituents. Kicking off this research tradition, Heinz Eulau and his colleagues (1959) used data from four states to observe that state legislators were apparently more likely to see themselves as trustees rather than as instructed delegates; this was especially true in the conservative southern state of Tennessee.

Other studies of elites, such as the landmark *Homestyle* by Richard Fenno (1978), sought to better understand how legislators see their roles as representatives of their constituents. Fenno argued that representatives adopt different "homestyles," or the presentation of themselves and their representational styles in their districts, in order to build trust so that they have a freer hand to act in D.C. with less monitoring by constituents (see also Bianco, 1994; Lipinski, 2002; Rosenthal, 1998).

A different, but related, research stream in representation studies examines "policy responsiveness," or the congruence between the voting behavior of legislators (or other policymaking behavior; see Arnold, 1992) and the opinions of constituents. With the publication of "Constituency Influence in Congress" (1963), Warren Miller and Donald Stokes ushered in a generation of research. They concluded that "the representative's roll call behavior is strongly influenced by both his own policy preferences and by his perception of preferences held by the constituency... the findings of this analysis heavily underscore the fact that no single tradition of representation fully accords with the realities of American legislative politics" (1963:56). More generally, the literature, taken as a whole, demonstrates that constituent influence varies considerably according to context and issue type, but seems to have steadily waned over the course of the past generation or so (see especially Jacobs & Shapiro, 2000).[5]

Interestingly, though, this empirical research tradition carries an unmistakable normative bent. That is, most contemporary examinations of representation start from the (often unstated) assumption that congruence between

[5] For good reviews, see Kuklinski and Segura, 1995, and Ansolabehere, 2010.

public opinion and policy outputs is one of the defining elements of any non-totalitarian form of government (e.g., Etzioni, 1968; May, 1978), and thus that democratic health can be gauged by the degree to which representatives respond to public demands (e.g., Erikson & Wright, 2000; Hill & Matsubayashi 2008; Jacobs & Shapiro, 2000; Stimson, Mackuen, & Erikson, 1995; Wlezien, 1995). Indeed, as Manin, Przeworski, and Stokes have put it, "The mandate [instructed delegate] conception of representation is widespread: scholars, journalists and ordinary citizens rely on it as if it were axiomatic" (1999:30). In other words, it is an implicitly understood assumption among most political scientists that representative government functions best when legislators act as instructed delegates (perhaps ignoring personal convictions) and that in some way the electoral connection has been short-circuited when representatives act and vote according to their internal judgment (neglecting constituent opinion).

But it does not take much looking before one realizes that, outside of the ivory tower, the instructed delegate-style model is anything but axiomatic. For example, the constitutions of many Western democracies (including Germany, France, Greece, and Spain) explicitly define members of parliament as independent and responsible only to their own consciences (see Weßels, 2007).

And anecdotally, we know that election campaigns in the United States are awash with candidates presenting themselves as "principled leaders" who will ignore public opinion. One of the most notable examples of this was Governor-then-President George W. Bush, whose proud reliance on principles over polls was part of his standard stump speech throughout his political life (Adler, 2004). On January 15, 2009, for instance, he gave his farewell address to the nation, saying,

> I have followed my conscience and done what I thought was right. You may not agree with some tough decisions I have made. But I hope you can agree that I was willing to make the tough decisions.

Moreover, a bit more than four years earlier (on Oct. 30, 2004), when he was running for reelection, Bush told a crowd in Orlando, Florida:

> I know how a President needs to lead. As Presidents from Lincoln to Roosevelt, to Reagan so clearly demonstrated, a President must not shift in the wind; a President has to make tough decisions and stand by them. The American President must not follow the path of the latest polls. The role of the President is to lead based on principle and conviction and conscience.

Here President Bush was linking himself with the classic examples of people he views as principled leaders—people who, as Bush also declared on many occasions, do not "need a poll or focus group to tell them what they believe."

To be sure, many a politician has been labeled weak and anchorless for appearing too responsive to public opinion. Indeed, Bush's (just mentioned) rhetorical flourishes were in part a calculated response to the widespread perception that President Bill Clinton had followed public opinion too closely (Luntz, 1994). As one Republican pollster noted, "[Bill Clinton] doesn't move a muscle, raise an eyebrow or bite a lip unless the idea, in every aspect, has been kid-tested and mother-approved in focus groups. I'm concerned that, in their current use, polls function more as a substitute for leadership, vision and responsible action" (Lehrer, 1998).

We may also recall how 2004 Democratic presidential nominee John Kerry was roundly criticized for appearing to pander to public opinion regarding the Iraq War, at one point famously claiming to have "voted for it [war funding] before I voted against it." We may also remember how much difficulty 2008 (and 2012) Republican presidential candidate Mitt Romney had with conservative pundits during the primary season(s) for having changed positions over time on a number of issues, in accordance with different constituencies.

So it would appear that elite perspectives (by lawmakers and philosophers) are anything but uniform or simple when it comes to how elected leaders (of various stripes) either should or do exercise their roles as representatives. But do ordinary *citizens* actually hold meaningful opinions on such things? What little systematic inquiry there has been on the subject suggests that, just like those of philosophers and elites, public preferences regarding styles of representation vary considerably as well.

For instance, whereas Cantril and Strunk (1951) found that preferences for the instructed delegate model outpaced preferences for the trustee model by more than two to one—a pattern that was replicated by both McMurray and Parsons (1965) and Davidson (1969, 1970)—Patterson, Hedlund, and Boynton (1975) concluded the opposite, observing that most respondents (in their Iowa sample) preferred to have representatives act as trustees. And Parker (1974) found responses to be evenly split on the subject. Then, for some inexplicable reason, even though no consensus was reached, scholars largely gave up directly studying this subject right about the time John Travolta taught the country how to do "The Hustle."

One notable exception (about 15 years later) was the innovative study put forward by Sigelman, Sigelman, and Walkosz (1992). Using an experimental design to gauge individual preferences within a specific context, as opposed to abstract measures that can sometimes mislead, Sigelman et al. found that preferences for one style of representation versus the other are dependent upon many contextual factors, such as the office the representative occupies (executive vs. legislative), the type of issue under consideration, and citizens' level of trust in government.

More recently, interest in mass attitudes pertaining to representation processes has experienced something of a resurgence, particularly by researchers outside the United States (e.g., Bengtsson & Wass, 2010; Carman, 2006; Esaiasson & Holmberg, 1996; Mendez-Lago & Martinez, 2002). As for American attitudes toward representation styles, Grill (2007) recently confirmed that many citizens do prefer representatives who exercise "independent thinking," and Fox and Shotts (2009) observed that citizens who prioritize candidates' personal qualities are more inclined to prefer trustee-style representation, even if that means giving up some things when it comes to policy.

A closely related stream of research has examined the degree of direct control citizens think the public should have over policy. Most notably, Hibbing and Theiss-Morse (2002) observed that most Americans do not feel comfortable with the idea of political decisions being made by "ordinary people like you and me," preferring to entrust such power to "elected officials and bureaucrats." Similarly, Bowler, Donovan, and Karp (2007) found that while a majority of Californians consider the voting public to be more trustworthy than are elected officials when it comes to "doing what's right," most of these same people believe that citizens often lack the requisite information needed to enact coherent policies.[6]

On the whole, the state of knowledge regarding how American citizens want to be represented is still pretty underdeveloped. In the remainder of this chapter, we describe the data that will inform our efforts (in later chapters) at remedying this problem.

---

[6] For an interesting new examination of citizen preferences regarding representation "focus" rather than "style" (i.e., whether legislators should focus on representing their district constituents or the country as a whole), see the stream of research by David Doherty (2010). In it, he demonstrates that (1) people prefer representatives who focus on their district to those who focus on responding to the nation, (2) understanding what representational ideals appeal to people (e.g., how they say they want representatives to behave "in general") is not the same as investigating how people respond to specific instances of a representative's behavior (e.g., the fact that many people say they want representatives to focus on the country as a whole doesn't mean they will reward a representative for doing that), and (3) people seem to understand that adopting a locally (rather than nationally) focused mode of representation is in representatives' political self-interest.

## OUR DATA: HOW ARE REPRESENTATION PREFERENCES DISTRIBUTED?

From 2006 to 2009, we fielded four surveys under the auspices of the Cooperative Election Study Project (CES).[7] The CES is a consortium of public opinion researchers in the United States that pools resources in order to monitor a wide array of opinions among a very large national sample of citizens. The CES relies upon YouGov/Polimetrix, Inc., to conduct the Computer-Assisted Internet Interviews (CAII). YouGov/Polimetrix combines quota and random probability sampling techniques to produce national samples that compare favorably in terms of their representativeness to samples collected using more traditional (telephone-based) methods.[8]

The most obvious place to begin empirically examining public preferences for the representational relationship shared with elected officials is to ask citizens directly how they think members of Congress should be representing their constituents. Specifically, the following question was put to respondents in each of our surveys:

> Some people believe that members of Congress should be listening carefully to the people in their district, and trying their hardest to give them the policies they want. Other people believe that members of Congress are chosen to lead, based on their values, and should stay true to those values, no matter what the polls might say. What about you?
>
> Using the scale below, where 1 means that you strongly believe that members of Congress should try their hardest to give the people in their district the policies they want, and 6 means that you strongly believe that members of Congress should stick to their principles, no matter what, where would you place yourself? You can choose any number in between, to indicate how strongly you feel about this.

| 1 | 2 | 3 | 4 | 5 | 6 |
|---|---|---|---|---|---|
| Strongly believe give what people want | | | | | Strongly believe follow own principles |

[7] The CES includes a two-wave panel: a pre-election and post-election wave. Across all years, our survey questions were placed on the pre-election wave.

[8] For details regarding the sampling methodology, see Ansolabehere (2009). For a good comparison of the pros and cons associated with telephone-based sampling techniques and different types of Internet-based techniques, see, for example, Chang and Krosnick (2009). And for a particularly colorful defense of at least some forms of Internet-based sampling techniques (in particular, those employed here), see Rivers (2009).

**TABLE 2.1** *LEGISLATIVE REPRESENTATION PREFERENCES, 2006–2009*

| | 2006 (%) | 2007 (%) | 2008 (%) | 2009 (%) |
|---|---|---|---|---|
| Delegate | 24.60 | 26.56 | 25.10 | 35.01 |
| 2 | 22.88 | 22.43 | 20.87 | 19.52 |
| 3 | 20.26 | 19.62 | 20.26 | 16.10 |
| 4 | 16.53 | 17.71 | 16.23 | 16.70 |
| 5 | 11.19 | 9.76 | 10.18 | 6.24 |
| Trustee | 4.54 | 2.73 | 7.36 | 6.44 |
| Mean | 2.80 | 2.73 | 2.87 | 2.59 |
| s.d. | 1.48 | 1.46 | 1.56 | 1.56 |
| N | 992 | 994 | 992 | 994 |

*Data Source*: CES 2006, 2007, 2008, 2009

Prior to collecting these data, we expected to find a distribution of opinion that would be far from uniform.[9] And as Table 2.1 shows, the data support that expectation—clearly, and not surprisingly, not everyone thinks the same. Across all four of our surveys, most of our respondents tended to prefer the instructed-delegate model, but many respondents seem to prefer the trustee model as well.

While the patterns witnessed across our four surveys tend to be relatively stable, we observe that the means tend to be slightly higher in national election years (2006 and 2008), indicating a slight shift in preferences toward the

[9] After a great deal of consideration, we decided to present respondents with a balanced, six-item response scale. Following Krosnick's (1999) review of the survey literature, we decided that a middle response category, if offered, might encourage respondents to engage in satisficing behavior and effectively offer "no opinion." By offering what is fundamentally a forced-choice set of response categories (respondents had to choose to place themselves on the delegate or trustee sides of the scale), we are able to gauge the extent to which respondents have an instinctual response to a question they have not pondered in depth and "lean" toward one representation style or the other (see also Johnston, 2008). Of course, one potential problem with the lack of a middle category is that in forcing respondents to place themselves on one side or the other, we may well increase the measurement error in our dependent variable. If this is the case, then we can expect that error will be randomly distributed, attenuate our findings and increase the risk of committing a type II error. That is, at the worst, we increase the chances that we will not detect a relationship that does actually exist.

trustee model in those years. To speculate, perhaps this has something to do with the context of election campaigns, where American politicians tend to discuss (and promote) their "values" and "principles," framing elections as a stark contrast between different moral visions.

Also, we notice that in 2009, there were quite a few more people who seemed to prefer instructed delegate-style representation in the strongest possible way, as compared to the other years. Maybe the jump can be explained as an "Obama" effect, or a reaction to what had been perceived as excessive trustee-style representation during the Bush years. That is, while this variable measures preferences as they pertain to congressional representation styles, not presidential ones, we would not be surprised if many citizens' preferences regarding political processes at any level or within any branch of government are shaded somewhat by who is in the White House and what is going on there. And as such, people may have had greater expectations that government would be responsive, once Obama was firmly entrenched. One might wonder if it was even a function of shattered expectations—people expecting greater responsiveness but being disappointed after nearly a year of Obama. Alas, our data do not support that conclusion. That is, other measures of citizen's *perceptions* regarding the representation styles they are actually getting, rather than preferences over those styles (which we will describe more fully in Chapter 6), reveal that in 2009, far more citizens perceived that their representatives were behaving like instructed delegates, which also means that a lot more citizens were satisfied with the style of representation they were getting than had been the case in the previous years.

Putting speculative tangents aside, we come back to our initial observation. Overall, a majority of Americans do seem to prefer the type of democracy observed in the instructed-delegate model. However, a sizeable minority of Americans would prefer for those they elect to lead based on internally held principles, rather than to follow public opinion. If forced to choose between the will of the public and internal guidance, many would prefer that their members of Congress look inward when deciding how to act in Congress. Later in this book, of course, we return to this with an eye to explaining these differences.

### *Differences According to Issue Type?*

There are, of course, plenty of reasons to think that in addition to finding evidence that different people think differently about representation, we should also find that people think differently about representation when they are considering different issues (see Cooper, 1999). Almost 50 years ago, Miller and Stokes observed that as well: given "the fact that no single tradition of representation" dominates in the United States, "variations in the representation relation are most likely to occur as we move from one policy domain to another" (1963:56). Of course, as we have already discussed, Miller and Stokes were looking at (dyadic) representation itself, not mass preferences toward it. That is, they were modeling the relationship between legislator's roll-call votes and the opinions of his or her constituents across different issue domains; however, we imagine that their intuition is likely to hold when we look at how individuals might think about representation when considering different issues.

To examine how representation preferences vary across different issue domains, in two of our four years (2006 and 2008) we followed up our general representation question with a series of question probing respondents' representation preferences when thinking about particular issues. All of the survey respondents were first presented with a common stem, which was followed by a series of questions asking respondents to consider the question as it pertains to particular issue areas, randomly ordered. Specifically:

> Of course some people want members of Congress to closely follow public opinion in the district when considering certain issues. On other issues some people think members of Congress should follow their personal values and principles when deciding what policy is best.
>
> For the following issues, please use the same scale to indicate whether you think your member of Congress should closely follow public opinion or decide issues based on his or her own values and principles.
>
> What if the issue is [insert issue]?

Respondents were presented with the same six-point response scale as in the general representation preferences question (shown earlier). In this brief section, we will discuss a few of the issues we raised with respondents. Table 2.2 presents the marginal statistics for the three issue-oriented questions discussed in this section.

First, one of Miller and Stokes' (1963) clearest findings would indicate that we should expect preferences toward representation relating to foreign-policy issues to differ from those preferences relating to issues of domestic policy. Looking at issues related to foreign policy, then, we can imagine that our survey respondents would be more likely to express a preference for members of Congress to use their judgment, based on their principles and values, rather than base decisions on public opinion. And when we ask our respondents, "What if the issue is whether (members of Congress should) authorize the

**TABLE 2.2** *LEGISLATIVE REPRESENTATION PREFERENCES BY ISSUE, 2006 AND 2008*

| | Authorize War | | Budget | | Taxes | |
|---|---|---|---|---|---|---|
| | 2006 (%) | 2008 (%) | 2006 (%) | 2008 (%) | 2006 (%) | 2008 (%) |
| Delegate | 24.82 | 26.70 | 20.93 | 24.09 | 25.30 | 28.95 |
| 2 | 18.44 | 14.92 | 20.12 | 15.28 | 23.37 | 20.85 |
| 3 | 21.07 | 17.77 | 25.78 | 21.15 | 23.17 | 19.33 |
| 4 | 16.41 | 16.35 | 18.20 | 19.03 | 14.74 | 13.87 |
| 5 | 12.56 | 11.68 | 9.20 | 11.94 | 8.84 | 10.32 |
| Trustee | 6.69 | 12.59 | 5.76 | 8.50 | 4.57 | 6.68 |
| Mean | 2.93** | 3.37** | 2.92** | 3.05** | 2.71** | 2.76** |
| s.d. | 1.56 | 1.72 | 1.45 | 1.59 | 1.44 | 1.57 |
| N | 987 | 985 | 989 | 988 | 984 | 988 |

*Data Source*: CES 2006, 2007, 2008, 2009
Difference of Means (*t*-test)—Issue Type vs. General—** $p \leq .01$

President to go to war?" this does seem to be the case. In both 2006 and 2008, survey respondents tended to shift toward preferring a trustee style of representation when the specific issue of authorizing the President to take the country to war was the issue. Comparing the responses when the issue was "authorizing war" to the general representation measures, we find statistically significant differences—though, to be sure, the shifts were not earth-shattering in terms of substantive significance (2006: $t = 3.01; p < 0.01$ and 2008: $t = 4.21; p < 0.00$).

In thinking about how these preferences may vary according to different types of domestic issues, it makes sense, as Sigelman et al. (1992) point out, to distinguish between what Carmines and Stimson (1980) refer to as "easy" and "hard" issues. Carmines and Stimson (1980:80) assert that easy issues are those satisfying three basic criteria: (1) they are "symbolic rather than technical," (2) they "would more likely deal with policy ends than means," and (3) they would have been on the political agenda for quite some time. Issues that fail to satisfy these criteria tend to fall into the "hard" issue category, implying that they are complex and technical, requiring some degree of specific, factual knowledge to grasp the policy alternatives. To quote them at length (since they are far more eloquent than are we), Sigelman et al. argue:

> On a hard issue, members of the public may have good reason to give their leaders ample room to maneuver. After all, the issue is complex, and the average citizen lacks the time, information and aptitude to formulate a meaningful position. Under these circumstances, it makes little sense to

> insist that a leader do what the majority seems to favor, since the chances are that the majority does not really know what it wants. By contrast, on an easy issue, positions are clearly drawn, and there is no compelling reason for citizens to suppose that a leader is in a better position to decide than are they themselves. It follows that the character of the issue under consideration, easy or hard, has the potential to shape public expectations concerning the behavior of elected officials. On easy issues, it seems likely that officials will be expected to act more as delegates, on hard issues, more as trustees. (1992:371)

To distinguish between a "hard" and an "easy" issue, we asked respondents about two different issue areas within the same (very broad) domain. For a hard issue, respondents were asked about their representation preferences on "The Budget." The federal budget is, of course a large, amorphous and highly abstract "issue" that includes a great many considerations and technical distinctions. We also view it as a safe assumption that public knowledge about the budgetary process and the budget itself is sketchy, at best (Delli Carpini & Keeter, 1996). While it is certainly the case that the "budget" is an issue that is regularly on the agenda and is raised in media discourse about politics and Washington, it is also the case that the specific context in which the budget is discussed, and the programs that serve as the focus of attention in any given year, are fluid.

In contrast, people tend to have an immediate "gut response" (Carmines & Stimson, 1980:80) to the issue of "Taxes." Taxes certainly can be seen as a symbolic issue, evoking either the progressive idea of an activist government seeking to share society's resources across all members of society, or the conservative notion of "big government" taking away part of an individual's hard-earned livelihood. To be sure, there are highly technical aspects of taxation policies, just as there are technical aspects of Carmines and Stimson's example of racial desegregation. As Carmines and Stimson said, "Although the policy conflicts involved in desegregation can be detailed in great complexity, we think it reasonable to assume that the typical voter sees in it a simple issue" (1980:80). We concur and would claim the same about "taxes."

In both 2006 and 2008, we uncover a similar pattern: the mean of the "hard" issue (the federal budget) is significantly above the mean of the general representation measure, indicating a shift toward preferring a trustee style of representation when the issue is complex and difficult to grasp fully. On the other hand, the mean of the "easy issue" (taxes) is significantly below the mean of the general representation item, indicating a shift toward preferring a delegate style of representation then the issue is symbolic and elicits "gut reactions." As before, while the substantive changes in the means are not exactly huge, we do find clear and distinct statistical differences (the *t*-test for difference in means between the budget and taxes items resulted in a *t*-value of 6.59 ($p < .001$) in 2006 and 8.20 ($p < .001$) in 2008). So in two different surveys in the field two years apart and with two different samples, we find consistent evidence that simply asking about a (relatively) "hard" issue versus a (relatively) "easy" issue results in shifting preferences between trustee and instructed-delegate representational styles.

In sum, to this point we have reasoned that when people are asked about their preferences for political representation—preferences to which, in all likelihood, they have not given a great deal of thought at all—their response might be some version of "well, that depends on the issue we are talking about."

Our findings support those expectations. Mirroring the findings of Miller and Stokes (1963), we find that people seem to offer the most deference to their representative's better judgment on issues of foreign policy—especially, as we measured it, issues of war and peace. Likewise, we also find some evidence that when issues are "hard," people are more willing to defer to their representatives to sort out the best policy. But when issues are easier to understand, and people are more likely to have a better sense of their own position on the issue at hand, then they are somewhat more likely to prefer their member of Congress to look to the opinion in his or her district for guidance on how to vote on the issue.

### *Differences According to the Representing Institution?*

Sigelman et al. (1992) also raise the question of whether individuals' preferences for how they want to be represented vary by the office the elected official occupies. Similarly, we designed questions in our surveys to allow us to consider the degree to which citizens tend to prefer a different style of representation out of their president than they do from their member of Congress. We, like Sigelman et al. (1992), had suspected that the answer is "yes," reasoning that the constitutional distinctions in responsibilities expected of the executive and legislative branches, coupled with the mythology that surrounds the presidency, may lead many citizens to crave and expect more "leadership" out of the chief executive and commander-in-chief—even if they prefer an instructed-delegate style of representation out of their legislators.

To be clear, we are not suggesting that the executive and legislative branches are or should be considered equivalent representative bodies. As all Americans learn in high-school civics courses, the legislature is the political institution that is supposed to represent the "voice of the people," whereas the Founders applied no such understanding to the executive branch.

That said, however, it is not unreasonable to think of the president as a national "representative," who must monitor opinion and act accordingly, at least sometimes (see Rehfeld, 2009; also Canes-Wrone, 2006; Druckman & Jacobs, 2011; Fox & Shotts, 2009; Geer, 1996; Sigelman et al., 1992; Wood, 2009). After all, the president *is* an elected official, and he or she is often portrayed as the only elected official charged with looking out for the interests of "all the people."

And over the course of the past 50 years or so, at least, presidents have certainly been willing to adopt this mantle (when it has been in their interest to do so, anyway), "going public" by taking issues directly to the people so as to circumvent or manipulate legislative prerogatives (e.g., Kernell, 1997; but see Canes-Wrone, 2006). Such behavior encourages the public to see the president as a national representative. Indeed, Geer (1996) has shown how modern presidents have both the tools and incentives to follow public opinion on major issues of the day, but to lead it on more minor issues.

Accordingly, we asked survey respondents to reconsider representation styles, this time explicitly instructing them to think about representation as it applies to the president rather than to Congress. Specifically, we put the following question to our respondents in each of our four surveys:

> Of course it is possible that you could expect one thing out of members of Congress and another thing out of the President. Using the same scale, please indicate whether you think the President should closely follow public opinion or decide issues based on his or her own values and principles.

Looking at the marginal statistics included in Table 2.3 and comparing them to those observed in Table 2.1, we see that in every one of our surveys people do indeed tend to demand more "principled leadership" out of the president than they do from Congress. Preferences for representation style vary by the office under consideration. Not unreasonably, people's representation-style preferences reflect the idea that the legislature should be tied more closely to public opinion and the executive branch should reflect more independent judgment and lead based on principles and values.

We also observe that representation preferences vary across years. Adding together respondents who expressed a preference for a delegate (values 1–3), we find that in 2006, 2007, and 2008, roughly similar percentages of respondents (54%, 55%, and 53%, respectively) preferred a presidential delegate, while in 2009, the first full year of the Obama administration, almost 64% expressed a preference for the president to follow public opinion. Again, we really can only speculate as to the reasons behind these differences between the years.[10] The most obvious explanation is that the public was responding to Obama's implicit and explicit messages that his administration would be responsive to the grassroots.

Does the type of issue being considered matter when it comes to presidential representation, as it did for congressional representation? We expected that because the president is given constitutional authority over the military as "commander-in-chief," citizens would tend to expect more conscience-based representation in matters of foreign policy than in matters of domestic policy—in which even unsophisticated citizens are somewhat likely to recognize that presidential power is shared with the legislature.

In our 2006 survey, after asking respondents to reveal their generalized presidential representation-style preferences, we followed up with two more questions—one asking about preferences "if the president is considering foreign policy issues" and another asking "if the president is considering domestic policy issues." As the data (displayed in Table 2.4) bear out, it does seem to be the case that when it comes to issues of foreign policy—just as was the case when we asked about members of Congress—respondents preferred for the president to decide issues based on values and principles. On the other hand, when dealing with domestic policy, the mean preference is for the president to base decisions on public opinion.

So, in contradistinction to the implicit assumptions underlying a great deal of the representation literature, namely that just about everyone would be happier if representatives behaved like instructed "delegates" (parroting majority opinion in their districts when standing on the House and Senate floors or sitting in the Oval Office), we find simple evidence that this is not the case at all. In fact, our data show that while some people prefer delegate-style representation, others prefer trustees—especially from the president and especially when it comes to non-economic issues—and that it also depends in part on the issues and institutions under consideration.

## CONCLUSION

So, to summarize, in this chapter we have provided a general overview of citizens' preferences regarding styles of representation. We have observed

[10] Ideally, we would like to have a longitudinal, multi-wave panel to measure individuals' reactions (in terms of representational preferences) to political context. We could certainly imagine, for instance, that there could be a "thermostatic" aspect (Wlezien, 1995) to preferences for representation. At this stage and with these data, though, it is unfortunately not possible to determine.

**TABLE 2.3** *PRESIDENTIAL REPRESENTATION PREFERENCES, 2006–2009*

| | 2006 (%) | 2007 (%) | 2008 (%) | 2009 (%) |
|---|---|---|---|---|
| Delegate | 19.94 | 21.23 | 16.77 | 25.20 |
| 2 | 19.33 | 16.70 | 14.55 | 18.35 |
| 3 | 14.43 | 17.40 | 21.72 | 20.16 |
| 4 | 16.79 | 18.61 | 21.32 | 19.15 |
| 5 | 14.85 | 16.50 | 13.33 | 10.48 |
| Trustee | 9.66 | 9.56 | 12.32 | 6.65 |
| Mean | 3.16 | 3.21 | 3.37 | 2.91 |
| s.d. | 1.61 | 1.64 | 1.59 | 1.55 |
| N | 983 | 994 | 990 | 992 |

*Data Source*: CES 2006, 2007, 2008, 2009

that, generally speaking, more than a majority of citizens seem to prefer the instructed-delegate style of representation, but a sizable minority prefer the trustee style. What this indicates to us is that if we are really going to try to understand the processes of political representation in the United States, we should develop better models explaining how people think representation should work. As we have said previously, if we are going to evaluate how well (or not) people are represented by elected officials, it would be a good idea to first understand what people want and expect. Thinking of this in the broadest way, if "representation" is some sort of relationship between constituents and their elected officials, in order to judge how well that relationship is working, we have to know what the people in that relationship hope to get out of it.

We have also seen that trustee-style preferences increase when citizens consider different types of issues and when citizens contemplate executive representation (especially in matters of foreign policy) rather than legislative representation. While the differences we found across different types of issues (whether they are "hard" or "easy," whether they pertain to foreign policy or domestic policy) were not substantively enormous, they were statistically significant (and thus generalizable to the general population). This means that although people do not wildly change the sort of representation they prefer according to the type of issue under consideration, such details do matter.

In the next chapter, we will provide a detailed theory of how we expect mass preferences over delegates versus trustees to differ systematically, according to differences in culture, values, religion, and (by extension) partisanship.

**TABLE 2.4** *PRESIDENTIAL REPRESENTATION PREFERENCES IN 2006, BY ISSUE TYPE*

| | General (%) | Domestic (%) | Foreign (%) |
|---|---|---|---|
| Delegate | 19.94 | 22.33 | 20.77 |
| 2 | 19.33 | 21.12 | 17.43 |
| 3 | 14.43 | 21.73 | 18.64 |
| 4 | 16.79 | 15.33 | 15.91 |
| 5 | 14.85 | 11.88 | 16.62 |
| Trustee | 9.66 | 7.72 | 10.64 |
| Mean | 3.16 | 2.97** | 3.22* |
| s.d. | 1.61 | 1.56 | 1.66 |
| N | 983 | 985 | 987 |

*Data Source*: CES 2006

Difference of Means (t-test)—Issue Type vs. General—* $p \leq .05$; ** $p \leq .01$

## CHAPTER 3

# Cultural Warfare and Styles of Representation in the United States

> The American people have spoken…now we can only hope that he [President Bush] will listen.
>
> *–Senator Hillary Clinton (April 27, 2007), in reference to the 2006 midterm elections, which were perceived to be a referendum on the Iraq War*

> I do not need to take your pulse before I know my own mind. I do not reinvent myself at every turn.
>
> *–Then-Governor George W. Bush, in his acceptance speech at the 2000 Republican National Convention*

As the literature we reviewed in Chapter 2 has shown (and as our data also revealed), people vary significantly in terms of the style of representation they prefer. Unfortunately, as many other scholars have critically noted (see, especially, Jewell, 1985, and Sigelman et al., 1992), existing scholarship offers little in terms of explaining *why* people prefer one style of representation rather than the other. That is to say, even on the relatively rare occasions during the past 35 years when scholars have examined differences in public preferences regarding the instructed delegate versus trustee question, they have almost never sought to actually *explain* the differences across individuals (but for recent exceptions, see Barker & Carman, 2009, 2010 and Carman, 2007).

In Chapter 2, we explored how individual preferences for either instructed delegates or trustees sometimes vary *within* individuals—how a single individual's preference might change depending on the institution doing the representing and the issues under consideration. In this chapter (which, we're warning you now, is quite long), we begin to explain how those preferences vary *across* individuals. That is, we seek to understand why, regardless of institution or issue type, some people might prefer representatives who listen to public opinion, while others prefer to entrust those representatives to "do what's right."

The (mostly dated) scholarship on this subject has pointed to social class as an important correlate of representation preference: as socioeconomic status increases, so does support for trustee-style representation (Carman, 2007; McMurray & Parsons, 1965 [cited in Lipinski, 2002]). Such findings certainly stand to reason: while the wealthy are a numerical minority, they hold a disproportionate share of power in society (especially in the economic sphere). It intuitively follows, then, that such people of means and influence might tend to resist the idea of the masses shaping policy outcomes.[1]

Also intuitive is the observation that African Americans are more likely than whites to prefer trustee-style representation when they live in districts represented by white legislators, but were more likely to prefer delegate-style representation when they live in districts represented by African American legislators (Carman, 2007).

Together, these race- and class-based findings suggest that representation preferences may be driven in part by individual perceptions of majority/minority status. That is, as we pointed out in the first paragraph of Chapter 1, and in keeping with rational choice theory and other interest-based models of mass preferences, individuals often want representatives to follow the will of the majority when they also perceive themselves to be part of the majority, but when the "other side" holds the numerical advantage, they may prefer "leaders who lead."

Alas, while it may provide intellectual comfort to know that citizens appear to apply some rationality when thinking about how they want to be represented, such interest-based findings do not leave us searching for the proverbial pen with which to write home. As such, those findings can go only so far in helping us identify generalizable patterns of preferences across individuals that could be applied over time to various contexts. In other words, if mass preferences toward representation style are really worthy of our attention, there must be more to such preferences than simple considerations of "what's in it for me."

That is why we argue that there are deeper (perhaps even intrinsic) motivations that lead some people to find the trustee style of representation more palatable than the instructed delegate style, and vice versa. The ultimate

---

[1] It is probably not a coincidence that just such class-based concerns shaped the debates between Federalists and Anti-Federalists to which we referred in Chapter 2. That is, Federalists desired institutional barriers that would, among other things, protect propertied interests from presumed populist impulses.

conclusion we draw in this chapter will be that, over the past 30 years or so, Republicans have been somewhat more inclined than Democrats to favor the trustee style of representation (on balance). The reason for that pattern, we argue, is that the Republican Party houses many more traditionalistic Christians (as well as other types of traditionalists) than does the Democratic Party.

To be somewhat more precise, we suggest that traditionalists—especially Christian traditionalists, and even more especially evangelical Christian traditionalists—often possess worldviews that are not particularly consistent with the values that underlie liberal popular democracy (that is, they are often somewhat more dogmatic and authoritarian, and somewhat less egalitarian and humanistic, than are other Americans). Accordingly, traditionalists tend to instinctively prefer trustees to instructed delegates. And because traditionalists are disproportionately Republican, partisan differences are also observable.

## A VALUE-BASED APPROACH

Our argument begins with the suggestion that representation preferences sometimes manifest differences in individual *value priorities* (e.g., Hurwitz & Peffley, 1987; Jacoby, 2006; Rokeach, 1973; Tetlock, 1986). For our purposes, we define values as *overarching, abstract, core beliefs about "right and wrong"—as distinct from considerations of self-interest or group identity/antipathy*. In the past 25 years, a flood of research has demonstrated that the way individuals prioritize some values over others goes a long way toward determining a wide array of policy opinions (for an excellent overview, see Feldman, 2003a). It only makes sense, then, to expect that values would also influence opinions pertaining to somewhat grander considerations such as the proper relationship between constituents and representatives.[2]

But if value priorities do in fact help to orient a person toward either instructed delegate-style or trustee-style representation preferences, just *which* values are doing the work? Our basic premise is the following: instinctive preferences for instructed delegates over trustees reflect, to some extent, heightened sympathies for "liberal popular democracy" itself. In other words, in our view, given that *democracy* literally translates as "people rule," one might

[2] At this point, we should reiterate that we do *not* imagine that the typical American citizen spends *any* time actually thinking about what style of representation he or she prefers, or why. Rather, stemming from particular deep-seated value orientations, we simply suggest that some people *instinctively* tend to sympathize more easily with the instructed delegate style of representation, while others naturally find themselves drawn toward the trustee-style alternative.

say that one's instinctive preference between instructed delegates and trustees comes down to the degree to which one thinks ordinary people are indeed fit to rule—not just indirectly and intermittently via the electoral process, but in actively shaping policy outcomes, year by year and even month by month.

If our contention is true—that is, if attitudes toward representation styles are really, to a considerable extent, attitudes toward liberal popular democracy itself—then perhaps a good strategy for pinpointing which values shape representation preferences would be to think about the values that underlie liberal popular democracy in the first place. To do so, we first need to make clear what liberal popular democracy actually is (at least how we are using the term), and then proceed to build our argument from there.

In the remainder of this chapter, then, we (a) distinguish our understanding of liberal popular democracy from other non-autocratic forms of government, (b) elaborate what we see as the clear connection between instructed delegate-style representation and liberal popular democracy, (c) distinguish the core values that, in our view, underlie liberal popular democracy (egalitarianism and humanism) from other orientations that oppose it (authoritarianism and dogmatism), (d) discuss how these orientations therefore also underlie the competing styles of representation, and (e) delineate the various reasons why evangelical Christians and other cultural traditionalists tend to disproportionately hold authoritarian and dogmatic worldviews, and to deprioritize humanistic and egalitarian ones, thereby inclining them to like trustee-style representation more than other Americans do.[3] From there, we (f) explain how these value-driven preferences manifest themselves in partisan differences, thereby representing a previously unconsidered front in the Red/Blue American Culture Wars.

## REPUBLICS, DIRECT DEMOCRACIES, AND LIBERAL POPULAR DEMOCRACIES

To be sure, settling upon a single understanding of "democratic" government has proven difficult, contentious, and ultimately elusive (for an overview, see Held, 1996). While an idealized "democracy" might demand any number of features, such as government transparency, a commitment to human rights,

[3] At different points in this chapter, we will use the terms "democratic," "Democratic," "republican" and "Republican." Following standard grammatical convention, the terms beginning with lowercase letters refer to classic political systems, whereas the capitalized terms refer to the American political parties. The exception to this rule, of course, occurs when one of these terms is used in a section header, in which case it will always be capitalized.

and a good many other things (e.g., Goodhart, 2005), perhaps the most fundamental element underlying any conception of democracy is some notion of self-governance. Unfortunately, "self-governance" has itself been interpreted pretty broadly as well. However, three basic models of self-government stand as those most commonly put forward—republics, direct democracies, and liberal popular democracies—and it is on those that we focus here. As we will describe, if the bare essence of democracy is this notion of citizens ruling themselves, we believe these three models of self-rule can be placed on a scale from least to most democratic.

According to the first model—a *republic* or *liberal republic*—self-government can be taken to simply mean that the reach of government should be institutionally limited, subject to the *consent* of the public, and governed by the rule of law, which thereby enables people to "rule" their personal and economic lives with as little government interference as possible. Such republics were first observed in the English "Glorious" Revolution of 1688 and especially in the United States following the Constitutional Convention (indeed, see *Federalist 10* for a defense of republicanism; for a broader overview of these historical roots, see Sabine, 1952). In such republics, individual citizens are protected from governmental tyranny, but their influence in policymaking is only sporadic (subject to the electoral calendar) and even then quite limited. The way individual rights are protected in this system is by simply limiting the reach and concentration of political power, rather than by instituting mechanisms through which individuals can actively shape policy outcomes on a regular basis. As such, while a republic takes care to protect individual rights, it also takes great care to insulate government from popular sentiment. Or, put differently, in a republic, government may be "for the people" and to some extent even "by the people" (because leaders are elected), but it is not really very much "*of* the people."

The second model of democratic politics views the words "people rule" in a much more active sense—to mean popular sovereignty; citizens actively shape policy itself. The most radical version of this is *direct democracy* (e.g., Dahl, 1989). The first attempt at direct democracy on a large scale grew out of the French Revolution of the late 18th century (Sabine, 1952). Of course, if direct democracy plays out in its most simplistic form, with the public just voting directly on policy through ballot initiatives and the like (without institutionalized protections of minority rights), it can quickly devolve into "mob rule," which silences all voices not included as part of the numerical majority (even if that majority is a mere 50.05%). We contend that when minority views are completely discarded in this way—a condition commonly known as "tyranny of the majority"—the system is (perhaps ironically) less "democratic" than the aforementioned republic. Such majoritarian tyranny is precisely what transpired in the aforementioned 18th-century France, paving the way for Napoleonic dictatorship.

So, whereas a republic institutionalizes the protection of individual rights but does not encourage popular sovereignty, direct democracy encourages popular sovereignty but only in the strictest majoritarian sense, which thereby limits it severely. We do not have to look back to 18th-century France to find clear instances of majoritarian democracy being used to restrict democratic rights. As just one example, the most recent decade saw a slew of states using ballot initiatives to ensure that gays and lesbians would not be extended certain equal protections under the law. These initiatives have faced stiff scrutiny from the institutionalized protector of minority rights—the judicial system. Indeed, on this matter, the courts have denied the "will of the people" repeatedly, just as they did during the Civil Rights era and have done on countless other occasions throughout American history. Our point is that when the judicial system frustrates the popular majority in the short term in order to expand popular sovereignty in the long term, it is *serving* democratic ends, not thwarting them. So, because the purest of direct democracies includes no such mechanism, its democratic capacity is limited.

Therefore, each of the prototypes of self-government we have discussed so far includes only half of the conditions necessary for the "people" to really "rule." For a political system to fully empower the masses, it must serve as an instrument of the popular will to as great of an extent as possible, but the popular will must also be checked against the trampling of minority voices. Systems that attempt to do both of these things simultaneously are usually called *liberal popular democracies*, and can be considered the most democratic of the three prototypes we have now discussed (republic, direct democracy, and liberal popular democracy).[4]

For our purposes, the relevant prototypes to compare are republics and liberal popular democracies, because in the next section we argue that the former demands trustee-style representation while the latter demands the instructed delegate style. Before getting to that, though, we need to make something clear: when we claim that liberal popular democracy is more democratic than is a republic, we are not trying to make a normative statement. We merely mean to convey that one type is, by definition, more encouraging of

---

[4] Of course, we are using the term "liberal" in the classic sense, as an adjective denoting the promotion of individual liberty, rather than in the contemporary sense, used in American politics to denote the policies of the ideological "left." The two meanings may or may not be consistent, depending on one's perspective.

active popular sovereignty *for everyone* across the political spectrum than the other. In the next section, we make the theoretical connection between liberal popular democracy and instructed delegate-style representation.

## LIBERAL POPULAR DEMOCRACY AND INSTRUCTED DELEGATE-STYLE REPRESENTATION

It is not difficult to see how the preceding brief discussion of the different democratic prototypes speaks to the competing styles of representation that are our focus. We assert that because instructed delegate-style representation affords citizens the most direct policymaking influence, while simultaneously making room for minority voices to be heard, it is the natural expression of liberal democratic sentiment in large societies. After all, a clear implication of the instructed delegate style of representation is that the decisions made by representatives are based exclusively on the representatives' understanding of constituent preferences—not just majority opinion, but the full distribution of opinion as it exists in the constituency.

Of course, a direct democracy that also includes constitutional protections of individual rights and a judicial system to enforce those protections would fit the description of a liberal popular democracy as well. And because such a system affords citizens the ability to vote directly on policy, one might expect that it would realize the liberal democratic vision better than does a representative democracy that relies on instructed delegates as representatives. We disagree, however, for a few reasons. First, minority *rights* may be protected through the rule of law, but (as we discussed in Chapter 2) when it comes to the amplification of minority *voices*, an idealized instructed delegate adjusts her positions to be in accord with the *distribution of opinion* in the constituency, not just the simple majority (i.e., not just her ideological comrades who elected her). Such full consideration is not the case in a direct democracy that makes policy via ballot initiatives, even if judicial protections are in place to preserve the majority from encroaching on fundamental civil liberties.

In this regard, it should also be remembered that representatives' tasks are not limited to voting on bills (or, when the representative in question is an executive, signing/vetoing bills), but include many other activities, such as setting the policy agenda, proposing/drafting legislation in the first place, adding amendments to legislation, negotiating to modify the size/scope of legislation, instructing the bureaucracy to administer policy in different ways (in the case of executive representatives), and working to obtain "pork" for the district (in the case of legislative representatives). It is in these capacities that an instructed delegate can serve as a mouthpiece not only for the majority will but for the full constituency. By contrast, it is hard to imagine how all of those things could play out via direct democracy. Perhaps, in theory, a direct democracy—using online interfaces or something—could enable citizens to write and propose legislation, deliberate collectively to set the agenda and amend legislation, and finally vote in massive roll calls, all in real time. But as things stand, and for the foreseeable future, direct policymaking on the part of citizens happens only one way, by voting on referenda and initiatives.

To press this point a bit further, we argue that even if the overriding goal of a popular democracy was to simply exercise the will of the majority, the dynamics associated with trying to carry out direct democracy via the electoral process can constrain popular sovereignty in at least two additional ways that might not be true of democracy via instructed delegate-style representation.

First, we must remember that winners of initiatives and referenda do not necessarily reflect the will of even the majority. Rather, they reflect the will of *the majority of those who voted that day, subject to the idiosyncrasies of particular electoral institutions, and so on*. They are influenced heavily by voter eligibility rules, each side's ability to mobilize supporters, systematic resource-based differences in participation, skillful campaign manipulation, the wording and placement of options on ballots, the ways that votes are counted, and so on. Taken collectively, these factors can lead to electoral outcomes that are not at all in keeping with what the majority of citizens truly want.

So, when it comes to ballot initiatives, winners are winners and losers are losers, with the policy spoils going to the victor—regardless of how the victory was achieved, and regardless of whether the victory is by 50 percentage points or only a single vote. This imprecision with which opinions get translated into votes, and those votes are translated into policy, is a problem for a system attempting to maximize popular sovereignty. Instructed delegates (those conforming to stereotype, anyway), on the other hand, use public opinion polls to monitor constituent preferences, priorities, and concerns more or less constantly. And while such polls certainly have their flaws, they can reflect citizens' sincere wishes more accurately than American elections can.

Secondly, the instructed delegate's monitoring of constituent opinion via scientific polling affords her the ability to monitor opinion *dynamics* as well. The committed instructed delegate can modulate her policymaking behavior constantly, in real time, in response to weekly polls—perhaps slightly emphasizing some things while deemphasizing others—in response to constantly changing nuances in constituent opinion. By contrast, elections are expensive and time-consuming to organize. As such, states cannot hold elections with the regularity that would be necessary to translate rapidly changing public opinion dynamics into public policy. Thus, unlike what the instructed delegate can do, a direct democracy reliant upon initiatives and/or referenda cannot reflect weekly or even monthly trends in constituent opinion.[5]

## TRUSTEES AND REPUBLICANISM

Whereas instructed delegate-style representation seems to conform best to the liberal popular democratic vision, trustee-style representation is much more in keeping with the popular sovereignty-limiting principles that characterize a republic (for a fuller argument of this point, see Miroff, Seidelman, & Swanstrom, 2009). Indeed, as we mentioned earlier, Edmund Burke argued that a legislature composed of instructed delegates would short-circuit the entire purpose of a legislature. In a manner that did not attempt to conceal his pessimism toward the decision-making capacity of the mass citizenry, Burke argued that a legislature of instructed delegates, which would be bound to the demands and preferences of constituents, would severely limit the ability of elected representatives to arrive at the best policy decisions.

It is also important to reiterate here that at the time of the American Founding, it was the Federalists who defeated proposed legislation that would have forced elected representatives to follow their constituents' wishes. If we linger for an additional moment on the general differences between these antagonists—the Federalists and Anti-Federalists—there can be little doubt as to which of these two groups was more philosophically committed to expanding democratic voice to citizens. It was the Federalists' Constitution, after all, that consciously restricted popular influence by creating such institutions as the electoral college, indirectly elected senators, and others. By contrast, Anti-Federalists feared that the Constitution's centralization of power would primarily serve the interests of propertied elites rather than the public at large (for an overview, see Main, 2004).

Indeed, when these Anti-Federalists eventually cohered into a functioning political party during the early years of the Republic (a.k.a. the "Jeffersonian" Republicans), their Federalist opponents dubbed them "democratic" as a term of derision—a label the Jeffersonians eventually embraced (some 20 years later) by dropping the "Republican" moniker altogether. In fact, the new Democratic Party that emerged at that time, under the leadership of Andrew

---

[5] To paraphrase David Judge (1999), in the United Kingdom a commonly heard refrain is that they live in a democracy every 5 years, or whenever an election is called, but not in between those times. We are suggesting that the same may be true on this side of the pond, when representatives do not behave as instructed delegates anyway.

Jackson and Martin Van Buren, is remembered for expanding popular sovereignty to a degree previously unseen in the United States (e.g., Reynolds, 2008). Such "Jacksonian Democracy" was one of the characteristics of Jackson's Democratic Party that its opponents, the (frequently pietistic) Whigs, fervently opposed.

*A Cautionary Tangent*: As the Whigs began to gray as a viable party, the political history becomes tricky. We certainly cannot say with confidence that either the Republican or Democratic parties of the 1850s through the 1970s, or the (various) ideological perspectives that they represented during those years, stood for liberal popular democracy any more consistently than the other one did.

To elaborate, if one were to perform a content analysis of all convention platforms, campaign speeches, State of the Union addresses, legislative milestones, and the like for the past 130 years, searching for patterns in terms of which political "teams" tended to stand more on the side of expanding popular sovereignty (including the power of minority voices), one would unearth a lot of contradictions. This is because all politicians naturally try to use whatever tools they have at their disposal to achieve desired policy goals. So if a party understands that it enjoys the sympathy of the majority on a given issue, it may evoke the wisdom of the "will of the people" in pushing its agenda or come election time. That same group of people, however, may often be heard bemoaning their opponents for "pandering to the public" when the roles reverse a couple of years later.

Complicating the issue even further, both parties have at different points in time sought to suppress the popular will in the short term, in moralistic and perhaps even elitist fashion, in service to liberal democratic principles, and vice versa. To provide just two rather obvious examples, the nation was of course split in half in the 1860s (and long afterward, really) because zealous Republicans sought to impose their abolitionistic will on the South (obviously over the objections of white Southerners), at least in part for moralistic reasons relating to expanding the rights, political and otherwise, of African Americans. On the other hand, roughly 100 years later, Democrats (though not in the South, and with the help of some Northern Republicans of course) sought to do roughly the same thing, for the same purpose, during the Civil Rights movement. Both the Republican abolitionists and the Democratic civil rights activists worked to get public opinion on their side (and they eventually succeeded), but their early efforts entailed pursuing liberal democratic goals (expanding the political power of those who had not had any) in spite of public opinion on the matter, not in service to it.

## "POPULISM"

Some readers may wonder why we have avoided using the term *populism* to describe an affinity for popular democracy, even though by some definitions it would seem appropriate. Indeed, in general, populism refers to any mode of thought that champions "the common person" over elites (Canovan, 1981). Accordingly, one could consider the attempt to expand popular sovereignty to be a form of democratic populism, because it elevates the decision-making power of common citizens. However, "championing the common person" can mean many different things, and the term has been used to characterize all kinds of perspectives that have nothing to do with expanding democratic voice, including some perspectives that actually undermine such expansion. The first problem with the term is that it has a specific historical reference point in the United States—to the Populist Party of the late 19th century. The Populist Party, centered in the South and Plains states, is perhaps remembered best for its crusading form of agrarianism and its charismatic leader, William Jennings Bryan (who is also famous for his fundamentalist opposition to the teaching of evolution during the Scopes trial of 1925). For readers who possess even a glancing familiarity with this history, use of the term could generate no small amount of confusion.

More generally speaking, people often use the term *populism* to describe macroeconomic perspectives that seek to benefit working-class interests at the expense of the wealthy. Such economic populism usually means reigning in the free market, and has been associated with the global ideological Left. By the same token, and perhaps even ironically, populism of a more cultural or nationalistic bent can refer to the authoritarian impulses that easily emerge among majorities to restrict the rights of racial, ethnic, religious, or sexual minorities, and is therefore associated with groups of the far ideological Right. Such populism may share some things in common with the strictest form of majoritarian direct democracy (as we mentioned earlier), but not of liberal popular democracy as we have been describing it. At any rate, the point here is that we do not want readers to confuse our discussion of popular sovereignty—and its advocacy through liberal democratic systems and instructed delegate-style representation—with 19th-century political parties, Marxism, fascism, religious fundamentalism, the silver standard, farming implements, or anything else.

Tangents aside, now that we have made the connection between styles of representation and forms of popular rule, the next section attempts to identify the essential values underlying liberal popular democracy, as well as the orientations that undermine it, so as to gain some specificity in terms of who we ultimately expect to prefer one style of representation or another.

## VALUES THAT PROMOTE/CONTRADICT LIBERAL DEMOCRACY AND STYLES OF REPRESENTATION

If preferences for instructed delegate-style representation are really (at least in part) a manifestation of an underlying orientation toward liberal popular democracy, as compared to its republican cousin, then we should be able to explain those preferences by identifying and measuring the specific values that underlie liberal popular democratic sentiment. So what are the essential values that make up the liberal popular democratic vision? Our reading of democratic theory leads us to focus on two: *egalitarianism* and *humanism*—which are themselves related.[6] We further suggest that two other belief systems, *authoritarianism* and *dogmatism* (also related), form the basis of anti-liberal popular democratic sentiment.[7] The next subsection fleshes out these claims—by (1) defining each of these orientations, (2) clarifying how each relates to liberal democratic sentiment, and therefore (3) explaining how each predicts preferences regarding styles or representation.

Before we get to that, though, we want to emphasize right off the bat that we are not suggesting authoritarianism or dogmatism are precursors of republicanism; we believe the natural governmental manifestation of authoritarianism would be a dictatorship or a monarchy, not a republic. However, we

[6] These are surely not the only important democratic values. We think, however, that they are undoubtedly two of the most fundamental (as we will discuss later, we consider liberty to be a subcategory of these, as we are defining them). We could expand our consideration to include other values as well, but the discussion would quickly become complicated in a way that no reader would welcome. Thus, in this book, we will focus on just these two democratic values.

[7] Most scholars would certainly not consider authoritarianism and dogmatism to be values, *per se*, and neither do we. They have often been treated in the literature as personality-based dispositions that stem as much or more from psychological needs as from conscious perspectives on right and wrong. We see them as orientations, belief systems, or worldviews that inhibit democratic values.

are saying that if the 20% to 40% of Americans who have strong authoritarian and/or dogmatic leanings (see Hetherington & Weiler, 2009) were forced to choose between either a liberal popular democratic system of government or a republican one, we suspect they would be inclined to choose the latter more often than the former (unless, of course, choosing the former served their instrumental ends).

*"Strong" Egalitarianism Versus Authoritarianism*: Many scholars have pointed out that liberal popular democracies (but not necessarily republics) flow naturally from an underlying belief in what Robert Dahl calls the Strong Principle of Equality (Dahl, 1989). This is the idea, in Jefferson's words, that "All men are created equal...endowed by their creator with certain unalienable rights." As Dahl elaborates:

> The members believe that no single member, and no minority of members, is so definitively better qualified to rule that the one or the few should be permitted to rule over the entire association. They believe, on the contrary, that all the members of the association are adequately qualified to participate on an equal footing with the others in the process of governing the association. (Dahl 1989:31)

From Dahl's words, we can infer that such "strong" egalitarianism (which should not be confused with other, more restrictive iterations of egalitarianism such as support for equality of condition, equality of opportunity, etc.) naturally leads to liberal popular democratic sentiment because it asserts that there are no systematic, innate differences in virtue or competence between classifications of people. To such an egalitarian, the collective wisdom of the citizenry can and should be trusted (so long, once again, as it does not devolve into tyranny of the majority, wherein minority rights are usurped, which thereby undermines the very principle of basic equality on which it is based).

The antithesis of this kind of egalitarianism is elitism, one form of which can also be called authoritarianism. Authoritarianism has been defined and measured in various ways, including a tripartite combination of submission, conventionalism, and aggression (Altemeyer, 1996), a disposition toward social uniformity (Stenner, 2005), the reliance on established authorities to satisfy a deep intolerance of ambiguity (Hetherington & Weiler, 2009), a pathological need to dominate (Ray, 1992), or what amounts to right-wing ideological conservatism (Adorno et al., 1950). We like the following definition best: *the belief that some people are simply smarter and more decent than others, that the smartest and best will (and should) naturally rise to the top, and that they should naturally exercise leadership over the masses (who should naturally submit to that leadership).* Or, to put it more simply, we take authoritarianism to mean *the belief that some are born to lead, by virtue of their superiority, while others are born to follow.*[8]

Thus, authoritarianism necessarily implies anti-egalitarianism. Indeed, as these things pertain to political governance at least, we can think of strong egalitarianism and authoritarianism as opposite poles of a single value-scale. If we picture the scale running from left to right, with the left pole marking egalitarianism and the right pole marking authoritarianism, we can easily map political systems onto the scale. Fully functioning liberal popular democracies would correspond to the left (egalitarian) end of the pole, while fascist dictatorships, monarchies, and other autocratic systems would mark the right (authoritarian) end of the pole. Somewhere left of the center, but nowhere near the leftward pole, we would find republican forms of government.

In the same way, this egalitarianism/authoritarianism scale can readily predict preferences for representation styles: strong egalitarianism implies that representatives should act as instructed delegates, because there is no reason to believe that the representative's internal judgment is inherently better, intellectually or morally, to that of her constituents. In fact, given that the distribution of opinion within a constituency reflects the collective wisdom of a large number of people, egalitarians should think that constituency opinion is usually superior to that of a single leader—because errors in judgment/reason cancel out on both sides of a debate, leaving a more carefully considered position at the mean (indeed, this is the one of the philosophical arguments for why the "marketplace of ideas" produces desirable outcomes within a participatory democracy).

By contrast, as mentioned above, while a republican system employing trustee-style representation does not reflect far-right authoritarian sentiment by any stretch of the imagination, the imagination need not be too limber to see how purist egalitarians would not feel terribly enthusiastic about the trustee-style system, relatively speaking. After all, trustee-style representation really makes sense only if the collective decision-making capacity of the

---

[8] To embed a detailed discussion of the extensive authoritarianism literature, and the related social dominance literature (see Sidanius & Pratto, 2001), into this chapter would, we fear, distract readers from the points on which we would like them to be focusing. This is not, after all, primarily a book about authoritarianism; we merely draw from that literature to inform part of our theory. For interested readers, an excellent overview of the literature can be found in Hetherington and Weiler (2009).

masses is quite suspect. It suggests that elites, whose capacities are presumed to be inherently greater, must exercise leadership in the best interests of their constituents—in a benevolent form of service—so as to protect an uninformed and inherently fickle public from its own foolish caprice.

*Humanism*: So egalitarianism and authoritarianism speak not only to one's beliefs regarding the idea that all opinions have equal merit, but also to how much *range* there is across human beings in terms of their decision-making fitness and natural capacities to lead. Egalitarians believe this range is small and authoritarians believe it is large. Another—related—dimension of belief concerns the inherent capacity of people to do much of anything competently and sincerely. Those with the most sanguine views of human capacity have been called *humanists*. By definition, then, humanism is *a system of thought that conscientiously affirms the ability of human beings to determine right and wrong for themselves, for their own ends, and to achieve social progress* (again, whatever that may mean to them) *via secular channels* (e.g., American Humanist Association, 1933).[9] Or, in simplest terms, humanism holds a positive view of innate human nature.

Those who hold less sanguine views of human nature, non-humanists, often do so in order to emphasize the gulf between humanity and the divine. Such non-humanists do not believe that humanity is valueless, only that it is weak and wicked in the absence of divine guidance. In other words, they believe that humans are capable of exercising good judgment when directed by the hand of God, but not otherwise—at least not consistently and reliably.

So humanism really has two components: it reflects not only a sanguine view toward human nature but also a resistance to certain religious perspectives that emphasize a gulf in value between God and humankind. Thus, in a way, anti-humanism is also anti-egalitarian—as applied in a framework where differences across individuals in terms of their tendencies to make good decisions are based on whether an individual has submitted to the Highest Authority for direction.

[9] In the same way that Jefferson's words in the Declaration of Independence epitomize basic egalitarian principles, they extol humanism as well, in the claim that among humans' natural inalienable rights is included "the pursuit of happiness." In the mid- to late 18th century, the presumption that humankind had a right to be happy and to pursue that happiness for its own sake was provocative, contradicting most views regarding the purpose of human existence, which held it to be for the glorification of God, not the pursuit of individual utility. Indeed, Jefferson's insertion of "the pursuit of happiness" redefined John Locke's understanding of fundamental rights (which had included *property*, not *happiness*).

Humanism, then, is instinctively anti-authoritarian. As such, it is a building block of liberal popular democracy. Indeed, in its earliest incarnations, during the European Renaissance (14th through 16th centuries), humanism as expressed in art was a reaction against what was perceived to be the stifling of human capacity as represented by the medieval Catholic Church. Similarly, during the Age of Enlightenment (17th through 18th centuries), humanism acted as a counterweight to what many saw as religious authoritarianism both in the Catholic Church and in the newly prevalent Calvinist and Counter-Reformation movements (Lamont, 1997).

Thus, it is pretty easy to see how differences in humanism would affect instincts toward liberal popular democracy and, therefore, preferences regarding representation styles. Indeed, if ordinary citizens are inherently weak, inept, or morally depraved without the guiding hand of God, then the idea of those ordinary citizens making decisions that are binding on society (as opposed to divinely inspired agents making those decisions) is ludicrous.[10]

Of course, it is certainly possible (and not at all uncommon, actually) to be both a Judeo-Christian *and* a humanist. Many Judeo-Christian tenets affirm the dignity and worth of humanity, and a good number of faith traditions work diligently to promote social progress through whatever channels are available, including secular ones. However, as the next few paragraphs discuss, it is probably difficult to be a humanist if one is truly *dogmatic* about a traditionalistic interpretation of Christianity.

*Dogmatism:* Dogmatism refers to *any absolute commitment to an idea or principle, which one does not question and from which one does not budge—an intolerance of moral ambiguity* (e.g., Rokeach, 1954). Some have treated dogmatism as the mindset that precedes authoritarianism (see Hetherington & Weiler, 2009), or as a non-ideologically tainted version of the authoritarian mindset (e.g., Altemeyer, 1996). While we strongly agree that the two concepts are clearly intertwined, we do not consider them to be the same thing. We see authoritarianism as being more about a preference for hierarchy among human relationships, whereas dogmatism is more about the absence of ambivalence.

---

[10] An exception to this rule would be under circumstances where anti-humanists believe that concentrated factions of ordinary citizens are the ones most inclined to rely on divine guidance. Under such conditions, one could imagine a locally focused, anti-humanistic populism. There seems to be an element of this behind some aspects of modern conservatism.

Dogmatism is also related, theoretically speaking, to almost all religious modes of thought—because, after all, one way that religion can be defined is as an absolute and faith-based belief. Having said that, dogmatism certainly does not require a belief in God, or the supernatural, and need not reflect any religiosity in the traditional sense. Its sense of absolutism can be in devotion to any particular perspective—Christian, Muslim, atheist, Marxist, free-market capitalist, environmentalist, or anything else.

Regardless of what the particular perspective is to which the dogmatist has committed, a dogmatic mindset clearly impedes his or her willingness to consider competing ideas fairly—and that is the key point as far as we are concerned. Those who view particular ideas as sacred and inviolable tend to see changes of mind not as rational responses to new information, but rather as moral and intellectual weakness (i.e., abandoning one's principles or "selling out"). Relatedly, to the dogmatist's way of thinking, compromise based on consideration of others' perspectives and political power is not a democratic superlative; it is a sin.

In that way, while dogmatism does not exactly represent the opposite end of a single scale from humanism, it is clearly antithetical to it. To elaborate, humanism values pursuits of happiness for their own sake; it encourages people to pursue their fulfillment however they may have defined it. And that definition is allowed to change over time, according to differences in context. Such open-mindedness implies a certain normative relativism; no ideas should be dismissed out of hand, and nothing is ever set in stone. Ends, as well as appropriate means, change—simply because human desires and priorities change. Accordingly, morality is contextual and relativistic, not eternal and absolute. Almost everything comes in shades of gray.

By extension, dogmatism also runs counter to the liberal popular democratic vision. That is because any absolute commitment to an idea or set of ideas naturally privileges those ideas when competing in the public square, and such competition is a basic precept of liberal popular democracy (for elaboration of this point, see Marietta, 2008). In other words, if certain ideas or sources enjoy a large *prima facie* advantage in the public square, then reasoned debate in that public square faces an uphill battle to endure. That is to say, if understandings of truth are absolute, unchanging, and faith-based, then the marketplace of ideas has little for sale.

What all of this means, of course, is that dogmatism on the part of elected officials would preclude them from exercising the instructed delegate style of representation, and dogmatism on the part of constituents would preclude them from preferring instructed delegates. The instructed delegate style presumes that different people, in different contexts and at different points in time, have different preferences that change based on conditions and new information, and that when those preferences change, so should government policy. Trustee-style leadership, on the other hand, presumes the opposite—that while public opinion is fickle, good judgment requires representatives to chart a consistent course and stand on principles in the face of public vacillation. Thus, it is easy to see how dogmatists would feel much more comfortable with trustee-style representation than with the instructed delegate alternative.

To summarize, in this section we have suggested that liberal popular democracy, and therefore instructed delegate-style representation, is rooted in the values of basic egalitarianism and humanism, and is contradicted by authoritarianism and dogmatism.[11] We consider these orientations to be very deeply rooted. In fact, we do not know how much more basic normative beliefs can get than considerations of whether humankind is essentially capable or incapable, whether it is equal or unequal, and whether morality is absolute or contextual. Therefore, these values (or dispositions) are very useful foundations on which to build our theory, because they are obviously so basic that we do not have to worry much about our theory suffering from questions relating to the direction of causality. That is, the notion that representation-style preferences could actually precede humanistic, egalitarian, authoritarian, or dogmatic worldviews—rather than the other way around—just does not make any sense.

[11] Some readers may object that we did not include libertarianism—a predisposition toward believing that humans should live their lives freely with as little interference from government as possible (so long as they are not harming others in the process)—as one of the basic values on which liberal democracies are built. We have omitted it because we consider it to be implied by the others, and subsequent to it. If one believes that human beings are basically good and capable, and that no class of people is inherently better than others, and therefore that people should not be expected to just submit to authority or to exercise it with impunity when given the chance, it logically follows that political systems should be structured in such a way as to enable people to live their lives—politically and otherwise—as freely as possible. On the other hand, if one believes in fundamental eternal principles that should never be violated, that most human beings are essentially weak and wicked when left to their own devices, but that some enlightened individuals are born to lead, then a political system built on the premise of ensuring liberty really makes no sense at all.

## A BIT MORE HISTORY

We said earlier that it would be ludicrous to entrust the masses to making decisions if one believes that those masses are intrinsically capricious, weak, and depraved. It would be equally ludicrous to do so if principles are absolute and knowable only by knowing God, particularly if one assumes that most people do not know God. And indeed, "ludicrous" is precisely what most civilizations throughout recorded human history have thought of the idea of a truly empowered mass public.

Indeed, as we mentioned earlier, due to a lack of faith in the capacity (both moral and rational) of citizens, the Constitutional founders designed a system that afforded citizens far more political rights than they had enjoyed as British subjects, but was more than careful to rein in popular sovereignty (e.g., Madison, 1787). It was just such thinking that led to the creation of (a) the electoral college, (b) indirect election of senators, and (c) judicial appointment (rather than election), among other institutional arrangements designed to create layers between the public and its representative government.

Such historical cynicism toward this notion of liberal popular democracy also stands to reason, because the Enlightenment-style humanism and strong egalitarianism that underlie liberal popular democracy are themselves radical ideas as well. Not only do those ideas stand in stark contrast to the authoritarian modes of thought that dominated most civilizations prior to the Enlightenment, but they have also offended the sensibilities of many historical vanguards of representative government.

Of course, as Western society has evolved over the course of the past two centuries, such leeriness toward liberal popular democracy has clearly fallen out of favor (especially rhetorically). Democracy has not only outgrown its pejorative connotation; it has grown exponentially. Without a doubt, the masses have substantially more policymaking influence in American politics now than they did in the early days of the Republic, a trend that grew steadily over time and is consistent with similar trends in most European and Latin American nations as well (with significant fits and starts, of course).

However, the apparent growth of liberal popular democracy, both in the United States and globally, masks a lingering skepticism toward the principle of humanism that underlies it—a skepticism that is distinctly pronounced in the United States. Furthermore, as has been demonstrated repeatedly, strong anti-democratic currents of dogmatism and authoritarianism remain in Western society, typically needing only the emergence of some significant perception of threat to surface and sometimes trigger the willing abandonment of many liberal democratic ideals (e.g., Hetherington & Weiler, 2009; Stenner, 2005).

In a nutshell, then, to this point we have argued that a general suspicion toward humanism and basic egalitarianism, along with an inclination toward dogmatism and authoritarianism, fosters an instinctive reluctance to embrace fully the principles of liberal popular democracy, which thereby leads to a preference for trustee-style representation. Conversely, the embrace of humanism and basic egalitarianism, at the expense of dogmatism and authoritarianism, should inspire liberal democratic sympathies—which are then manifested in preferences for instructed delegate-style representation.

This leads us to the next stage of our argument, which is that prioritizing humanistic and egalitarian beliefs over authoritarian and dogmatic ones is something that can be observed more regularly in some sectors of the population than in others. So who are these people? In the next section, we point to secular and religiously progressive citizens as that group of Americans most likely to decry dogmatic authoritarianism and embrace egalitarian humanism (and therefore prefer instructed delegates), while cultural traditionalists and especially evangelical Christians are the ones most likely to do the opposite. We discuss several reasons why we expect this to be the case.

## CHRISTIAN TRADITIONALISM AND TRUSTEE-STYLE REPRESENTATION

There are several characteristics of traditionalistic Christian belief and culture, and especially evangelical Christian belief and culture, that may diminish believers' enthusiasm toward some of the values that underpin liberal popular democracy. By extension, those aspects of belief and culture would also engender preferences for trustee-style representation. We begin by explaining why authoritarianism, anti-egalitarianism, and especially dogmatism may be more frequently observed among traditionalists than among many other Christians or secular people. From there, we consider a few doctrinal beliefs held by many evangelicals that dispose them to resist humanistic modes of thought, thereby inclining them even further toward the trustee style of representation.[12]

[12] Of course, religious differences routinely influence politics in ways that have nothing to do with differences in traditionalism. For perhaps the most careful and thorough explication of these dynamics, see Djupe and Gilbert (2009).

## DISTINGUISHING EVANGELICAL AND TRADITIONALISTIC CHRISTIANS FROM OTHER CHRISTIANS

Before we can proceed to fleshing out our argument, we must clarify what we mean by "cultural traditionalists and especially evangelical Christians." Evangelical Christianity can be distinguished from Catholicism or mainline Protestantism in several ways.[13] First, evangelicals place greater focus on the idea of salvation, or an individual's eternal life after death in heaven, as opposed to improving social conditions in this life. Second, they believe that to achieve that salvation, one *must* have a "born-again" experience, consciously deciding to give one's life (or heart) to Jesus at some point of awareness, as opposed to being nurtured in the faith from birth. Third, this decision *must* be made for Christ specifically—not for God in general, or to any other figure; Jesus is the *only* way. Fourth, evangelicals believe that if one does not make such a decision, one is automatically subject to eternal damnation, regardless of one's behavior. That is, everything is dependent on the decision that one makes, thereby making the religion quite individualistic in that sense. Fifth, they believe that upon making that decision, they are able to have an intense personal relationship (through prayer, Bible study, and meditation) with what they consider to be a living Christ. Sixth, because salvation achieved via the born-again experience is the primary focus of the faith, they place much greater efforts on proselytizing (e.g., evangelism, missions, or "witnessing") than do other Christians.[14]

The Protestant denominations that are usually classified as evangelical include Southern Baptists and most other Baptists (but not the American Baptists), charismatic/Pentecostal traditions such as the Assemblies of God, Church of God, and many others, Wisconsin/Missouri Synod Lutherans, some small sects of Presbyterians (but not the largest sect, the Presbyterian Church of the USA), some Methodists (but not very many outside the South), and many other independent "Bible

[13] The following distinctions between contemporary evangelical Christians, fundamentalists, and other types of Christians are drawn from several sources (Fowler et al., 2010; Marsden, 2006; Williams, 2008), all of which reinforce each other and our own understanding of this subject.

[14] Of course, not all evangelicals necessarily subscribe to each and every one of these things. But each of them is part of what scholars would include as part of the distinction. What we have done, then, is describe the "ideal type."

churches," "Alliance churches," etc., that proudly claim to be "nondenominational."

*However*, one can now find evangelicals (as we have defined them) sitting in the pews of virtually any Protestant church (whether traditionally characterized as "evangelical" or not) on most Sundays, and anywhere in the country (but especially in the South and Midwest). By most estimates, if evangelicals are identified according to belief/practice, as we have here, rather than by denominational affiliation, they represent somewhere between 30% and 35% of the U.S. population (e.g., Pew, 2008).

Many (perhaps most) evangelicals are also *biblical fundamentalists*, who believe that a particular interpretation of the Bible is absolutely inerrant and completely authoritative (though not necessarily literal), even in matters pertaining to history or science, and focus on uncompromising adherence in certain particulars of dogma as being essential to the Faith (e.g., Original Sin, Virgin Birth, Substitutionary Atonement for sin, Resurrection, Second Coming).

However, and importantly, it is certainly possible to be a fundamentalist without being an evangelical, and vice versa. Indeed, many Catholics, Mormons, and Jewish people can be classified as fundamentalists in the sense that they hold absolute and uncompromising interpretations of scripture (whether the Bible, the Book of Mormon, the Tanakh or Talmud), even though they would not necessarily abide by many other aspects of evangelicalism, such as the emphasis on being born again.

Because the term "fundamentalist" has become somewhat pejorative in common parlance, and because it does have a historical reference point within Protestantism (dating to the early 20th century), we use the term "traditionalistic" Christian when referring to the larger group of Christians that includes most evangelicals but also those kindred spirits within other Christian (and even Jewish) traditions who hold uncompromising doctrinal views and emphasize them as the essence of their faith.

Christian traditionalists, whether evangelical Protestants or conservative Catholics, also tend to attend church more "religiously" than do nontraditionalistic Christians (e.g., Pew, 2008), though this is certainly not always the case.

### *Penchant Toward Dogmatism*

Perhaps the most obvious reason evangelicals and some other Christian traditionalists may at times resist instructed delegate-style representation is that they are disproportionately predisposed toward dogmatic modes of thought, which as we discussed earlier, contradict the liberal popular democratic vision of self-government. While traditionalistic Christian readers may find that statement provocative, upon inspection we think it cannot really be denied. As we noted earlier, religion is by definition faith-based, which means (also by definition) that it demands adherence based on an absolute commitment to certain beliefs, many of which cannot be put to empirical test. Indeed, if a set of beliefs has been arrived at entirely by reason, or after careful empirical testing—with no faith component—it is not really a religion at all. It may be an ideology, or perhaps a philosophy, but it is not a religion. Religious dogma is called "dogma" for a reason. Furthermore, if one *is* willing to compromise one's religious principles, then those principles were not really adhered to religiously in the first place—because, again, that is part of the definition of religion.

Of course, this is not to say that traditionalistic religious doctrine has no grounding in reason, or that people who are religious in this traditionalistic sense do not use reason when deciding what they believe. To be sure, many faith traditions have long histories of connecting faith to reason. It is merely to say that when all is said and done, religious faith must include an element of dogmatism for it to properly be considered religious faith. And so, by extension, those who practice that faith in a serious way necessarily adopt a dogmatic point of view to at least some extent.

So if religious faith has an element of dogmatism to it by definition, why do we single out traditionalistic Christians from other Christians or other religious adherents as those most inclined toward dogmatism? Well, first of all, our argument does not exclude traditionalistic adherents of other religions. Indeed, if the United States contained large numbers of Orthodox Muslims or Orthodox Jews, they would be included in our argument and our analysis. But the United States does not, and so we do not.[15] As for why we single out traditionalistic Christians from other Christians when it comes to dogmatism, we consider it a matter of degree. That is, as mentioned above, while all religious

[15] To be sure, the United States does include concentrated populations of Orthodox Jewish Americans. However, concentrated populations in particular geographical areas would still not produce enough respondents in representative survey samples of U.S. citizens to conduct meaningful statistical tests. We could in theory oversample such populations, but that would be prohibitively expensive.

faith must by definition include an element of dogmatism, some religious varieties are undeniably more dogmatic than others. Christian traditionalists, in particular, include elements of dogmatism *as part of their definition of what it means to be a Christian*, in ways that other Christians do not. For example, as listed above, part of evangelical dogma is a belief that people *must* go to either heaven or hell after they die, and that they *must* make a decision for Christ at some point in their lives if they want to be "saved." In this worldview, no other path to salvation exists. These positions are nothing if not black and white.

Furthermore, Protestant fundamentalism as a historical movement (out of which modern evangelicals grew) arose specifically so as to emphasize the absolute commitment to certain elements of Christian dogma as the essence of Christianity—in response to progressive Christian groups who were trying to emphasize discipleship or were applying intellectual skepticism to some pieces of scripture. In that way, evangelical Christianity, as distinct from other types of Christian belief and practice, is rooted in dogmatism.

That said, we want to reiterate once more that dogmatism is far from unique to religious traditionalists. One can be absolutely committed to and unwilling to compromise on any number of beliefs or ideas. We can easily identify plenty of people who are dogmatic in their defense of liberalism, the scientific method, or the Steelers. However, belief in or support for these principles is not dogmatic by definition, in the same way that Christian traditionalism is, and so if we are trying to identify particular demographic groups that are most likely to exhibit dogmatic habits of thought, Christian traditionalists stand out.

### *Disposition Toward Authoritarianism and Anti-Egalitarianism*

While Christian traditionalists are certainly not authoritarian by definition in the same way that they are dogmatic by definition, they have been shown to hold hierarchical views of humanity, crave leadership, admire the military, and employ authoritarian parenting styles more frequently than do secular citizens or other types of religious adherents (e.g., Altemeyer, 1996).[16]

[16] It is important to point out that we are not implying that traditionalistic Christian religiosity *causes* authoritarianism (or dogmatism, for that matter). If anything, we suspect that the causal arrow runs in the opposite direction, given that these orientations are probably deep-seated personality traits that may even be transmitted genetically, in part (e.g., Alford, Funk, & Hibbing, 2005; Gerber et al., 2010). Thus, in discussing these correlations, we are merely pointing out that we can expect to observe authoritarian tendencies more readily among traditionalistic Christians than among seculars or nontraditionalistic Christians.

Moreover, such a tendency to submit to authority can be seen in studies revealing that within different types of church congregations, traditionalists are far more uniform in their attitudes, congregation-wide, than are nontraditionalists (e.g., Pew, 2008)—perhaps in part because they are more likely than nontraditionalists to adopt the theological and political views of the pastor (see Fowler et al., 2010).[17]

By extension, then, traditionalists necessarily also tend to feel some relative discomfort toward at least some forms of strong egalitarianism. Again, they certainly do not see other religious beliefs as equal to their own, and so those who hold those other beliefs cannot possibly be equally capable of leadership or decision-making. It is certainly possible, however, and perhaps likely, that anti-egalitarian sentiment on the part of traditionalistic Christians may be restricted to perceived differences between *believers* and *nonbelievers*. That is, within the traditionalistic community, fellow congregants may be viewed as equals and treated as such. By extension, it is highly unlikely that traditionalistic Christians tend to perceive hierarchical differences between persons as innate. Rather, it stands to reason that such believers would attribute differences across individuals to either the choice to reject the faith or the lack of an opportunity to embrace it.

### *Anti-Humanism*

The factors linking evangelicals, in particular, to anti-humanism are stronger, and more numerous, than those linking evangelicals to authoritarianism, dogmatism, or anti-egalitarianism. The reason is that there are several anti-humanistic doctrinal beliefs held disproportionately by evangelicals, which do not necessarily extend to other Christian traditionalists. Hence, it is really based on the anti-humanistic aspect of evangelical Christianity, rather than the dogmatic, authoritarian, or anti-egalitarian tendencies of evangelical Christians, that lead us to expect evangelicals (in the aggregate) to be especially sympathetic toward the trustee style of representation—even more so than mainline Protestant traditionalists, Catholic traditionalists, other religious traditionalists, or nonreligious traditionalists.

*1. Belief in a Hard-Edged Version of Original Sin*: Although evangelicals certainly champion humanity as having inherent (even precious) value, they take as an article of faith that humanity is anything but intrinsically capable and good. Dating back to the Calvinists's Synod of Dordt (1618–9), conservative

[17] Of the Christian traditions, Catholicism is perhaps the most hierarchically organized. It may be the case, then, that the authoritarian stream of influence is more pronounced among Catholic, rather than Protestant, traditionalists.

Protestants have held that original sin renders human nature not just fallible with good intentions (as Catholics, mainline Protestants, and other Christians tend to believe), but *utterly depraved* and helpless without the hand of God to guide them. Furthermore, this belief is considered one of the fundamental tenets of the faith for evangelical Protestants (Dixon, 1910–1915). Naturally, then, many traditionalistic Christians are deeply suspicious of secular human motives, or the ability of secular efforts to improve society through science, higher learning, media dissemination of information, or (especially) the government (e.g., Williams, 2008). Such a perspective is, by definition, at odds with the more sanguine views of human nature and secular institutions that are embodied in humanism.

It is not difficult, then, to see how such a cynical view of human nature would disincline one from intuitively trusting the instructed delegate model of representative democracy. After all, if ordinary citizens and the institutions designed to represent them are inherently wicked, then the idea of granting them the power to make binding decisions on society, based on nothing more than their caprice, sounds like a ridiculous recipe for disaster. It obviously makes much more sense, assuming this interpretation of original sin, to do everything in one's power to identify leaders who are inspired by God, elect them, and entrust them to make decisions that are guided by those eternal principles.

2. *Focus on Individual Salvation*: As noted in the textbox above, while evangelicals participate regularly in charitable activities, the focus of the faith is on saving individual souls from eternal damnation. Indeed, although evangelicals continually reach out to their local communities (as well as to the world more broadly), the primary aim underlying such efforts is typically evangelism rather than general community-building or the promotion of social progress. Again, it is not that evangelicals do not care about "making the world a better place"; they simply do not place nearly as much emphasis on such worldly pursuits as do the Catholic, Jewish, and mainline/progressive Christian traditions (e.g., Wald, 2003; Wuthnow, 1999)—believing instead that worldly problems would take care of themselves if more people would accept Jesus as savior. Indeed, fundamentalism as a Protestant movement (which eventually morphed into contemporary evangelicalism) began as a reaction in part to what they saw as the heresy of the Social Gospel movement, which had aimed to place greater focus on collective, worldly goals rather than soul-saving (e.g., Marsden, 2006).

Such religious individualism—a focus on the next life, as opposed to this one, and on individual souls, rather than collective social progress—is nearly the antithesis of humanism, and easily lends itself to a preference for trustee-style representation. As Putnam (2000) has argued, religious individualism leads to "bonding-group social capital," or within-group solidarity, which is detrimental to social trust, solidarity, and reciprocity across the larger community. Religious collectivism, on the other hand, which focuses on collective social betterment rather than soul-saving, and is practiced by more mainline Protestant, Catholic, and Jewish believers, generates "bridging-group social capital," which then serves to enhance the democratic building blocks of trust, reciprocity, and so forth across members of different social groups. Such bridging social capital enhances the same democratic building blocks that religious individualism dilutes.

Putnam further argues that as bonding-group capital grows at the expense of bridging-group capital, general interest in other citizens' policy preferences plummets—especially those considered to be non-Christians, a conclusion that Wuthnow (1999) also reaches. This dynamic would also suggest greater trustee-style representation. Hill and Matsubayashi (2008) put this idea to a direct empirical test, finding that community leaders are in fact less responsive to citizen demands in communities containing large concentrations of evangelicals and other traditionalists, and more responsive in communities containing large numbers of mainline Protestants.

3. *Quasi-Calvinistic Faith in God's Will:* As we just mentioned, evangelicals tend to focus on what they believe will happen in the next life rather than in this one. However, when they do consider the goings-on of *this* life, they tend to believe, more so than do other Christians (and than seculars, obviously), in the idea that God has a very specific plan for both individuals and nations—a historical blueprint of how events should unfold to everyone's benefit, if people choose to follow that will.

This notion of God being actively involved in even the smallest minutiae of human endeavors manifests the Calvinistic roots of conservative Protestantism. While evangelicals reject the traditional Calvinist doctrine that humans lack any capacity whatsoever to determine their fate, they do believe that God's plan for one's life will be carried out if one is willing to surrender one's will to God. Such thoroughgoing belief in the doctrine of God's will completely contradicts humanism's assertions of man's independence and capacity. The doctrine also contradicts egalitarianism's claims, by the way, to human capacity being roughly comparable across individuals, because (according to the doctrine) some people choose to follow God's will and some do not; those who do not would not be considered equally trustworthy to those who do.

These contradictions provide another reason to expect that traditionalistic Christians should tend to resist humanism as a value and thus to like trustee-style representation more than other Americans do. After all, why should we want lawmakers to pay much attention to the wishes of constituents if we think that those constituents largely reflect a fallen world (including not only the unchurched but also liberal Catholics, mainline Protestants, and followers of other religions)—meaning their wishes reflect the foolishness of their "fallen natures" and would thereby thwart God's will if they were to be enacted into law? Better to play it safe and trust the lawmaker's internal judgment (assuming the lawmaker in question is trusted as "one of our own," of course).[18]

## SUMMARY AND CAVEATS, SO FAR

So, to summarize the chapter to this point, we have argued that preferences for instructed delegate-style representation are partially a function of an underlying penchant for liberal popular democracy (rather than republicanism), which is itself predicated on the values of humanism and basic egalitarianism. These values, or aspects of them at least, contradict authoritarian and dogmatic modes of thought, which are the orientations that dampen one's enthusiasm for the more democratic model. Therefore, we posit that individuals who instinctively prioritize humanistic and egalitarian visions over certainty, authority, and sacred moral traditions are more likely to prefer instructed delegate-style representation to its trustee-style alternative. Finally, we suggest that while such people may come in many stripes, one place to find a lot of them is in traditionalistic Christian churches (especially those traditionally labeled as "evangelical," but also within many United Methodist and Presbyterian traditions, among others).

For the purposes of trying to achieve some semblance of clarity and to minimize tedium, our argument may at times have included less discussion of the nuances, exceptions, and contradictions inherent in human behavior

[18] As Fenno (1978), Fiorina (1989), and especially Bianco (1994) have pointed out, many if not most politicians put enormous amounts of effort into constituency casework (if we are talking about legislators) and other non-policy-related activities that are designed to build trust within their constituencies, so that they can then exercise independent judgment on policy without worrying as much about suffering a backlash when that judgment contradicts their constituents' wishes. We suspect that those politicians who represent traditionalistic Christian constituencies are just as skilled at doing this as are politicians representing any other type of constituency, and that such constituencies are just as likely as others to be convinced. Accordingly, we suggest that most traditionalistic Christians come to see their personal representative as a trusted ally and kindred spirit, and are therefore willing to trust him or her with policy decisions.

than a wide-lens picture of such behavior would reveal. There are, however, a couple of caveats that are very important for us to mention. Most importantly, we are absolutely *not* claiming that Christianity *per se*—or even evangelical Christianity—necessarily contradicts the principles underlying liberal popular democracy. In fact, there are a good many reasons to think precisely the opposite. Indeed, many have interpreted the teachings of Jesus as radically egalitarian (e.g., Crossan, 1994). Furthermore, solid evidence exists that the rise of Christianity in the 4th century contributed greatly to an expanded recognition of human rights (e.g., Stark, 1996). And to be sure, one of the notions underlying the Protestant Reformation was that everyone has the capacity to interpret the Bible for oneself, which is certainly consistent with the principles of the Enlightenment and the representative forms of government that followed (Mitchell, 1992). What is more, in colonial America, the congregationalism of the Puritan church may have laid the foundation for some popular democracy (relatively speaking) in the colonies (Miller, 1991). And throughout American history, Christians (including many evangelicals) have had a major hand in several egalitarian movements, including abolitionism, "free-silver" populism, women's suffrage, and agitation for African American civil rights. Finally, as we mentioned above, to the extent that traditionalistic Christianity is empirically correlated with "the common man," in contradistinction to "secular elites," traditionalistic movements may draw upon popular democratic methods and rhetoric. To be absolutely clear, then, we want to emphasize that we do *not* claim Christianity itself to be inherently unreasonable, antithetical to democracy, or anything else like that.

What we *are* saying, rather, is that authoritarian and/or dogmatic mindsets *of almost any kind* steer people away from the desire to maximize popular sovereignty, which we argue is best manifested in instructed delegate-style representation. And so, because *a particular brand* of devotion—what we have called Christian traditionalism—tends to correlate with authoritarianism and is by definition dogmatic, we suggest that such traditionalistic believers instinctively tend to prefer trustee-style representation to the instructed delegate style. We further argue that particular doctrinal elements of the evangelical version of the faith—especially when adhered to in an absolutist way—logically lead believers even further away from the values of liberal popular democracy, and by extension the instructed delegate model of representation.

Additionally, we do not contend that antipathy toward humanism and egalitarianism, or sympathy toward dogmatism or authoritarianism, are the only worldview-based factors that might matter in the shaping of instinctive preferences for one style of representation or the other. We do, however, see these as the most readily identifiable and theoretically justifiable factors—as we discussed in the previous section—and so we think focusing on them is simply a good way to kick off what is this inaugural attempt at understanding the intrinsic underpinnings of representation-style preferences.

To conclude this series of caveats, then, we want to make clear that if one were to use our theory to predict the representation-style preferences of any single individual—evangelical or not, Christian or not—there would be a lot of "misses" associated with that prediction. However, once those errors cancel out, we think certain *patterns* of behavior will stand out—that evangelicals and other cultural traditionalists tend to prefer trustee-style representation more often than do other citizens. As a byproduct of those patterns, we suggest that trustee-style representation is also associated with modern conservative Republicanism. In the next section, we flesh out that claim.

## THE PARTISAN CONNECTION AND THE RED/BLUE CULTURE WARS

Historically speaking or in the abstract, there are no strong reasons to believe that support for trustee-style representation should necessarily reflect ideologically conservative goals more often than ideologically liberal ones. After all, while authoritarianism is correlated with modern *cultural* conservatism to some degree (see, especially, Hetherington & Weiler, 2009), it is not automatically correlated with free-market conservatism. Dogmatism bears even less of a necessary correlation to economic conservatism (but see Jost et al., 2003). And when it comes to traditionalistic Christianity, it was certainly not always associated with the ideological Right in the way it is now. Many progressives were moralistic in their inspiration—reflecting not a faith in the will of the public but rather a desire to do "the right thing," policy-wise, in spite of public opinion.[19] And in that sense, such examples would support our basic theory that traditionalistic Christians tend to prefer a republic of trustees, not a democracy of instructed delegates, regardless of whether their policy interests

[19] A particularly useful modern example of an evangelical politician who tended to behave as a trustee, but in pursuit of more liberal causes, can be observed in the presidency of Jimmy Carter—a Sunday School teacher and the first American president to openly identify as a "born-again" Christian. Carter repeatedly made policy decisions that were not very popular with the public, including the attempted switch to the metric system, a more sustainable energy policy, a foreign policy centered on human rights, and the boycotting of the 1980 Summer Olympics.

align with the ideological Left or Right, and regardless of whether they tend to identify as Democrats or Republicans.[20]

However, while it is true that at different points in American political history, traditionalistic Christians have served as loyal foot-soldiers marching for both progressive and conservative armies (and, as such, for both the Democratic and Republican parties), the partisan identities of traditionalistic Christians have become much more one-sided over the course of the past generation or so. They have become the most reliable Republican constituency in the country, by far. Given that recent trend, we must ask whether the religious and value-based connections to one or the other style of representation have had partisan repercussions over the course of the past 30 years.

The answer, from our perspective, is "of course." As a great deal of research has made abundantly clear (for a good starting point, see Layman, 2001), the Republican Party began attracting Christian traditionalists during the 1960s and gradually established control of this constituency during the course of the next 40 years. Simultaneously, the ever-rising numbers of secular Americans started flocking to the Democratic Party. This pattern culminated in the now-famous Red and Blue electoral maps that characterized the elections of 1988 through 2008, in which electoral victory for Republicans corresponded very closely to the percentage of traditionalistic Christians in a given county or state. Therefore, if such GOP-leaning traditionalists tend to prefer trustees—as we have been arguing is the case—it would mean that over the past 30 years or so (and especially over the past 10), Republican leadership would equal trustee-style leadership more times than not.

At this point we should note that the clash between Christian traditionalists and seculars/religious progressives (and its implications for partisan politics) is at the heart of the Culture Wars thesis (e.g., Hunter, 1991). As we mentioned in Chapter 1, Hunter has explicitly claimed that the preeminent modern political cleavage in the United States is no less than a conflict over whether the Enlightenment should be repealed, with Republican Christian traditionalists waving the banner for its repeal. And in many ways, Hunter's bold claim has received considerable empirical support (e.g., Abramowitz

[20] Some readers might wonder where Jerry Falwell's "Moral Majority" (1970s–80s) fits into this discussion. Importantly, it is not clear that the leaders of the organization used the term "majority" to suggest that the conservative views they espoused on public education, abortion, women's rights, gay rights, and foreign policy were necessarily reflective of the numerical majority of U.S. citizens. Rather, the term "majority" may have referred to a period of maturity, such as when a child reaches adulthood, or the "age of majority."

& Saunders, 1998; Barker & Tinnick, 2005; Hetherington & Weiler, 2009; Layman, 2001).[21]

As we also pointed out in Chapter 1, some scholars have argued that such "Culture War" language is too hyperbolic, rightfully pointing out that the country is not nearly as polarized along these dimensions as Hunter and some others would have us believe (see Bartels, 2006; Fiorina et al., 2005; Gelman et al., 2008). And other scholars have demonstrated how the cultural conflict that does exist in the United States forms along quite a few other fronts besides the religious ones to which Hunter points (e.g., Leege et al., 2001). It is not in dispute, however, that the dimensions of political conflict in the United States have been extended to include cultural matters, and that partisanship and electoral outcomes have become quite predictable based on those matters, especially differences in religious perspective. In fact, the movement of religious traditionalists into the Republican fold is one of the most easily recognizable developments within American politics over the course of the past 40 years.

If our theoretical argument is borne out empirically, we will have uncovered evidence that cultural conflict in the United States extends well beyond what Hunter or anyone else has envisioned. Indeed, we will have discovered that "Red America" and "Blue America" differ in ways that are significantly more consequential than tastes in beer, Sunday habits, or even electoral choices; we may need to stop talking about Red and Blue states on the electoral map and start talking about Red and Blue styles of governance.

While our suggestion that political representation now comes in Red and Blue partisan shades is new, some earlier work has foreshadowed it. Broadly, historians Isserman and Kazin (2007) go so far as to claim that the Burkean understanding of trustee-style representation actually undergirds contemporary American conservatism. Furthermore, Hacker and Pierson (2005) show empirically that conservative Republican governance tends to not reflect constituent opinion very well. Additionally, in keeping with the particular religious-cultural underpinnings of our argument, Rosenthal (2009) observes that state legislators tend to say they are not particularly interested in constituent

[21] This perspective is also consistent with the work of Jonathan Haidt and his colleagues, who in various books and articles have shown that liberals and conservatives have different habits of moral reasoning, with conservatives moralizing across five dimensions (harm/care, fairness/reciprocity, ingroup/loyalty, authority/respect, and purity/sanctity), whereas liberals tend to focus only on the first two, and often view injunctions regarding ingroup loyalty, authority, and purity as immoral. For an overview of the various studies, and accompanying references, see Kessebir and Haidt (2010).

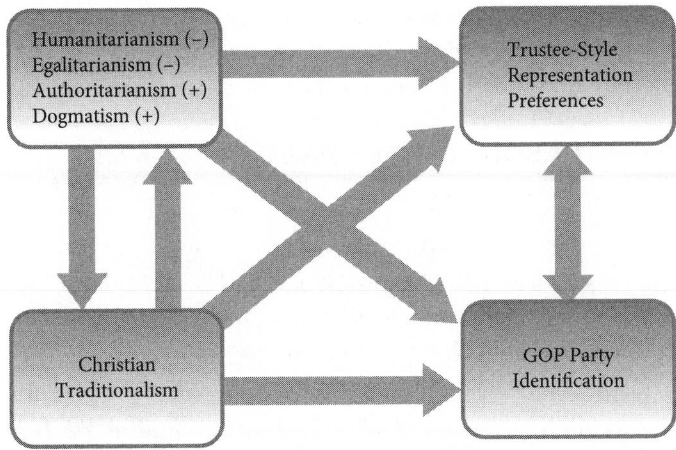


*Figure 3.1* Theoretical Path Model of Democratic Values, Cultural Orientation, Representation Preference, and Political Alignment

opinion when it comes to Culture War issues like abortion and gay rights, preferring to follow their own judgment on such issues.[22] And in support of our larger claim that cultural traditionalism is associated with suspicion toward some liberal popular democratic principles, Hibbing and Theiss-Morse (2002) report that apathy for democratic processes is statistically associated with policy conservatism and Republican partisanship. Hibbing and Theiss-Morse did not attempt to explain this finding (which was, after all, tangential to their analysis), but they noted that the explanation must stem from "deeper reasons" not articulated in their main thesis. We may have identified at least one of those deeper reasons.

Figure 3.1 presents a graphical summary of the theoretical argument we have laid out in this chapter. As the figure tries to show, we want to reemphasize that our theory does not suggest a clear, unidirectional causal relationship between secular progressivism and the values of liberal popular democracy. As we have discussed, we imagine the causality flowing in both directions between these concepts. All that matters, for our theory, is that there is a relationship. Moreover, we do not suggest a causal relationship at all between

[22] Rosenthal does not examine differences between Republican and Democratic legislators in this regard, but we think the fact that the prototypical Culture Wars issues are the ones legislators mention as the ones about which they are more likely to follow their consciences is at least suggestive that the process we have described is at work.

delegate-style representation preferences and Democratic partisanship. We merely suggest that the two are empirically associated because of their shared predictability according to cultural progressivism.

## CONCLUSION: WHAT ABOUT THE TEA PARTY?

To be clear, as we mentioned earlier, we see no reason to expect the less culturally traditionalistic wings of the Republican Party to be any more inclined toward trustee-style representation than anyone else would be. Indeed, our theory does not envision any kind of independent association between economic attitudes (pro-market vs. pro-labor) and representation-style preferences.

Again, we can even imagine that a relationship *in the opposite direction* could emerge: the more committed one is to *laissez-faire* capitalism, the more one might prefer instructed delegate-style representation, because both perspectives share a humanistic foundation. That is, the theory underlying a capitalist system—which really did not catch fire until the Age of Enlightenment—depends upon individual human beings being capable of making sound economic decisions, disciplined enough to pursue their goals with vigor, and decent enough to not simply lie, cheat, and steal one's way to maximizing profit. It also rests, normatively speaking, on the notion that individuals are innately equal to enough of a degree that most can achieve success if they are willing to sweat, save, and think. Thus, it stems from some of the same underlying values that liberal democracy does. Indeed, it would not surprise us if libertarian Republicans—those who embrace free-market capitalism but reject cultural traditionalism—actually tend to prefer instructed delegates.

So what to make of those who are *both* economically conservative and culturally conservative? Given that we already know such "ideological constraint" across issue realms is highly predicated on a predisposition toward dogmatism and/or authoritarianism (e.g., Barker & Tinnick, 2005), we predict that such individuals do tend to prefer trustee-style leadership in the same way that other cultural traditionalists do, for the same reasons that we discussed above pertaining to authoritarianism and dogmatism.

We think the conservative Tea Party movement illustrates this point well. We have watched the movement with great fascination since its inception in 2009. It began, ostensibly at least, as a movement by fed-up citizens who were primarily upset about fiscal issues—the growth of the federal debt and the size of government in general. In that way, it was characterized in its early days as a libertarian crusade, and therefore as distinct from the Religious Right and other culturally traditionalistic wings of the conservative "family." But as time has passed, it has become clear that the Tea Party and the Christian Right have joined forces, morphing into more or less the same movement (for all practical purposes, at least). That is, while the Tea Party still contains some libertarian elements, it is made up, for the most part, by ideologically constrained conservatives who are far more likely than other Americans to identify as evangelicals, to believe the Bible is inerrant, and to report that religion is the most important factor in determining their issue attitudes (e.g., Clement & Green, 2011).

As such, the patterns of behavior we have observed by Tea Party activists—and especially Tea Party legislators—have not been surprising; indeed, they strike us as very consistent with the story we have been telling. During repeated policy debates during 2009 through 2011, at both the national and state levels, Tea Party caucusers demonstrated that compromise with Democrats (or even with moderate Republicans) was anathema, even though they had public opinion working decidedly against them. Indeed, many of them were ready (eager, even) to (a) strip public employees of collective bargaining rights (fall of 2010), (b) let the government shut down over budget disagreements (spring of 2011), or even (c) let the United States default on its debts (summer of 2011) rather than cave to pressure from the public at large (which was so strong, at the end of the debt default issue, that Internet servers on Capitol Hill crashed from the volume of incoming e-mails). Why? Because they believed that standing firm was the "right" thing to do (e.g., Howe, 2011).

On the other hand, given the ideological character of many of the constituencies represented by Tea Party conservatives, perhaps the legislators were not really bucking majority opinion *in their particular districts* (even as they were clearly defying national opinion polls). If so, it would be hard to really classify their behavior as either instructed delegate style or trustee style. Perhaps, though, it didn't matter too much to these representatives whether their local constituencies agreed with them or not on the merits of those policies; these lawmakers may have recognized that their constituents would view apparent wishy-washiness more unfavorably than they would view policy disagreement. That scenario is one of the possibilities we will consider in the next couple of chapters. Generally, in Chapter 4, we will begin putting the theory we have laid out in this chapter to empirical test, focusing on the values and preferences of citizens. In later chapters, we then connect the dots between citizens and lawmakers, and ultimately examine how successfully the representation styles of lawmakers can be predicted based on this theory.

CHAPTER 4

# Mapping the Cultural and Partisan Divide in Representation Preferences

In the previous chapter, we provided the theoretical rationale for why we expect cultural traditionalists (and especially evangelical Christians) to prefer trustee-style representation more instinctively than do other types of Americans. In this chapter, we consider the extent to which these hypothesized linkages stand up to empirical scrutiny.

To perform all the analyses described in this chapter, we rely upon national survey data collected under the auspices of the 2006–9 Cooperative Election Study (CES), which we described in Chapter 2.[1] The following sections describe the results from a series of multiple regression analyses, each one predicting preferences for either instructed delegates or trustees from, in turn, (1) measures of the value orientations we described in Chapter 3, (2) measures of traditionalistic Christian religiosity, which we have argued bring these value priorities together, and (3) party identification.[2] All of our models control for the standard demographic variables that sometimes predict public opinion as

[1] Details regarding the 2006, 2007, 2008, and 2009 CES data collections can be found at http://projects.iq.harvard.edu/cces/data.

[2] While we were fortunate to obtain enough funding to purchase "modules" on the CES in each of these four years, the number of questions we actually had at our disposal, to place on these surveys, was limited (more so in some years than in others). Accordingly, to test all of our ideas, we had to pick and choose which questions we would place on which years' surveys. We would have obviously preferred to place all of our questions on all of the surveys, but we had to rely on this second-best option. What this means is that, unfortunately, in the analyses we describe below, some of our hypotheses could only be tested with one or two years' worth of survey data, making the results obtained from those particular hypothesis tests somewhat less generalizable than those that were tested with all four years of survey data. It is our hope that other scholars will examine those relationships, especially, with more years of survey data, to see how well the results we have observed stand up over time.

it pertains to political issues: race, gender, age, income, education, and living in the South. The models also control for Catholic identity, so as to ensure our religion-based findings are not somehow being driven by Catholics.[3]

To capture *general* orientations toward preferring one or the other representation style, as opposed to those that might be affected by idiosyncrasies relating to a specific issue under consideration, a specific year, or the specific institution being considered (executive vs. legislative), we did not use any of the measures described in Chapter 2 that asked respondents to consider representation as it pertained to a specific issue area; we focused our analyses on the general representation preference items.[4] Furthermore, we combined the presidential and legislative preference items into a single scale. To enhance the clarity of our discussion and graphical presentation below, we trichotomized the variable so that "zero" means the respondent consistently prefers for both legislators and presidents to behave like instructed delegates, "one" means that the respondent wants representatives from only one of the institutions to behave like a trustee, and "two" equals a preference that both act as trustees.[5]

---

3 In alternate specifications of our models, we also included variables for the particular year in which the interview took place, whether the respondent viewed herself as part of the political majority in her district, and whether her preferred partisan "team" was in control of Congress at the time of the interview. As expected, viewing oneself as part of the majority is associated with instructed delegate-style preferences, whereas trustee-style preferences are associated with being represented by someone of the same partisan identity. We did not expect these variables to share much variance with our variables of interest, which they did not. As such, we also did not expect them to meaningfully affect the relationships we describe in this chapter—and our expectations were confirmed in that regard as well. Therefore, given that a couple of the models we discuss could not include one or another of these controls (based on differences across years in terms of exactly which items were included on our surveys), we decided to just leave them out of all the models we actually discuss, to maintain consistency across models.

4 In alternate models, we created a large index that combined all of the measures (both the general and those asking about specific issue areas) into a single scale. Those models produced results that are similar to those we report below. We have chosen to report and discuss results from the simpler models here because the items are identical across all four years (which was not the case with the issue-specific representation preference items). We believe that using all four years of data enhances the generalizability of our results.

5 This was the cleanest way we could think of to capture, to some extent at least, preferences for Eulau's (1959) famous vision of "politico"-style representation, which combines elements of the instructed delegate and trustee styles.

This measure serves as the "dependent variable" in all the models we discuss below.[6]

We use multinomial logistic regression to estimate our relationships. We asked ourselves whether it was fair to say that those who express consistent preferences for trustees really want "more" or "less" representation (in such a way as it can be expressed in a quantitatively meaningful way on an ordinal scale) from those who express a preference for delegates. Certainly they want a different style of representation, but not necessarily "more" or "less." Thus, after much consideration, we decided that we needed to treat our trichotomized scale as a nominal variable. As such, the multinomial estimator is the safest choice.[7]

For readers of a more technical bent, all the statistical results from these equations can be observed in the Appendix. Here, though, to make things a little more clear for most readers, we focus our presentation of results on the changes in predicted probabilities of preferring one or the other of the representation styles, according to changes in our various measures of value priorities and religious orientations.[8] In that regard, we tend to focus most on changes associated with the predicted probability that someone would prefer instructed delegate-style representation consistently versus being willing to entrust at least one institutional representative to make choices for her. Thus, one might say that we are interested in knowing how differences in value priorities affect someone's willingness to give away a significant portion of her political voice—even if only to one of the branches of government.

---

[6] There are also statistical reasons for collapsing the scales into dichotomies and then combining them into a trichotomous measure. A 12-point scale is too large to perform an ordered regression technique; at the same time, the Ordinary Least Squares regression assumption of interval-level measurement would have been violated (e.g., on this 12-point scale, there is no reason to believe that the difference between a "3" and a "4" is the same as that between a "9" and a "10"). By contrast, in our 3-point measure, each category is clearly distinct.

[7] We should note, however, that any of these choices we have just discussed, pertaining to measurement of the dependent variable and the statistical estimation technique, do not affect the size or statistical significance of the relationships we report below in any meaningful way. Furthermore, Hausman tests reveal that the independence of irrelevant alternatives assumption—on which multinomial logistic regression depends—is not violated in any of the relationships that we discuss below.

[8] All the results we report are statistically significant at the <.05 level or better. We computed changes in predicted probabilities using the SPOST family of commands in STATA (Long & Freese, 2006).

## THE VALUES OF LIBERAL POPULAR DEMOCRACY AND PREFERENCES REGARDING REPRESENTATION STYLES

The first step in the process is to test our value-based hypotheses that humanists and egalitarians tend to prefer instructed delegates, and that authoritarians and dogmatists tend to prefer trustees. The following subsections test each of these hypotheses, in turn.

*Humanism*: Recall that humanism reflects the degree to which one believes that people are intrinsically decent and capable of making good decisions without the omniscient hand of God to guide them. Accordingly, to measure this concept, we put two questions to respondents.

We begin by looking at an item that gets at the concept directly:

> Please tell us the degree to which you agree or disagree with the following statement: Most ordinary people are naturally capable of making good and wise decisions; they don't necessarily need religion to guide them. Do you strongly agree, agree, disagree, or strongly disagree?

We call this variable *People Not Capable*. Responses were coded on a scale ranging from 0 to 3; the mean is 1.76, meaning that responses skew slightly to the non-humanist side—but only slightly.

Figure 4.1 shows us that those who strongly agree that people are naturally capable of making good decisions without God's help are around 9% more inclined to prefer instructed delegates consistently, and about 12% less inclined

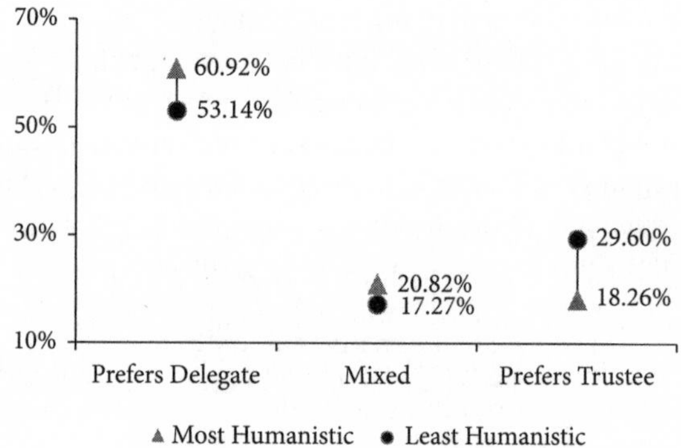


*Figure 4.1* Changes in Delegate/Trustee Preferences by Humanism (Humans Capable)

to prefer trustees consistently, than are those who strongly disagree with the statement. These are not some of the larger effects that we observe in our analysis, but they are meaningful and strongly significant, statistically speaking.

Unfortunately, we were able to include this question only in the 2009 wave of our data collection. As such, the results cannot be considered as generalizable as some others we will report in this chapter.

Fortunately, we were able to ask the following question across all the years in our data collection:

> If you HAD to choose, what would you say is more important to making really important decisions: Faith or Reason? Use the scale below to indicate how strongly you feel about this. You can choose any number on the scale. Please make a choice, even if it is difficult.

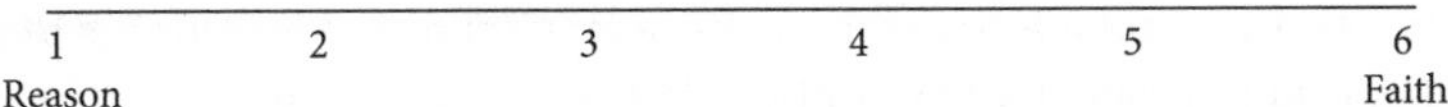


We call this variable *Faith Over Reason*. The responses skew somewhat to the "Reason" side, with the mean falling at 2.9, with a standard deviation of .39.

Figure 4.2 displays the relationship between humanism (or anti-humanism), measured in this way, and representation-style preferences. Strongly preferring faith to reason reduces the probability of preferring instructed delegates, consistently, by almost 16%. Furthermore, this effect is more meaningful than its magnitude would initially suggest because it crosses the magical 50% threshold. That is, while the probability of preferring instructed delegates is .58 for those who indicate that they strongly prefer reason to faith, it is only .42 for those who strongly prefer faith to reason.

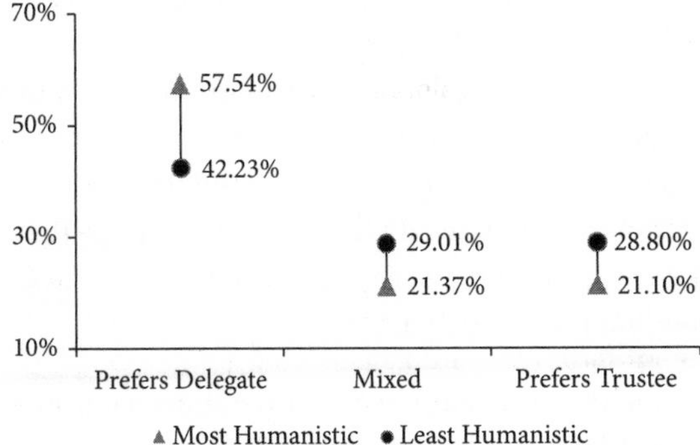


*Figure 4.2* Changes in Delegate/Trustee Preferences by Humanism (Reason vs. Faith)

*Dogmatism*: Another way to interpret the results of this relationship is to see preferences for faith over reason as indicators of dogmatism, or at least dogmatism of a certain religious orientation. Indeed, as we discussed in Chapter 3, while dogmatism and anti-humanism are not the exact same thing (one could be dogmatically humanistic), the two concepts do overlap to some degree, theoretically speaking. More times than not, we expect that anti-humanists would also be dogmatic. So, again, one could choose to interpret the results displayed in Figure 4.2 as evidence of the role that dogmatism plays in orienting citizens toward trustee-style representation.

But we have other survey items that we believe measure dogmatism more directly—at least a form of moral dogmatism. Due to constraints in resources, we were not able to ask these questions on all four years of the surveys we fielded. However, we were able to include them on two of the waves, in 2007 and 2008. The first of these questions asks respondents to consider the degree to which morality is absolute or relativistic. It reads as follows:

> Which of the following two statements best captures your feelings about right and wrong?
>
> 0 = Right and wrong sometimes depend on one's point of view. As society evolves, so should society's view of what is right and wrong.
>
> 1 = Some things are just plain right and others are just plain wrong. This will never change.

Response option "1" corresponds to a black/white or dogmatic mindset, whereas response option "0" captures the perspective of one who sees morality in more contextualistic terms.

The second question is similar, but rather than focusing on whether morality is unchanging, it asks respondents to consider whether morality either is simple or complicated:

> Again, which of the following statements best captures your feelings about right and wrong?
>
> 0 = Right and wrong are sometimes complicated. Reason and science can sometimes help us to determine whether certain things are right or wrong.
>
> 1 = Right and wrong are not complicated and things like science and reason don't have anything to do with it.

Again, we have counted those who chose response option "1" as being more dogmatic than those who chose option "0."

To try to minimize the amount of measurement error associated with our construct, we simply summed responses to these questions. On this resulting 0-to-2 scale, the mean is .93, with a standard deviation of .85, indicating that

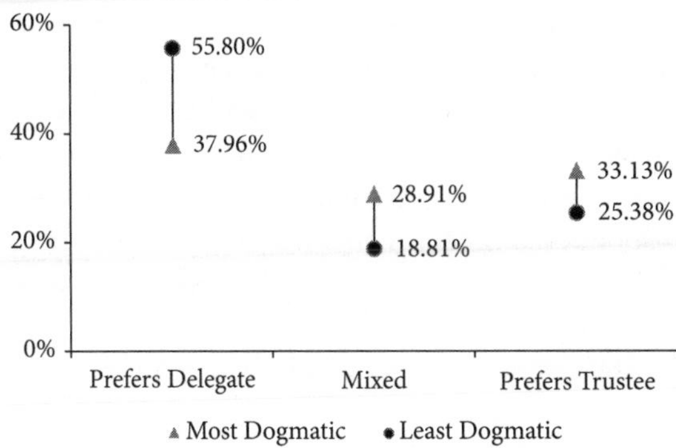


*Figure 4.3* Changes in Delegate/Trustee Preferences by Dogmatism

responses skew slightly toward the non-dogmatic end of the scale, but that there are large numbers of respondents (roughly a third) who fall into the most dogmatic category.

Figure 4.3 displays the degree to which representation preferences are predictable according to different levels of moral dogmatism, as we have measured it.

These models are the most compelling yet: while the probability of consistently preferring instructed delegates is .56 among the least dogmatic respondents, it is only .38 among the most dogmatic, a difference of more than 18%. Even more dramatically, if we look just at the least dogmatic group of respondents, the difference in the probability of consistently preferring instructed delegates over trustees is an impressive 31% (from .56 to .25), while the difference among the most dogmatic is only 5% (from .38 to .33).

*Egalitarianism*: The second value orientation that we identified in Chapter 3 as underlying the liberal popular democratic vision is the degree to which one believes that people are born more or less equal in terms of their ability to be self-determining, and therefore all deserve to have the same political rights. The first way that we attempted to capture such sentiment, which we did in both 2006 and 2008, was by simply asking respondents to indicate the degree to which they believe more needs to be done to ensure equal rights in the United States. Specifically, we asked them to consider the following statement and response scale:

We have gone too far pushing equal rights in this country.

| 1<br>Strongly<br>Agree | 2 | 3 | 4 | 5 | 6<br>Strongly<br>Disagree |
|---|---|---|---|---|---|

Naturally, we chose to label this variable *Equal Rights*. The more a respondent disagrees with the statement, the more egalitarian we consider him or her. The mean is 3.76, almost right at the midpoint, with a standard deviation of 1.81. However, the mean masks the fact that response option 6 was the most popular choice by a fair margin (506 as compared to the next closest option, option 1, which 323 respondents chose). Thus, while there appears to be significant variance in egalitarianism across the American mass public, there are quite a few more egalitarians than not.

Figure 4.4 displays the results of our model, using this item to predict representation preferences.

As the figure shows, these results are also compelling. The most egalitarian of respondents were roughly 16% more likely to consistently prefer instructed delegate-style representation to trustee-style representation than were the least egalitarian respondents (.58 to .42). As a reminder, these results hold up (as do the others presented in this chapter) in the face of a wide swath of control variables traditionally used to predict individual-level attitudes toward political phenomena and leaders.

In an effort to link up our measure to the idea of liberal democracy in a slightly more precise way, in one year of our data collection (2007) we were able to gauge the degree to which citizens seek greater equality of voice in presidential elections. Specifically, we asked respondents to consider the continued utility of electoral college, which as an institution epitomizes the Madisonian vision of a republic that conscientiously restricts popular sovereignty.

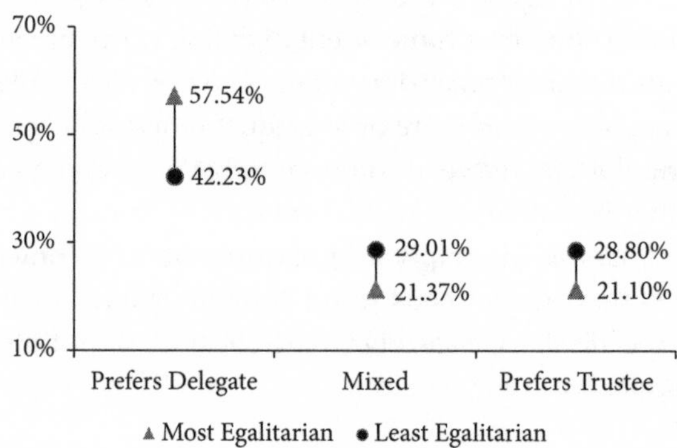


*Figure 4.4* Changes in Delegate/Trustee Preferences by Egalitarianism (Equal Rights)

Specifically, the electoral college clearly gives some citizens more say over who becomes president than other citizens, not only because of differences across states in electors, which do not correspond perfectly to state population, but also because the winner-take-all system of allocating electoral votes (used by all states except Nebraska and Maine) means that every vote for a candidate beyond that one that enables a majority in a given state is worthless to determining the outcome. This reality leads campaigns to focus their energy almost exclusively on swing states, because they know that funds spent in the states that are either safely Democratic or Republican are wasted funds. As such, citizens living in safe states do not get as much of an opportunity to meet candidates and try to influence them.

Without a doubt, then, eliminating the electoral college as the means by which Americans choose presidents and replacing it with a direct popular vote would not only represent a significant expansion of popular sovereignty in the United States, just as moving to directly elected Senators did in 1913 with the ratification of the Seventeenth Amendment, but it would also make the distribution of electoral power across citizens considerably more equal.

To capture attitudes toward the electoral college, we asked respondents the following question:

> There has been a lot of talk about whether the United States should elect the president with a direct popular vote, whereby the candidate with the most votes would become president, thereby eliminating the electoral college. How do you feel about this?
>
> 0 = I am strongly opposed to eliminating the electoral college and electing the president by popular vote.
>
> 1 = I am somewhat opposed to eliminating the electoral college and electing the president by popular vote.
>
> 2 = I somewhat support eliminating the electoral college and electing the president by popular vote.
>
> 3 = I strongly support eliminating the electoral college and electing the president by popular vote.

The mean of this variable, which we chose to label *Eliminate Electoral College,* is 1.78, with a standard deviation of 1.15—meaning, again, that responses skew in an egalitarian direction, but not by that much.

As Figure 4.5 displays, these are by far the strongest results that we have reported so far. Those who strongly support eliminating the electoral college are

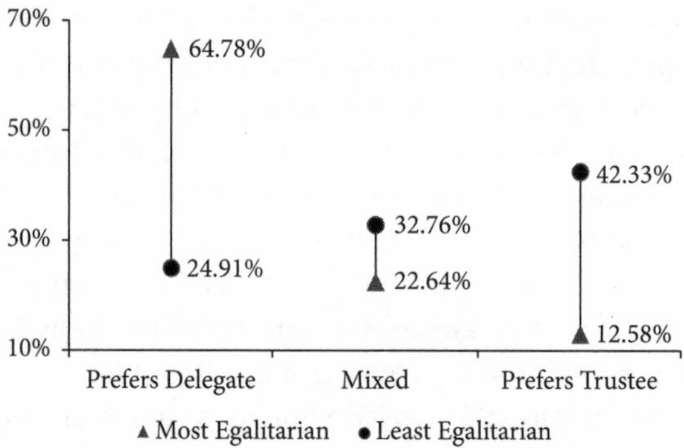


*Figure 4.5* Changes in Delegate/Trustee Preferences by Egalitarianism (Eliminate Electoral College)

40% more likely than those who strongly oppose that idea to prefer instructed delegates consistently (.65 to .25).[9] They are also 29% less likely to prefer trustees consistently (.13 to .42). These results suggest that when people are asked to consider matters of equality specifically as they apply to the political process, egalitarianism is overwhelmingly predictive of instructed delegate-style representation preferences. Ideally, as was the case with one of our humanism measures, we would have preferred to include this measure in all years of our survey data collection, so as to increase our confidence in this relationship's generalizability across time. Space limitations prevented us from doing so. For now, though, we can say that in this one year at least, these results strongly support our hypothesis.

*Authoritarianism*: As we discussed in Chapter 3, we expect authoritarianism to be another orientation that is associated with a preference for trustees, rather than instructed delegates. As we also discussed, authoritarianism can be thought of in some ways as the antithesis of egalitarianism, but not entirely—or else there would be no reason to include a separate analysis of its effects here. Authoritarianism is anti-egalitarianism of a particular sort—the sort that is applied to leadership. It is the belief that people are not equal—either inherently or by circumstance—and therefore that those who are weaker should naturally submit to the leadership of those who are stronger.

To measure this concept, we have followed the emerging conventional wisdom among political psychologists (Feldman, 2003b; Hetherington & Weiler,

[9] Because of the 2000 electoral anomaly, when Democrat Al Gore won the popular vote but Republican George W. Bush won the electoral vote and therefore the presidency, we checked whether additional controls for party identification are required in this model. In short, they are not. Including party identification in the model does not change the findings in any appreciable manner.

2009; Stenner, 2005) and have created an index of attitudes towards child-rearing styles—how important it is that children be raised to respect authority and submit to it. This child-rearing index avoids the pitfalls that befell authoritarianism research of previous decades because these child-rearing attitudes would clearly precede considerations of political issues, causally speaking. To elaborate slightly, if one tends to believe that the most important trait to be developed in children is submission to their authority figures, it is not because one wants to deny civil rights to religious minorities (original measures of authoritarianism were subject to such fallacies in logic).

Thus, our index of authoritarianism, as measured by attitudes towards the important traits to be developed in children, begins with the following question stem and the four sets of choice-pairs:

> Although there are a number of qualities that people feel that children should have, every person thinks that some are more important than others. Listed below are pairs of desirable qualities. For each pair, please indicate which one you think is more important for a child to have, as well as how strongly you feel about that. Please make a choice, even if it is difficult.

*Independence or respect for elders?*

0 = Strongly prefer independence
1 = Somewhat prefer independence
2 = Somewhat prefer respect elders
3 = Strongly prefer respect elders

*Obedience or self-reliance?*

0 = Strongly prefer self-reliance
1 = Somewhat prefer self-reliance
2 = Somewhat prefer obedience
3 = Strongly prefer obedience

*Curiosity or good manners?*

0 = Strongly prefer curiosity
1 = Somewhat prefer curiosity
2 = Somewhat prefer good manners
3 = Strongly prefer good manners

*Being well-behaved or considerate?*

0 = Strongly prefer considerate
1 = Somewhat prefer considerate
2 = Somewhat prefer well-behaved
3 = Strongly prefer well-behaved

Preferences for children who are well-behaved, well-mannered, obedient, and respectful of elders—rather than considerate, curious, self-reliant, or independent—have shown, in other research cited above, a capacity to reflect an authoritarian mindset.

However, there is some controversy in the literature about whether the child-rearing items *best* capture authoritarianism or a somewhat different (albeit related) orientation toward defining morality in terms of either discipline or compassion (see Barker & Tinnick, 2006).

Accordingly, to try to enhance the reliability of our measure, we then added a fifth item to the index; staying with the theme of considering relations within the family unit, this item asks respondents to consider the degree to which husbands and wives should be truly equal partners within a family unit, or if traditional gender roles should be respected. The survey item read as follows:

> Which of the following statements best captures your feelings about authority and roles within a family?
> 0 = The husband is the head of the household, and should therefore make all the decisions.
> 1 = The husband should consult his wife and listen to her opinion, but ultimately he should make the important decisions.
> 2 = Because of their different natural roles, husbands should make some types of important decisions, and wives should make others.
> 3 = Husbands and wives are completely equal, and should jointly share all decisions, chores, parenting responsibilities, and "bread-winning" responsibilities.

We used factor analysis to construct the index. Factor analysis is a useful tool for generating measurement indexes because it analyzes the intercorrelations among individual items within the index to produce an overall measure that is stripped of some of the error associated with each individual item, to better gauge the latent concept being measured (e.g., Kim & Mueller, 1978).[10]

[10] The authoritarian factor was created by applying a maximum likelihood extraction technique to the now-standard parenting items along with an additional item assessing the individual's attitudes toward marital gender roles. We extracted one factor with an eigenvalue of .98. While we fully recognize that this factor is on the cusp of the rule of thumb that eigenvalues should be >=1.0, we feel confident in the validity and reliability of this measure, given that the child-rearing items have become the industry standard when it comes to assessing individual-level attitudes toward authoritarianism.

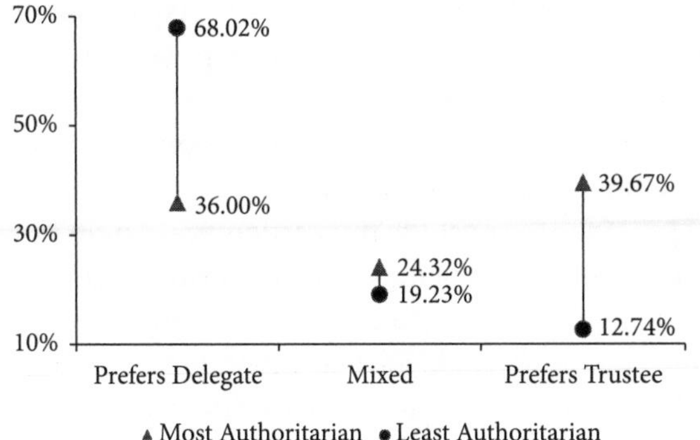


*Figure 4.6* Changes in Delegate/Trustee Preferences by Degree of Authoritarianism

Factor scales are expressed in standard deviation units, so our measure ranges from –1.71 to 1.42, with a mean of zero and a standard deviation of .69.[11]

As Figure 4.6 displays, the most authoritarian respondents were roughly 32% less inclined to prefer delegates consistently (.36 to .68) than were the least authoritarian respondents, and 27% more inclined to consistently prefer trustees (.13 to .40).[12]

As was the case with a couple of our other measures, constraints in resources did not enable us to measure authoritarianism on any of our surveys after 2006. As such, the results we just discussed are limited to that single year. Accordingly, and again, unlike some of the other results we have described, we cannot feel as confident that these results would generalize across time. Still, we are encouraged that the data we were able to collect provide support for our hypothesis and the theoretical perspective it represents.

[11] Including the gender roles item in the scale increases the eigenvalue associated with the extracted factor (from .90 to .98), and strengthens the item's overall predictive capacity. However, the statistical significance of authoritarianism as a predictor does not depend on the inclusion of the gender roles item in the measure.

[12] As several authors have observed, authoritarianism is associated with perceptions of threat (e.g., Altemeyer, 1996; Hetherington & Weiler, 2009; Stenner, 2005). That is, as people become threatened, they are more likely to reveal authoritarian tendencies. One measure of threat is the degree to which citizens are willing to support government wiretapping of private citizens for the purpose of monitoring terrorist activity, thereby sacrificing privacy rights. Our models reveal that such willingness is indeed associated with our measure of authoritarianism, and is also predictive of trustee-style representation preferences—providing new support for the relationship between threat and authoritarianism, while also providing evidence supporting the validity of our concepts and measures.

Overall, then, the statistical models that we have discussed strongly support the story we are trying to tell. Liberal popular democratic principles such as basic egalitarianism and humanism seem to undergird preferences for instructed delegate-style representation, while orientations that contradict liberal democracy in certain ways are associated with preferences for trustees, relatively speaking. To conclude this section, we should point out that the measures we have been discussing (for humanism, egalitarianism, authoritarianism, and dogmatism) tend to correlate strongly and significantly ($p < .001$), and in the ways expected. That is, the humanism measures are positively associated with the egalitarianism ones, and negatively associated with the authoritarianism and dogmatism items.[13]

The next section of this chapter takes the next step in putting our theory to the test, by examining the extent to which these values and orientations correspond to differences in religious perspectives, as our theory suggests they should, and then considering the extent to which those religious-identity measures predict representation preferences.

## RELIGIOUS TRADITIONALISM AND PREFERENCES REGARDING REPRESENTATION STYLES

Having demonstrated that the values associated with liberal popular democracy (basic egalitarianism, humanism) are predictive of preferences for the instructed delegate style of representation, and that those that are not associated with it (dogmatism, authoritarianism) are predictive of preferences for the trustee style, we have laid the proper foundation to see the degree to which traditionalistic Christian religiosity (especially that of an evangelical bent) also predicts trustee-style preferences. Given, as we discussed in the previous chapter, that such traditionalism captures elements of both dogmatism and authoritarianism, while eschewing humanism and basic egalitarianism

[13] This is also true as it pertains to the Christian traditionalism and party identification items that we describe below. That is, the authoritarianism, dogmatism, Christian traditionalism, and Republican Party identification items are highly correlated, and negatively correlated with the humanism and egalitarianism items. The one exception to this rule has to do with the *People Not Capable* variable, which was collected only in 2009. It was actually negatively associated with the other humanism and egalitarianism measures. Accordingly, we think readers should place less stock in the results obtained from that particular model than from the others.

(at least in some ways), we expect to find a strong association between such religiosity and trustee-style preferences.

To measure traditionalistic evangelical religiosity, then, we again used factor analysis to create an index comprising three items: (1) belief in biblical inerrancy/authority, (2) "born-again" Christian identity, and (3) regular church attendance.[14] Fortunately, in this case, we were able to measure these items in all four years of our data collection. We measured the first item, *Belief in Biblical Inerrancy/Authority*, with the following survey question:

> Which of the following comes CLOSEST to your view of the Bible?
>
> 0 = The Bible was written by men who lived so long ago that it is worth very little today.
>
> 1 = The Bible is a good book because it was written by wise men, but God had nothing to do with it.
>
> 2 = The Bible is a good book because it was written by wise men, inspired by God, but it is not the actual Word of God.
>
> 3 = The Bible is God's Word and conveys spiritual truth, but because it was written by men, it contains some human errors.
>
> 4 = The Bible is God's Word and all it says is true, but not everything in it should be taken literally, word for word.
>
> 5 = The Bible is the actual Word of God and is to be taken literally, word for word.

The mean for this variable is 2.40, with a standard deviation of 1.35.

We measured the second item in the index, *Born-Again Identity*, dichotomously, with the simple survey item:

> Do you consider yourself a born-again Christian?
>
> 0 = No
>
> 1 = Yes

The resulting variable has a mean of .34 and a standard deviation of .47.

---

[14] The latter item, by itself, would not have been a good measure of traditionalism, because many regular church attenders practice more progressive versions of the faith. Fortunately, the factor analysis technique creates the index by using only the portion of the variance in each item that is shared—or capturing the same underlying concept. As such, in this case, the variable includes the portion of the variance in the church attendance measure that correlates with traditionalistic beliefs, while discarding that which does not correlate with traditionalism.

We measured the final item in our index, *Church Attendance*, with the following survey question:

> How often do you attend religious services?
>
> 0 = never or almost never
>
> 1 = once a month or less
>
> 2 = a few times a month
>
> 3 = once a week
>
> 4 = more than once a week

This variable has a mean of 2.59 and a standard deviation of 1.59.

The factor analysis produced a standardized variable (as it always does), with a mean of 0 and standard deviation of 1, ranging (in this case) from –1.31 to 1.31.

Figure 4.7 displays the efficacy with which this *Christian Traditionalism* index predicts representation preferences, using the same statistical estimation procedure as we reported earlier (just substituting *Christian Traditionalism* for the respective value orientations). As the figure makes clear, these results provide strong evidence in support of our hypothesis. Specifically, those with the highest traditionalism scores were 24% less likely to consistently prefer instructed delegates (38% to 62%) than were those with the lowest traditionalism scores. Furthermore, if we focus on those with the lowest scores, the difference in their probability of consistently preferring delegates to consistently preferring trustees was 43 percentage points (.19 to .62), while the same difference for the most traditionalistic respondents was only 9 percentage points (.29 to .38).[15]

In separate models (not shown) that interact Christian traditionalism with humanism, dogmatism, or egalitarianism (separately, and in turn), we observe that the effect of Christian traditionalism is either enhanced or entirely dependent upon the dispositions. Specifically, when either dogmatism or humanism is included the model, along with an interaction term that multiplies the value by Christian traditionalism, the effect of humanism or dogmatism is robust, but the effect of Christian traditionalism disappears among those for whom dogmatism is low or humanism is high. A similar pattern is observed when egalitarianism is the value in question, but the independent effect for egalitarianism is weaker and not quite

15 In one year (2007), we were able to perform a robustness check by performing the same analysis with a different measure of traditionalistic religiosity, which simply asked respondents the degree to which they believed that "Belief in Jesus Christ is the *only path* to salvation." Remarkably, this model produced statistical results identical to those reported above.

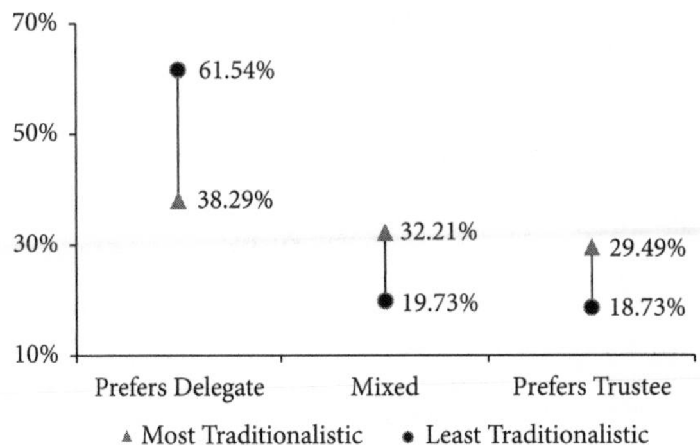


*Figure 4.7* Changes in Delegate/Trustee Preferences by Christian Traditionalism

statistically significant ($p < .16$). Authoritarianism proves to be an exception to this pattern: it is not robust to the absence of Christian traditionalism, whereas Christian traditionalism is a strong predictor even in the absence of authoritarianism.

In sum, then, we can say that the capacity of Christian traditionalism to predict trustee-style representation preferences is a byproduct of dogmatism, anti-humanism, and to a lesser extent anti-egalitarianism, which is in keeping with the value-based theoretical story we have spun. However, the Christian traditionalism effect is not a function of authoritarianism—in fact the reverse may be true. We suspect that authoritarianism and Christian traditionalism may both be functions of dogmatism—which is itself very close to representing the opposite end of the scale from humanism.

## PARTISAN IDENTITIES AND REPRESENTATION PREFERENCES

At this point, we have laid the proper theoretical groundwork to provide expectations regarding how and why representation preferences could come in Red or Blue partisan hues. In this short section, we describe our efforts to put that hypothesis directly to the test. This time, we predicted representation preferences according to differences across individuals in terms of party identification, measured on a simple 3-point scale: Democrats and Democratic "leaners"/pure Independents/Republicans and Republican "leaners" (see Keith et al., 1992).

As was the case with our Traditionalistic Religiosity index items, this measure has the benefit of being included in all four years of our data collection.

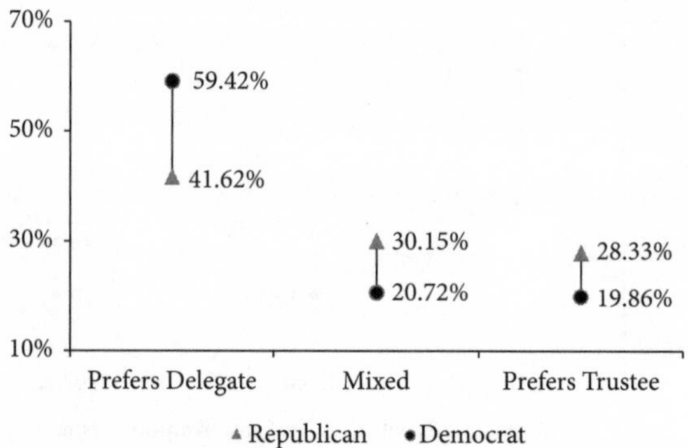


*Figure 4.8* Changes in Delegate/Trustee Preferences by Party ID

And just like all the other models discussed in this chapter, this model controls for age, race, gender, income, education, marital status, Catholic identification, and Southern regional identity. And again, for those who are interested, the Appendix provides the full statistical results.

We see in Figure 4.8 that Democrats are 17% more likely to consistently prefer instructed delegates as representatives than are Republicans (.59 to .42). Furthermore, Democrats are almost three times as likely to consistently prefer instructed delegates than to consistently prefer trustees (.59 to .20), whereas Republicans are only 14% more inclined to do so (.42 to .28).[16]

Because we do not have measures of all the value orientations across the different years, we cannot simultaneously enter everything into the model, in order to find out which of these various mechanisms "win the race" in terms of influence. We can, however, include Christian traditionalism and party identification simultaneously. When we do this, we observe that both variables remain highly statistically significant, but that traditionalistic religiosity does heavier lifting. The substantive effect associated with party identification gets cut in approximately half, while the effect of Christian traditionalism diminishes only slightly. This result supports our contention that the attitudinal consequences of traditionalistic orientations are not only to be observed among evangelical Christians,

[16] Alternate models that predict representation preferences with (a) the variance in ideological identification (liberal/moderate/conservative) or (b) approval of President Bush (5-point scale, strongly disapprove to strongly approve) reveal very similar results.

nor only among Republicans—but they are observed among those groups more regularly.[17]

## CONCLUSION

In sum, as can be easily observed by the models we have discussed in this chapter, these data provide strong evidence in support of our hypothesis that (a) the values of liberal popular democracy help explain the variance in citizens' attitudes toward representation styles, (b) because those values manifest secular and progressive worldviews, the variance in such worldviews also explains representation preferences, and finally (c) all of this ultimately translates into Democrats preferring instructed delegates more consistently than Republicans do.[18]

These findings provide the first stage of evidence in support of our ultimate contention that political representation in the United States tends to look differently, depending on the dominant cultural orientation or partisan shade of the locality.

### *Some Caveats, Additional Details, and Speculation*

Before moving on, we should reiterate that the results we have reported here are robust to changes in the measurement of our dependent variable. That is, the results hold regardless of whether we measure representation preferences in the most general way (as we have discussed) or if we measure them more restrictively—by focusing on one institution or the other (the president or Congress), or by focusing on representation attitudes as they pertain to particular issue types (see Chapter 2).

[17] Interestingly, unlike the Christian traditionalism effect, the party identification effect is robust to the inclusion of egalitarianism, humanism, dogmatism, or authoritarianism, and to the inclusion of interaction terms multiplying any of these values/orientations. Given that we view the party identification effect as capturing the *collective* effect of the values/dispositions, it stands to reason that controlling for any individual value does not wash out the collective effect of the ones left over, which are still being captured in party identification.

[18] These results are also consistent with those derived from national opinion data collected from two sources in the late 1970s (the 1977 Commission on Administrative Review [a.k.a. Obey Commission] data and the 1978 American National Election Study), which showed (between the two of them) that Republicans and especially Southern Democrats (where cultural traditionalists live in large numbers) are more likely to prefer trustee-style representation than are Democrats who resided outside of the South (Carman, 2007).

That being said, some differences in the size of the estimated relationships do emerge across the different institutional and issue-based contexts. Specifically, the relationships tend to be a little stronger when the issues under consideration are cultural issues (such as abortion or gay rights) rather than economic issues (such as taxes or the federal budget). We attribute this to the fact that such cultural issues are strongly associated with the Culture War mechanism underlying our theory. That is, if it is religious and cultural traditionalism that produces trustee-style preferences, it stands to reason that issues clearly dividing Americans along such religious and cultural lines would also be the ones for which we would observe the starkest differences in terms of whether Americans want their representatives to listen or lead. If traditionalists want their representatives to "stick to their principles" above all else, then that should be especially true with regard to issues that are thought of as more principle-based (such as abortion rights).

Furthermore, the relationships tend to be two to three times as strong when the political representative in question is the president, rather than Congress. Perhaps this relates to the fact that more citizens can readily identify the president and understand what he does than can do the same regarding their Congressional representatives, which may lead to responses that are more systematically predictable according to theory. Another explanation could be that there is simply more variation in representation preferences as they pertain to the president, meaning there is more opportunity for statistical associations to emerge between such attitudes and measures of traditionalism (or anything else).

In the next chapter, we explore the degree to which the dynamics described in this chapter bear relevance in the voting booth. That is, do representation preferences exert an independent influence over vote choices, thereby producing systematic differences in the types of lawmakers that different constituencies get?

# 11

## The Fine Art of Pandering

Performing the job of an elected representative is something like buying beer for your little brother and his friends on his 21st birthday (you're the only one with more than a dollar of gas in the tank. Besides, it's his birthday, and you're nice). None of them have been of age for very long, and so they are...shall we say...eager. As they scrounge for dollars and cents, they start arguing—animatedly—about what they want you to bring back home. Your kin casts the first ballot for Guinness, because "black beer is manly" (your eyes roll). His cooler-than-thou history-major friend insists on some IPA out of Fort Collins or somewhere that no one has ever heard of (and that he just read about yesterday). The new kid (who is wearing sandals, even though it is February) votes for Smirnoff Ice or some such thing (blank stares all around). And of course Mr. Pi Kappa Alpha lobbies for the 30-pack of Pabst Blue Ribbon (good thing he only gave you about three bucks). Eventually, three of them form a coalition in favor of the cheap stuff, and you have a majority. So off you go to get this over with. As you drive to the store, though, ambivalence sets in. You're pretty sure their best bet would be something like a twelve-pack of Bud: classic, palatable enough to the newly initiated, and reasonably priced—but not *so* affordable as to land anyone in jail or the ER later on tonight (which mom would surely blame on you). So what to do? Do you give the majority what it wants, turn off your phone, and hope for the best? Or do you follow your own instincts, knowing that as a consequence they might all curse you and demand their money back when you return?

This is usually where the complications end when students of politics contemplate representative decision making. But it shouldn't be. Maybe some of those birthday revelers actually hope you will follow your better judgment when you get to the store. Your election as beer runner was no coincidence, after all: you are the oldest and you have the most relevant expertise. If you instinctively understand that some of your thirsty constituents want you to use that expertise, rather than just following what the majority wants, your choice of social lubricant becomes a lot easier, and probably turns out differently than it otherwise would. As obvious as this sounds, it has not been so obvious to most people who have analyzed political representation over the years. The previous section gave us some idea about what types of citizens are most likely to prefer trustees rather than instructed delegates. This section focuses on the ways those preferences may affect actual representative behavior.

CHAPTER 5

# Representation Styles, Candidate Cues, and the Voting Booth

In the first half of this book, we showed that individual citizens vary systematically when it comes to the style of representation that they would like to see exercised by their elected officials. We provided evidence supporting our contention that the variation in such preferences is predicated, in part, on the degree to which citizens instinctively embrace the values associated with liberal popular democracy (egalitarianism, humanism), on the one hand, or those that contradict it (dogmatism, authoritarianism), on the other. We also showed that "Blue America" (whether defined in cultural, religious, or partisan terms) seems to prefer instructed delegates more consistently than does "Red America."

In the remainder of the book, we make a case for why any of that matters. Our eventual claim is that the citizens of Red America tend to get what they want, style-wise: representatives who, when making policy, listen to their internal compasses more than they listen to public opinion. Ironically, then, Red American politicians who "shirk" public opinion can sometimes also be called panderers…just of a different sort. Instead of pandering to constituents' policy preferences, they pander to constituents' preferences for the trustee style of representation.

But for our claim to be true—that is, if representatives really can pander in this unconventional and artful way—we must identify the process(es) through which citizens' preferences for either trustees or instructed delegates get communicated to representatives and ultimately affect the policymaking behavior of representatives. We envision that process as being dual-pronged, and reinforcing. In this chapter, we focus on what we see as the first, and primary, part of that process—electoral politics.

## PANDERING 2.0

When we hear of a politician "pandering," we think we know what it means. It means that the politician sticks her finger in the proverbial wind, in order to figure out which direction constituent opinion is blowing on some policy issue, and will modify her position on the issue so as to cater to those constituents... right? Well, that certainly is one example of pandering. Spun more positively, as we have argued earlier, that type of pandering is also an example of the instructed delegate style of representation. Or we might even say that it is liberal popular democracy in action. However, we want to make the case that there are other ways that representatives can pander to their constituents. Specifically, we suggest that representatives pick up cues from constituents about not only policy preferences but also whether the constituency, by and large, prefers instructed delegate-style representation or trustee-style representation. We then suggest that an adroit politician can skillfully use that information to give constituents what they want, style-wise. We call this type of behavior "Pandering 2.0." So, when constituents send cues that they prefer instructed delegate-style representation, old-fashioned pandering and Pandering 2.0 are the same thing. However, when constituents somehow signal that they prefer trustee-style representation, clever politicians will respond to those cues by paying *less* attention to public opinion on policy issues. Or one could say that by making a show of not pandering in the traditional way, they are really pandering in a new way.

In short, we suggest that political candidates who pride themselves on their willingness to buck public opinion in service to internal principles (the trustee style) are more likely to find sympathetic ears within culturally traditionalistic audiences—which also happen to be Republican ears more often than not (among white voters, anyway). As such, we hypothesize that trustee-style preferences are associated with Republican voting, at all levels of government, and that this association extends beyond that which would be expected due to the partisanship-based associations we have already uncovered.

We test this hypothesis in a few different ways. We begin by examining the 2008 presidential election. We test whether those who prefer trustees also tended to prefer Senator McCain to Senator Obama—even after taking party identification and ideology into account. Next, we take a look at House, Senate, and gubernatorial elections. Drawing upon data collected in both 2006 and 2008, we examine how robust our hypothesized relationship is across these different electoral contests.

Finally, in an attempt at enhancing our ability to draw causal inferences from our data, we describe a controlled experiment, executed in 2006 and replicated in 2008, in which we manipulated the campaign rhetoric of legislative candidates so that voters received either instructed delegate-style or trustee-style representation cues. We observe the extent to which voters' evaluations of these hypothetical candidates vary according to the interaction between the voter's partisanship (as well as her cultural identity) and the type of rhetorical cue (delegate or trustee) that she received.

## REPRESENTATION PREFERENCES AND THE 2008 PRESIDENTIAL ELECTION

The 2008 presidential election is a pretty good case study in which to examine the extent to which citizens' preferences regarding different representation styles might have had bearing on their candidate preferences. When it comes to John McCain, in particular, the senator went out of his way to create a persona of a principled politician who would ignore public opinion if he thought it was the "right thing" to do. For example, in 2007 and 2008, he ignored the wishes of many conservatives (infuriating the talk-radio crowd and right-wing blogosphere) by prominently backing immigration reform. At the same time, he proudly alienated most liberals with his staunch advocacy of a troop surge in Iraq at a time when large majorities of Americans just wanted to bring the troops home. Indeed, a Pew-sponsored survey conducted February 8–11, 2008, revealed that despite being "evenly divided" over whether McCain was a "true conservative," 75% of Republicans thought McCain "has an admirable character," with nearly as many calling him "honest and trustworthy" (Pew, 2008).

These survey findings are of course in keeping with the longstanding media narrative about McCain: that he is a "maverick" who offers "straight talk" instead of following his party or the public. In fact, one content analysis found that in 2000, the words "maverick" and "McCain" appeared within 10 words of each other no less than 2,114 times, a practice that generally continued over the decade (Brock & Waldman, 2008). For more on how McCain used much more absolutist, principle-oriented rhetoric during the campaign than did Obama, see Marietta (2008). This is not to suggest, of course, that McCain's actual record of stances on issues is any more (or less) consistent or "principle-based" than any other politician. The veracity of McCain's reputation, as of

November 2008, is not our concern; all that matters is that the media narrative was in place.

As for Obama, it would certainly be a stretch to argue that he honed an image that clearly emphasized an instructed governing philosophy (though we suppose the "Yes We Can" mantra might imply something like that). However, given McCain's carefully cultivated reputation (at the time), we suggest that many voters should have had little trouble differentiating candidates on this dimension (again, presumably on some instinctive or subconscious level).

We tested this hypothesis using the same data that we described in previous chapters. Figure 5.1 displays the results from a statistical (probit) model that regressed the 2008 presidential vote (McCain = 1, Obama = 0) on presidential representation preferences (0–1, trustee = 1), and the familiar sociodemographic control variables (age, race, gender identity, income education, marital status, Catholic identity, Southern regional identity). *We restricted our sample of respondents to those who identify as political independents, to make sure that our observed electoral connection is providing information beyond that which we already established in the previous chapter.*

As the figure shows, those who prefer trustees were 23% more inclined to vote for McCain, even after accounting for the association between representation preferences and longstanding political predispositions.[1,2]

---

[1] In separate analyses, we also showed that independents and even Democrats who prefer the trustee style of representation are more likely to have voted in one of the Republican nominating contests than in a Democratic one (see Barker & Carman, 2010).

[2] Using a different dataset of national survey opinion that we collected in 2004, we also found support for the hypothesis that those who prefer trustee-style representation (along with Christian traditionalists, conservatives, and Republicans) are more likely to say that a presidential candidate's "personal traits" are more important to determining their vote choices than are his "policy plans." This is consistent with our theory because it presumably requires representatives of requisite character in order to make principled decisions that may defy public opinion. This might also explain why, in 2012, Mitt Romney had such a difficult time winning over conservatives in his quest for the Republican presidential nomination, while Ron Paul did better than expected. Romney holds conservative issue positions across the board, but has a reputation (deserved or not) as an opportunistic flip-flopper who lacks conviction. Paul, on the other hand, holds many positions that are anathema to the conservative Republican base, but has honed a persona (again, deserved or not) of a principled, consistent libertarian who will not yield from those positions no matter what the public may want (i.e., being a trustee).

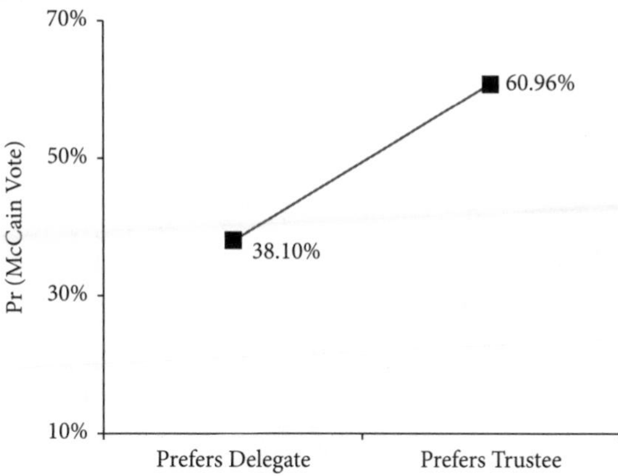


*Figure 5.1* Changes in Predicted Probability of McCain Vote by Presidential Representation Preferences, Among Independents

But is the electoral connection restricted to presidential contests, or perhaps even just to those presidential contests where there are clear distinctions between candidates in terms of the representation styles they project? In the next section, we consider this question directly.

## REPRESENTATION PREFERENCES AND ELECTORAL BEHAVIOR IN HOUSE, SENATE, AND GUBERNATORIAL ELECTIONS

First, we consider electoral contests for the House of Representatives. Conducting content analyses of candidates' rhetoric in each House race, to ascertain whether some candidates tended to provide "trustee" cues while others provided "instructed delegate" cues, would have been too unwieldy; accordingly, for this set of analyses (and those that follow), we draw upon the evidence that we have already brought to bear to suggest that Republican candidates tend to provide more "trustee" cues, on average, than do Democratic candidates. If they do, and if voters pick up those cues, then we should observe patterns similar to that which we just discussed. That is, we should see an independent association between mass preferences for congressional "trustees" and Republican votes for House candidates in 2006 and 2008 (n = 1,499), controlling for the same variables that have now become familiar.

Figure 5.2 displays the results of this test, which we estimated using multinomial logistic regression (similar to the procedure used in Chapter 4).

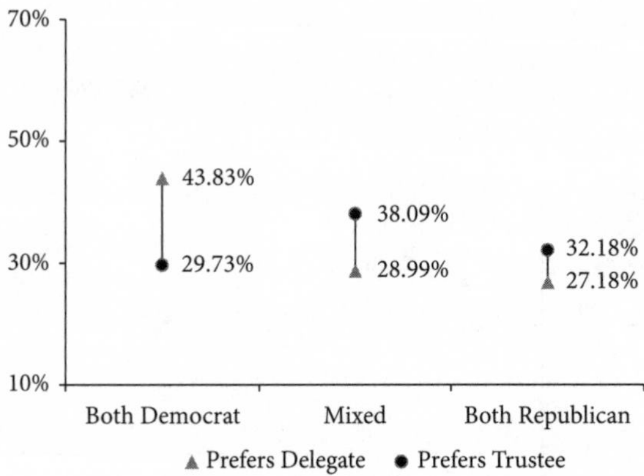


*Figure 5.2* House Vote Choice (2006 & 2008), by Congressional Delegate/Trustee Preference, Independents Only

Specifically, the dependent variable equals "0" if a voter chose a Democrat in both 2006 and 2008, "1" if the voter chose a Democrat in just one of the years, and "2" if the voter chose a Republican in both years. As can be easily observed, independent voters who prefer trustees to instructed delegates are about 14% more inclined to vote for a Republican in at least one of the two elections, all else being equal.

This result is somewhat weaker than the presidential finding, of course, which would be expected given the fact that there is surely considerable variance across Democratic and Republican candidates in terms of the degree to which they differ on the instructed delegate versus trustee dimension, or the degree to which they successfully communicate that to voters. Furthermore, as we discussed earlier, we would not expect *all* Republican candidates or voters to be more inclined toward the trustee style; rather, we primarily expect the relationship to be observed among religious and cultural traditionalists. The point is that there is surely considerable "noise" across these many House races, which might account for the smaller association. Still, 9% could make the difference in a tight election.

What about Senate elections? Our next model repeats the analysis, exchanging vote choices in House contests for vote choices in Senate contests. Unfortunately, because of space limitations in our surveys, we could not ask respondents for their representation preferences as they specifically pertain to senators (unlike what we were able to do for House members and presidents). Thus, instead of randomly picking either the House representation preferences measure (just described) or the presidential representation preferences measure (described in the previous section) and just plugging it into this model as our independent variable, we decided that the safest thing to do would be to combine the two measures—in order to capture a more "general" orientation toward one style of representation or another. This approach also makes some conceptual sense, we believe, because senators are much more visible than House members, but not so visible as presidents (e.g., Lee & Oppenheimer, 1999).

As Figure 5.3 displays, the now-familiar pattern emerges again—and this time, a bit more strongly. Those who consistently prefer instructed delegates are about 31% less likely to have voted for a Republican Senate candidate in at least one of those years.

The final type of electoral contest we consider is that for picking governors. Because governors are executives, we expect that citizens view them the same way they view presidents when it comes to preferred representation styles. As such, we use the presidential representation preference measure in this model to predict gubernatorial vote choices, to see if those who prefer their presidents to be trustees are more likely to vote for Republican governors. Figure 5.4 shows the results of this analysis, after controlling for all of the familiar variables that have appeared in every other model we have discussed (and again restricting our sample to political independents).

These results are the strongest yet. In fact, the magnitude of the relationship is almost shocking. Those who prefer trustee-style representation out of

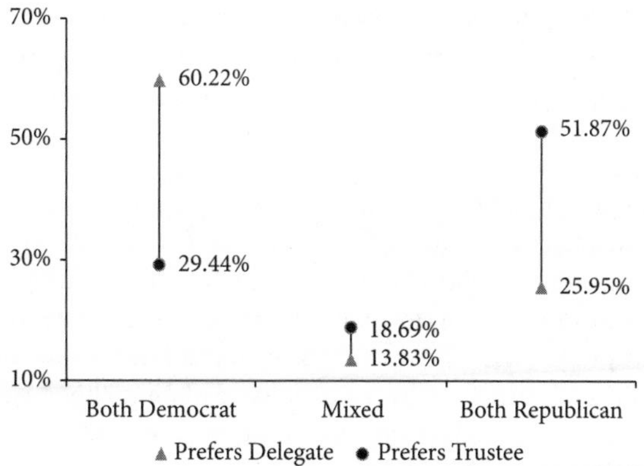


*Figure 5.3* Senate Vote Choice (2006 & 2008), by Delegate vs. Trustee Preferences, Independents Only

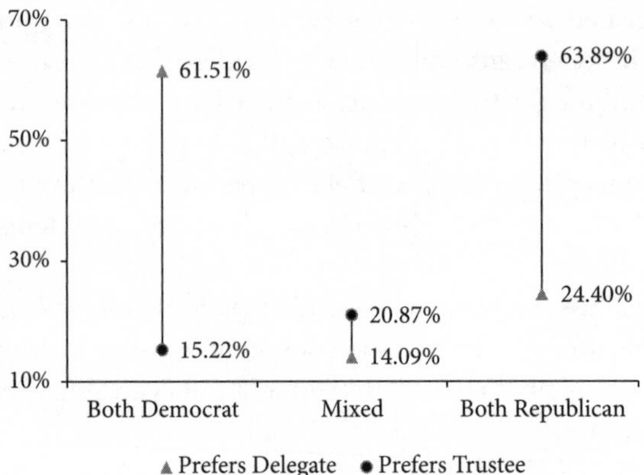


*Figure 5.4* Gubernatorial Vote Choice (2006 & 2008), by Delegate vs. Trustee Preferences, Independents Only

the national executive appear to have been a whopping 46% less likely to vote for Democratic state executives, on average, in 2006 and 2008.[3]

Why are the effects regarding gubernatorial elections so much stronger than the others? One place to start probably has to do with the fact that there is more variance in mass preferences toward representation styles when the targeted elected official under consideration is an executive, rather than a legislator. We observed that in Chapter 2. There are simply more people who want to see their executives acting as trustees than want to see the same thing from their legislators. As such, it creates more of an opportunity for a strong relationship to emerge. Indeed, our presidential model revealed the second-strongest set of results.

But that still does not explain why the findings in the gubernatorial vote choice model were so much stronger than even those in the presidential vote choice model. One option, of course, is that this is just an outlier effect—a

[3] Our results remain statistically significant even when we control for ideological identification (0 = liberal; 1 = moderate; 2 = conservative). We do not include this control in the models we report because it actually captures a significant portion of the theoretical rationale underlying our hypothesized relationship between representation preferences and vote choices (orientations toward cultural and religious traditionalism), thereby artificially deflating the magnitude of our results. In other words, it gives an inaccurate portrayal of a relationship if the researchers control away their proposed theoretical mechanism. We mention it here to say that, even when we radically overspecify our models, we *still* obtain statistically significant results.

one-time effect that is either a statistical anomaly or a function of some particular aspect of the gubernatorial races in those years. However, it is worth at least speculating as to possible explanations that are more systematic and would be more generalizable. Perhaps the reason has something to do with visibility. Gubernatorial elections are visible—visible enough that voters probably pick up on candidate cues relatively easily—but they are nowhere near as visible as presidential election results. The campaigns and media coverage of presidential elections are so overpowering that most votes get determined relatively early on, even among independents, and more or less come down to partisan "leanings," performance evaluations of the incumbent administration (especially economic evaluations), and other longstanding predispositions. Given that presidential election campaign environment, we would certainly not expect something like mass preferences regarding representation styles to have *too big* of an effect over vote choices. What we are saying is that perhaps if presidential elections were not quite so saturated with media coverage and campaign expenditures, we would observe an association between representation preferences and presidential vote choices that would rival those observed in the gubernatorial vote choice model.

It is also worth offering up some conjecture as to why the role of representation preferences in predicting House vote choices seems to be considerably weaker than that in any of the other contests. Again, the most obvious culprit probably is the lack of visibility. As we already noted, presidential races are incredibly visible, and gubernatorial races are very visible. Senatorial races are also fairly high-visibility contests. By comparison, House contests are barely a blip on most voters' radar screens. Many voters will never notice an ad or a speech by a House candidate (especially challengers) or see/read/hear any news coverage of the race. Indeed, a good many voters will probably not even know the names of the candidates who are vying for the seat. As such, voters' ability to pick up candidate cues as to what style of representation the representative would follow is surely quite muted. Furthermore, and somewhat relatedly, with over 90% of incumbents routinely being elected to the House, the role of incumbency in determining House contests is so overwhelmingly strong that there simply is not much room left for anything else (like preferred representation styles) to have much of an impact over vote choices.

In the end, of course, we can only go so far in explaining the fact that, in our data at least, the capacity of mass representation preferences to predict vote choices is so much weaker in House contests than in any other electoral context that we have observed. Fortunately, while it is fun to offer up some conjecture, the reasons for the disparity are not really all that relevant to our purposes. The point to take away from this little discussion of the differences that appear across different governing institutions is that any relationships that may actually exist between the way legislators govern and the styles of representation that their constituents prefer could very well be weaker than those between constituents and senators, governors, and presidents.

The main point to emphasize from this chapter, so far, is that voters may choose between candidates in part based on recognizable differences in representation style. By uncovering this evidence, we have not only established a potential voting determinant that has yet to be recognized in the political science canon; we also take a suggestive first step toward establishing that representation preferences may translate into identifiable differences in governing between Republican and Democratic representatives.

Still, we must be careful to not get too far ahead of ourselves at this point. Non-experimental research designs such as the one we have described so far (those that do not include random assignment of subjects to receive either a treatment or a placebo) do not enable researchers to make claims as strong as those that can be taken away from controlled experimental designs (e.g., Shadish, Cook, & Campbell, 2001). In light of this, the following section describes just such a set of experiments, for the purpose of retesting our main hypotheses in a way that harnesses the benefits afforded by experimental designs.

## MAXIMIZING CAUSAL VALIDITY: RESULTS FROM A CONTROLLED SURVEY EXPERIMENT

To gain further purchase over whether voters might actually recognize different representation styles in candidates and use that information to evaluate those candidates, we designed and executed a controlled experiment, which was imbedded within our survey modules in the 2006 and 2008 CES.

To simplify our presentation of these models and results, and to avoid redundancy, we focus our discussion on the 2006 experiment. Importantly, though, the 2008 results are nearly identical to the 2006 results, statistically speaking, and very similar to these in terms of their substantive strength.

The experimental procedure begins when survey respondents were asked to consider the following question stem:

> The following statement was recently made by one of the candidates for the House of Representatives from your region of the country. We cannot tell you whether this candidate is from your district, or whether he or she is the challenger or the incumbent. However, we can tell you that this candidate is the nominee of one of the major parties and is in a competitive race, according to the polls.

> As you read this statement, think about how well this candidate would represent his/her district. We realize that this is difficult with so little information, but we want your gut reaction.

Following the stem, respondents were randomly assigned to receive one of three treatments. We designed the first treatment so as to characterize a representative who was pledging to follow the instructed delegate representation style:

> My only priority is working hard to SERVE the people in this district. I will be your MOUTHPIECE. I'm not interested in cameras or cocktail parties. You see, I'm not so arrogant as to think that I know better than you what's best for you. That's why I'll really LISTEN to you, and the folks in Washington are going to hear YOUR VOICE, for once.

This treatment was randomly assigned to 348 respondents in 2006. The items that appear in all capital letters (which is also the way they appeared to our experimental subjects) are the key to this treatment. Instructed delegate-style representatives SERVE as their constituents' MOUTHPIECE, LISTENING to them so they can function as a simple conduit for constituent VOICES.

By contrast, we designed the second treatment (randomly assigned to 303 subjects) so as to characterize a representative who was pledging to embrace a trustee representation style:

> My only priority is working hard to DO WHAT'S RIGHT for the people in this district. I will be your ADVOCATE. I'm not interested in cameras, or cocktail parties. You see, I believe that leaders should LEAD, guided by firm PRINCIPLES that don't change every time the polls do. The folks in Washington are going to see what that looks like, for once.

By calling attention to DOING WHAT'S RIGHT and being an ADVOCATE as opposed to a mouthpiece, this hypothetical representative is trying to show that he or she is more of a LEADER than a listener—committed to PRINCIPLE more than to public opinion.

The third and final treatment (randomly assigned to 349 subjects) conscientiously prompts neither trustee nor instructed delegate representation styles; respondents who received this "placebo" treatment serve as the control group in this experiment:

> My only priority is working hard. I'm not interested in the cameras or the cocktail parties. The folks in Washington are going to see what that looks like, for once.

After being exposed to one of the three treatments, all respondents were asked the following question:

> Assuming this candidate is sincere, how well do you think this candidate would perform for the people living in the district? Use the scale below to indicate how you feel. You can choose any number on the scale. Please make a choice, even though it is difficult.

| 1 | 2 | 3 | 4 | 5 | 6 |
|---|---|---|---|---|---|
| Not at all | | | | | Perfectly |

This 6-point scale was converted to a 0-to-1 scale (0, .2, .4, .6, .8, 1) to ease interpretation of the results (enabling us to speak in terms of the percentage difference in support for the hypothetical candidate in questions associated with unit differences in our independent variables).

It should be noted that the prompts associated with the instructed delegate-style and trustee-style treatments were designed to be very similar in every respect except for the representation style they advocate. We also took great pains to ensure that each prompt is intuitively appealing, in roughly equal measure. By using short prompts, with relatively subtle cues, we made a conscious decision to err on the side of cautiousness. That is, we could have made the prompts much more dramatic, which would have ensured that the experimental subjects picked up on the message that was intended. However, we decided against that strategy because we did not deem it sufficiently realistic.

By the same token, our decision to tell the experimental subjects that these were real statements, made by real candidates, in real time—as opposed to creating a "game" experiment with fake elections—was also made with realism in mind. The consequence of these efforts to inspire as much realism as possible is that we risked not making the treatments strong enough to produce effects. As such, we should emphasize that we do not expect to observe large substantive effects to emerge from this experiment; any statistically significant findings that emerge at all will have swum upstream to do so.

We told respondents that the candidate was not necessarily from their own district for ethical purposes. We did not want respondents trying to infer who the candidate was and forming judgments about a real candidate on the basis of a misattribution. Of course, we debriefed all respondents at the conclusion of the survey, informing them that the attributions were a ruse. Still, we wanted to be very careful on this score, which is again why we chose to be vague about the geographical proximity of the hypothetical candidate.

Our first task is to test whether Christian traditionalists tended to evaluate the hypothetical candidate differently than nontraditionalists, based on whether the candidate was providing either instructed delegate-style or trustee-style rhetorical cues. We therefore used the same Christian traditionalism measure that we described earlier as our independent variable. As Figure 5.5 shows, these results are pretty similar to those reported earlier. The most traditionalistic subjects in the sample were about 26% more supportive of the candidate espousing trustee-style rhetoric than they were of the candidate espousing instructed delegate-style rhetoric; they were also about 25% more supportive of the trustee-style candidate than were the least traditionalistic subjects. When it came to evaluating the instructed delegate-style candidate, however, support did not depend on subjects' level of Christian traditionalism.

Next, we need to see whether those Christian traditionalism effects also translate into political identity effects. In other words, do conservative Republicans tend to support the trustee-style candidate more readily than do liberal Democrats, and more than they support the instructed delegate-style candidate? To test this hypothesis, we again relied on factor analysis to create an index of three items—party identification (as described earlier), ideological identification (again, as described earlier) and support for President Bush on

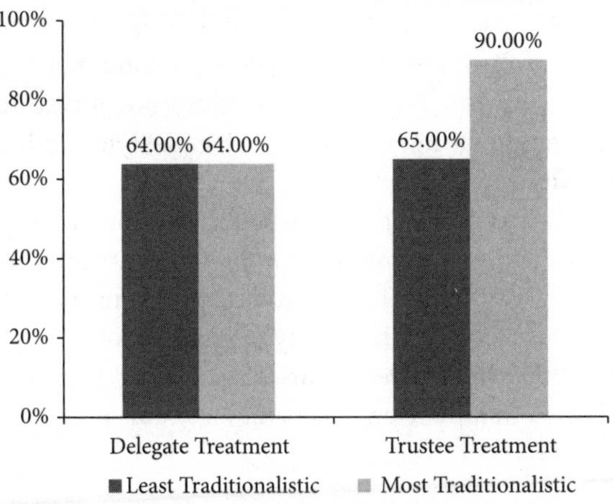


*Figure 5.5* Differences in Level of Hypothetical Candidate Support by Degree of Christian Traditionalism

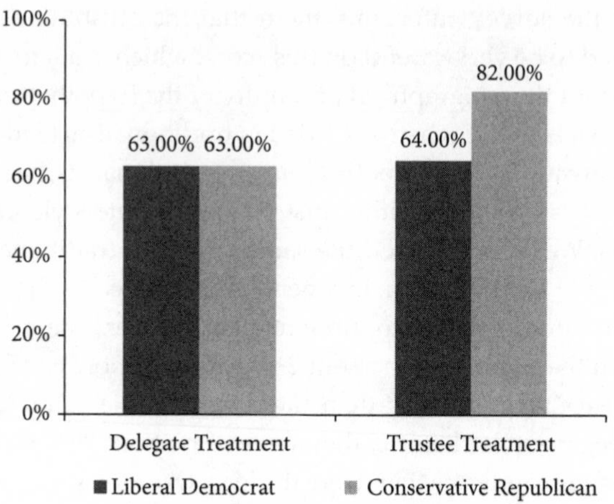


*Figure 5.6* Differences in Level of Hypothetical Candidate Support by Ideology/Partisanship

a 0- to 100-point feeling thermometer (eigenvalue = 1.93). We then plugged this index into the model, in place of the traditionalism index.

As Figure 5.6 reveals, the relationship is somewhat weaker, as we expected, but still strong. The most conservative Republicans in the sample were about 18% more supportive of the trustee-style candidate than were the most liberal Democrats, which was also about 20% more supportive than conservative Republicans were of the instructed delegate-style candidate.[4] Again, though, in something of a surprise, liberal Democrats did not appear to be any more supportive, on average, of the instructed delegate-style candidate than were conservative Republicans.

Thus, within the confines of this particular experiment at least, the ideological and religious face of representation preferences appears largely unidirectional: Christian traditionalists and some other conservative Republicans seem to evaluate instructed delegate-style legislators the same way secular progressives and other liberal Democrats do. However, for trustee-style politicians, it would seem that their prospects for electoral success tend to be quite

[4] It appears that the political identity results are a function of Christian traditionalism among many conservative Republicans. When both variables are entered into the model at the same time, the political identity finding disappears, while the Christian traditionalism finding stays the same, both statistically and substantively.

a bit more promising when their electoral constituencies are loaded with conservative Republicans—Christian traditionalists, in particular.[5]

Given, as we mentioned earlier, that this experiment was deliberately designed to err on the side of underestimating statistical associations, these effects are quite compelling. They augment the observational results discussed earlier, providing another layer of support for our theoretical argument.[6]

Why are our findings one-sided? That is, in our experiment, why did traditionalists evaluate the trustee-style candidate so much more favorably than did nontraditionalists, whereas everyone seemed to like the instructed delegate-style candidate about equally? One possible explanation might be that our trustee-style treatment contained less measurement error than our instructed delegate-style treatment. But maybe the true relationship really is mostly one-sided. After all, it is hard to reject a candidate who is claiming that she is going to listen to her constituents—regardless of who you are. It may be that traditionalists just like "principled leaders" all the more.

Another (not mutually exclusive) possibility is that traditionalists tended to like the instructed delegate-style candidate a little less than they let on in the survey; they may have felt silly indicating that they opposed a candidate who said he or she was going to listen to constituents—even though in their gut they may not have felt entirely comfortable with that candidate.

For our purposes, the one-sided nature of the results—and the reasons for it—do not really matter. All that matters is that, in the end, traditionalists were more supportive than nontraditionalists of the trustee-style candidate; these findings provide further evidence suggesting that trustee-style candidates fare quite a bit better, on average, when campaigning to traditionalistic constituencies than to nontraditionalistic ones.

---

5 Exact statistical models, with N's, standard errors, etc. can be found in the Appendix.

6 In other models that are not shown, we also found that the least egalitarian and humanistic respondents (using measures discussed in Chapter 4) tended to view the hypothetical trustee-style candidate much more favorably than did their more egalitarian and humanistic counterparts. Likewise, the more authoritarian respondents were more supportive of the trustee-style candidate than were the more libertarian respondents (unfortunately, we could not evaluate differences in support for the hypothetical candidate based on the variance in respondent dogmatism, because it was not measured as part of our survey data collection in 2006 or 2008, the years we conducted our experiments). These results are also in keeping with the theory we laid out in Chapter 3, and provide another layer of "robustness" to the findings we report here.

## CONCLUSION

So to summarize, in this chapter we have provided substantial evidence to support the idea that mass preferences regarding representation styles independently affect individual vote choices across various types of electoral contests. We have provided direct evidence of a candidate (albeit a hypothetical one) successfully pandering to a set of conservative Christian constituents (and by extension, to Republicans as well) by telling them that they need not worry about her pandering to public opinion on policy matters.

At this point it is perhaps useful to restate the essential claim that motivates our entire effort. In this book we are not merely suggesting that perspectives associated with the current political context in the United States lead Republicans to prefer trustee-style representation (and vice versa). Such perspectives and context can and will change, after all. Rather, we are proposing something much more theoretically consequential: that those with faith-based worldviews have always and will always tend toward trustee-style representation, while "secular humanists" will tend toward instructed delegate-style representation. Hence, so long as the Culture Wars rage: in American politics—that is, so long as the Democratic Party remains the party associated with Enlightenment values—we would expect the Democratic Party to also remain the party of instructed delegate-style representation (but not for a minute longer).

So do the Culture Wars actually produce casualties in terms of democratic governance? We of course do not yet know, based on the evidence we have discussed so far. We take up that question directly in Chapter 7. In this chapter, though, we have provided an important link in the theoretical chain—via the ballot box—giving us greater confidence that "Red" lawmakers do tend to govern with a different style than do their colleagues on the other side of the aisle. In Chapter 6, we explore other, non-electoral ways that conservative constituencies might send lawmakers the message that they crave principled leadership more than policy responsiveness.

CHAPTER 6

# Constituent Perceptions of Representation Styles and Democratic Accountability

In Chapter 5 we started connecting the dots, empirically, between constituency preferences for either instructed delegates or trustees and the degree to which elected representatives actually adhere to one of those representation styles or the other. By showing that representation preferences can independently predict candidate preferences and vote choices, we provided a causal mechanism—the ballot box—to underlie our argument that representation in "Red America" differs systematically from that in "Blue America." Essentially, it would appear that trustee-style lawmakers are more likely to get elected in the first place in Red America than they are in Blue America.

But that part of the story renders the individual citizen a somewhat passive character in this story. Sure, she has her role to play in the electoral booth every couple of years, but she does not otherwise really have much influence over her representatives' representation styles. In this brief chapter, we try to find out whether there could be additional constituency-driven enticements for Red American lawmakers to govern like trustees, and for Blue American lawmakers to govern like instructed delegates, *after having gained office*. Specifically, we want to see if citizens have opinions about the way they *are* being represented, relative to how they *want* to be represented, and whether that perception/preference gap is predictive of a legislator's approval rate. If so, we will have provided evidence that regardless of how they get elected in the first place, legislators have a continued incentive to give constituents the style of representation they prefer—lest they risk putting their reelection bids in jeopardy. In other words, representatives have additional reasons, once elected, to engage in what we described in Chapter 5 as "Pandering 2.0"—pandering to voters' representation-style preferences, rather than to their policy preferences, which would actually require eschewing such traditional policy pandering.

Based on the theory we presented in Chapter 3, and now buttressed by evidence presented in Chapters 4 and 5, we hypothesize that the gaps between the style of representation constituents prefer and the style they think they are getting influences congressional approval in uneven ways. Namely, we suggest that Democratic citizens tend to hold legislators' feet to the fire when they think those legislators are not listening to public opinion enough, but do not similarly punish lawmakers for listening *too* intently. Conversely, we anticipate Republican citizens holding members of Congress (MCs) accountable when those MCs follow public opinion too eagerly, but not when the MCs dig in their heels too much.

If the data support our hypotheses, we will have shown that Republican and Democratic lawmakers tend to face different types of pressure from constituents, which therefore provides them with different incentives. Essentially, Democrats would have extra incentives to pander to changes in constituents' policy preferences, while Republicans would face inordinate pressure to ignore any such changes. If lawmakers respond to those pressures accordingly, as we would expect them to, then we would expect to observe considerably more trustee-style behavior on the part of Republican lawmakers.

Having said all that, if constituents have no sense of whether their lawmakers are behaving like trustees or instructed delegates, then lawmakers' efforts at pandering in this reconceptualized way would be wasted. To gain a sense of whether this is the case, the final thing we do in this chapter is analyze whether citizens' perceptions of the type of representation they are actually getting are predictable based on whether the MC in question is a Democrat or a Republican. We expect that citizens who are represented by Republicans are more likely to say that they are getting trustee-style representation than are those who are represented by Democrats.[1]

The first step in this entire process, then, is to look at the simple distribution of opinions as they pertain to the style of representation citizens think they are getting, and compare those to the type they want.

[1] As we have noted at other points in this book, we do not actually expect most citizens to really know all that much about what their representatives are doing. Thus, we think that whatever perceptions that citizens have about the style they are getting are more about "gut feelings," based on rhetorical cues, images, general reputations, and the like. Now, a good many citizens won't even pay enough attention to pick up those cues. But we expect that enough of them will to reveal a significant relationship.

## WHAT CITIZENS WANT VERSUS WHAT THEY THINK THEY GET

To measure such perceptions, we again relied on the survey questions we were able to add to the CES surveys. In 2006, 2007, and 2009 we put the following question to respondents (which immediately followed the representation *preference* questions described in Chapter 2, and were used in the analysis described in Chapters 4 and 5):

> Now we want you to consider how you believe things actually are, which of course may or may not be the way you think they ought to be. Using the scale below, where "1" means that you strongly believe that your member of Congress tries his or her hardest to give the people in your district the policies they want, and "6" means that you strongly believe that your member of Congress sticks to his or her principles, no matter what, where would you place yourself? You can choose any number in between, to indicate how strongly you feel about this.

| 0 | 1 | 2 | 3 | 4 | 5 |
|---|---|---|---|---|---|
| Strongly believe gives what people want | | | | | Strongly believe follows own principles |

Do citizens' perceptions regarding representation styles match their expectations? This question is important because if the answer is "no," it would suggest widespread discontent regarding what is perhaps the most fundamental characteristic of republican governance. To find out, we compared responses to the survey question measuring legislative representation preferences to those for the question displayed above.

Specifically, we created a variable that subtracted each survey respondent's attitude about what "ought to be" from her perception of what is. The resulting variables range from –5 to 5. Positive scores capture gaps that favor the instructed delegate style. That is, they indicate that the respondent wants more instructed delegate-style representation than she thinks she is getting. A score of 1 or 2 means that the respondent would like the representative to be a little more responsive, whereas a score of 3, 4, or 5 suggests that the respondent would like the representative to be a lot more responsive. Negative scores therefore indicate the opposite—the respondent perceives the representative to be too quick to follow the public's whims instead of standing on principle.

**TABLE 6.1** *DISTRIBUTION OF RELATIVE REPRESENTATION PREFERENCES (HOW REPRESENTATION "IS"—HOW REPRESENTATION "OUGHT" TO BE)*

| | Value | Frequency | Percent |
|---|---|---|---|
| Wants MCs to be more Trustees | –5 | 20 | 0.68 |
| | –4 | 22 | 0.75 |
| | –3 | 59 | 2 |
| | –2 | 146 | 4.95 |
| | –1 | 326 | 11.06 |
| | 0 | 1012 | 34.34 |
| | 1 | 405 | 13.74 |
| | 2 | 335 | 11.37 |
| | 3 | 296 | 10.04 |
| Wants MCs to be | 4 | 156 | 5.29 |
| more Delegates | 5 | 170 | 5.77 |
| | Total | 2947 | 100 |

Table 6.1 shows the distribution of this variable. As can easily be seen, and as we expected, there are a lot more people who would like to see their representatives listening more to public opinion than those who would like to see them listening less. However, the gap is not entirely one-sided: there are significant numbers of citizens who would like their representatives to pay less attention to public opinion.

So given this significant gap that tends to exist between what citizens want and what they think they are getting, representation-wise, does such citizen dissatisfaction translate into citizens punishing representatives whom they perceive to be giving them the "wrong" style of representation, by expressing their disapproval on surveys of public opinion? Or are preferences regarding representation style such a low priority for voters that they are outweighed by other factors, leaving overall approval rates unaffected? And is the answer to that question contingent upon the *direction* of the gap (too much trustee style vs. too much instructed delegate style)? If so, is that contingency itself dependent on the political orientation of citizens? It is to these questions that we now turn.

## MC APPROVAL AND PERCEPTIONS OF REPRESENTATION STYLE

To find out the degree to which dissatisfaction regarding the representation style one thinks one is getting translates into overall disapproval toward one's

MC, we simply regressed the latter on the "absolute" version of the former (ranging from 0 to 5).[2] The dependent variable, then, is also a 5-point scale, recoded to range from 0 to 1, where 0 = strong approval and 1 = strong disapproval (mean = .45; standard deviation = .34).

The representation dissatisfaction variable in this equation, then, is the variable we described above, but folded so that all expressions of dissatisfaction (regardless of whether the respondent desires more delegate-style representation or more trustee-style representation) take on positive values.

We included the usual demographic suspects as control variables (age, gender, race, income, education), as well as party identification (0 to 2; 2 = Republican). We also control for the "directional" representation dissatisfaction variable (the one shown in Table 6.1), to make sure that one type of dissatisfaction is not driving the entire relationship. Finally, as we have done in all the models discussed in this book to this point, we again clustered the standard errors of the estimates according to the particular district in which citizens lived, to account statistically for other district-specific variation across years and reduce heteroskedasticity.

Table 6.2 shows that, not surprisingly, dissatisfaction relating to the style of representation one perceives one's MC to be practicing is significantly associated with disapproval toward that MC. In fact, if we multiply the regression coefficient associated with the variable in question (.032) times the full range of the variable (5 points), we see that those who perceive there to be the largest gap between the style they want and the style they think they get tend to be more than 16% less approving of their MC than are those who perceive no gap at all.

What is actually somewhat surprising is that this relationship is not larger. Wondering if this weaker-than-expected relationship could be explained by the direction of citizens' perception gaps (i.e., wanting more trustee-style representation than one thinks one is getting vs. wanting more instructed delegate-style representation than one thinks one is getting), we split the file according to this direction, and repeated the analysis for each group.

The second column of Table 6.2 displays the relationship among people who want greater delegate-style representation, and the third column displays the relationship among people who want greater trustee-style representation.

---

[2] We used Ordinary Least Squares (OLS) regression to estimate the models with this dependent variable, but we obtain the same substantive and statistical results when we use ordered logistic regression as the estimation technique.

**TABLE 6.2** *OLS REGRESSIONS OF DISAPPROVAL OF MEMBER OF CONGRESS ON REPRESENTATION GAP ("IS"—"OUGHT") AND CONTROLS*

| | All Respondents | Respondents who want more Delegate | Respondents who want more Trustee |
|---|---|---|---|
| Representation Gap (Directional) | –0.00558 | | |
| | (0.00477) | | |
| Representation Gap (Absolute) | 0.0324** | 0.0411** | 0.0571** |
| | (0.00558) | (0.00881) | (0.0122) |
| Party Identification (GOP high) | –0.0664* | –0.122** | –0.0367 |
| | (0.0254) | (0.0352) | (0.0477) |
| Women | 0.0235 | 0.0354 | 0.0391 |
| | (0.0177) | (0.0268) | (0.0413) |
| Whites | –0.0237 | 0.0143 | –0.0478 |
| | (0.0181) | (0.0232) | (0.0399) |
| Education | –0.00137 | 0.00722 | –0.000882 |
| | (0.00671) | (0.00765) | (0.0139) |
| Income | –5.91e–06 | –0.000500 | –0.00203 |
| | (0.00204) | (0.00326) | (0.00530) |
| Resides in South | –0.00154 | 0.00372 | –0.0187 |
| | (0.0155) | (0.0247) | (0.0335) |
| Married | –0.0225 | –0.00943 | –0.0196 |
| | (0.0218) | (0.0254) | (0.0457) |
| Birth Year | 0.00359** | 0.00275* | 0.00390** |
| | (0.000637) | (0.00107) | (0.00117) |
| Catholic | –0.00848 | –0.0414* | –0.00522 |
| | (0.0151) | (0.0196) | (0.0291) |
| Constant | –6.572** | –4.995* | –7.214** |
| | (1.240) | (2.087) | (2.268) |
| Observations | 2,679 | 1,243 | 528 |
| R-squared | 0.057 | 0.068 | 0.073 |

Robust standard errors in parentheses. Data: CES 2006, 2007, 2009
** $p < .01$, * $p < .05$

As can be seen, while those who want greater trustee-style representation might be a little more likely to punish their MC than are those who want greater delegate-style representation, the difference is not substantial. Thus, we can conclude, based on this set of analyses at least, that the relationship between MC approval/disapproval and dissatisfaction over the MC's style of representation is not one-sided. Both those who would like to see more following of public opinion and those would like to see more independent judgment are likely to punish the MC in roughly equal proportions.

But that might not be the end of the story. The inclusion of the party identification variable as a simple control in the previous model might be clouding our perception. Perhaps party identification actually *conditions* our relationship of interest. To find out, we reanalyzed the previous model, after also dividing the sample according to whether respondents identified as Republicans (recall that the file had already been split according to the *direction* of respondent dissatisfaction with the MC's representation style [too much trustee style vs. too much instructed delegate style]).

We hypothesize that Republican respondents tend to express greater disapproval toward representatives whom they see as excessively prone to following public opinion than they do toward representatives who they see as exhibiting too much trustee-style behavior. On the other hand, we expect to see exactly the opposite pattern among non-Republicans. That is, Democrats and independents should express greater disapproval toward representatives who seem to be too stubbornly resistant to constituent demands than they do toward representatives who seem too eager to please.

Table 6.3 displays the results. Our expectations were borne out rather convincingly. Looking at the first two columns of results, which focus on respondents who see their representatives as exhibiting more instructed delegate-style behavior than they would necessarily see as ideal, we can see that when Republicans see their representatives as following public opinion too closely, they really don't like it. Those who think they are getting the least trustee-style representation, relative to what they want, are around 50% less supportive of that MC, on average. But while that relationship is impressive, what is perhaps more interesting is that among non-Republicans, MC approval is not affected at all by perceptions of too much policy pandering. That is, while some non-Republican respondents may see their representative as too eager to please the public, it doesn't really translate into a significantly lower approval rate, overall.

Looking now at the third and fourth columns of results in the table, which focus on the subsample of respondents across the three years who see their representative as demonstrating too much trustee-style representation, we observe the same pattern as above but in reverse. Non-Republicans who perceive themselves to be getting the least amount of instructed delegate-style representation, relative to what they would like, tend to be about 23% less supportive of their representative, generally speaking. The same relationship does not hold for Republicans, however.

At this point, some readers might wonder if these results suffer from a problem of reverse causality. In other words, one might wonder if citizens who do not like their MC very much, for any reason or set of reasons, are just

**TABLE 6.3** *OLS REGRESSIONS OF DISAPPROVAL OF MEMBER OF CONGRESS ON REPRESENTATION GAP ("IS"—"OUGHT") AND CONTROLS, BY PARTY IDENTIFICATION*

| | Want More Trustee | | Want More Delegate | |
|---|---|---|---|---|
| | **Republicans** | **Democrats and Independents** | **Republicans** | **Democrats and Independents** |
| Representation Gap (Absolute) | 0.0987** | 0.0294 | 0.0207 | 0.0460** |
| | (0.0204) | (0.0189) | (0.0170) | (0.0105) |
| Married | –0.134* | 0.0491 | –0.00356 | –0.000897 |
| | (0.0549) | (0.0525) | (0.0479) | (0.0287) |
| Resides in South | 0.0407 | –0.0389 | 0.00597 | 0.00664 |
| | (0.0616) | (0.0329) | (0.0434) | (0.0236) |
| Birth Year | 0.00325** | 0.00435** | 0.00243 | 0.00292* |
| | (0.00113) | (0.00153) | (0.00192) | (0.00114) |
| Income | –0.0129 | 0.00261 | –0.00466 | 0.000965 |
| | (0.00811) | (0.00636) | (0.00689) | (0.00376) |
| Education | 0.00317 | –0.00372 | 0.00802 | 0.00409 |
| | (0.0163) | (0.0174) | (0.0174) | (0.00788) |
| Whites | –0.138 | –0.0316 | 0.00975 | 0.0105 |
| | (0.0784) | (0.0467) | (0.0613) | (0.0222) |
| Women | 0.0803 | 0.0182 | 0.0325 | 0.0475 |
| | (0.0723) | (0.0497) | (0.0467) | (0.0345) |
| Catholic | –0.0129 | –0.0155 | –0.0516 | –0.0364 |
| | (0.0563) | (0.0280) | (0.0433) | (0.0266) |
| Constant | –5.852* | –8.103** | –4.439 | –5.366* |
| | (2.229) | (2.973) | (3.781) | (2.208) |
| Observations | 193 | 335 | 344 | 899 |
| R-squared | 0.227 | 0.043 | 0.027 | 0.057 |

Robust standard errors in parentheses. Data: CES 2006, 2007, 2009
** p < .01, * p < .05

more likely to say that their representative is practicing the opposite style of representation from that which they prefer. And given that Republicans are generally more likely to prefer trustees than are Democrats, the particular pattern of partisanship-contingent results that we have uncovered might be a simple manifestation of those prior attitudes toward the MC. The analytical problem is that the main independent variable of interest—the gap between representation-style preferences and representation-style perceptions—is itself a measure of satisfaction/dissatisfaction. So, given that the dependent variable (MC approval/disapproval) is also a measure of satisfaction/dissatisfaction, it is hard to really know what is causing what here.

Thus, to make sure that this potential endogeneity problem is not accounting for our findings, we also pursued an alternate (and simpler) modeling strategy: we just used respondent perceptions of whether the MC is a trustee or an instructed delegate as the main variable predicting MC approval/disapproval (trichotomized), and we then compared the direction, magnitude, and significance of this relationship among Republicans to that among non-Republicans.

As Figures 6.1 and 6.2 show, these results tell the same basic tale: Democrats and independents who think their representative is a trustee are quite a bit less likely to approve of the job that representative is doing than they are if they see the representative as an instructed delegate, but Republicans who see their representative as a trustee are actually more likely to express *support* for that representative (though this latter relationship is rather small).[3]

While these results do not provide as much detailed information about this pattern of relationships as do the previous models (revealed in Table 6.2), and thus should not *replace* those models, these results do have the advantage

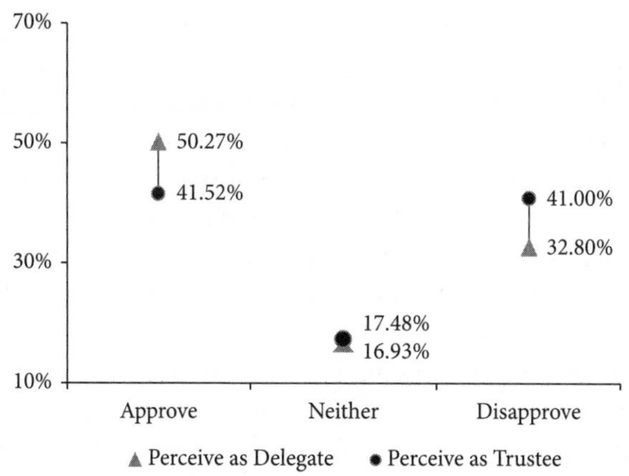


*Figure 6.1* MC Approval, by Perceived Representation Style: Among Non-Republican Respondents

[3] As has been the case throughout this book, the exact statistical relationships for the next two figures, with all appropriate inferential statistics, are included in the Appendix.

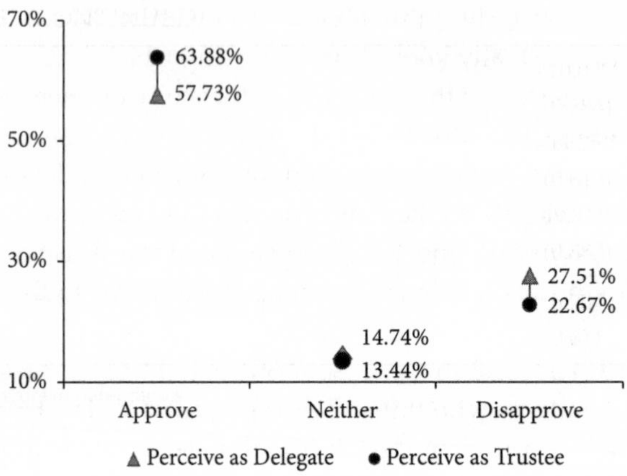


*Figure 6.2* MC Approval, by Perceived Representation Style: Among Republican Respondents

of not being contaminated by as many worries about reciprocal causality—because the independent variable is the simple perception of the MC's representation style, which is not in itself an evaluative statement.

Taken together, these two sets of results (revealed in the last two figures and the previous table) raise our level of confidence that perception/preference gaps among citizens in terms of MC representation styles do have bearing on approval rates, in ways that are consistent with the broader argument that we have been making in this book. This pattern of findings is important because it reveals, first of all, that the style of representation that lawmakers practice *does* matter to citizens. When representatives practice the wrong style, in the eyes of citizens, the approval rates of those representatives suffer.

However, what is more relevant to the main argument we craft in this book is that citizens of different partisan stripes do not view all representation-style sins the same way. Thus, representatives who do not have too many Republicans in their districts can try to appeal to a broader ideological constituency by following public opinion, without worrying too much about their core ideological supporters feeling like they are being sold out. Those same legislators, however, must be mindful to not ignore changes in public opinion, or they will surely hear about it. Those who do have a lot of Republicans in their districts, on the other hand, don't need to pay so much attention to changes in constituent opinion. In fact, they had better not change their policy positions too readily in response to public outcries, or else they are actually likely to see their popularity dwindle.

The implications of this pattern we have uncovered are clear: if representatives in Red America want to stay popular (so they can keep their jobs), the smartest move they can make is toward ideological "purity." They should stick to their guns when it comes to policymaking and resist the temptation to compromise with the other side or give in to majoritarian demands for change. Those who represent Blue America, however, have just the opposite incentive structure: they had better listen to majoritarian demands for change, or they will probably face a tougher reelection challenge.

## MC PARTISANSHIP AND PERCEPTIONS OF REPRESENTATION STYLE

In this chapter and the previous one, we have provided good reasons to expect that mass preferences regarding representation styles affect the way lawmakers behave. But as we all know, just because something makes sense does not mean that it actually occurs. Thus, in Chapter 7, we will use very different data to see if MCs seem to behave in ways that square with the electoral dynamics and "Pandering 2.0" strategic incentives that we have worked to establish.

Before we attempt to crown things in that way, though, there is one more possible relationship that we can eye up, which will help set the table for that final test. If, as we think they should, Republican legislators tend to act more like trustees than Democratic legislators do, and if they try to do so in ways that make constituents notice (in order to maintain their approval rates and appeal to the right reelection constituencies), then at least some constituents should be able to tell. While most constituents will surely not pay close enough attention to legislative rhetoric (let alone legislative behavior) to clearly recognize legislators' attempts at providing one or the other style of representation, we think some will. In fact, we expect that enough of them will so as to establish a relationship (albeit a weak one, perhaps) between the legislator's party identification and citizens' perceptions of that legislator's representation style.

Accordingly, we test the hypothesis that Republican legislators are more likely to be perceived as trustees than are Democratic legislators. Fortunately for us, in 2006 and 2007 (but unfortunately not in 2008 or 2009), the CES paired up each survey respondent with his or her MC, and listed the MC names as a variable in the data, along with another measure that identified each representative's party identification. This MC party identification measure became the dependent variable in a probit regression model in which the main explanatory variable is the representation-style perception measure described at the beginning of this chapter.

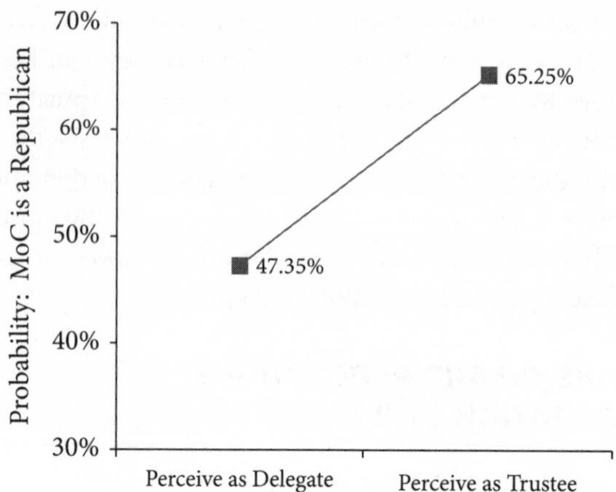


*Figure 6.3* MC Party Identification, by Perceived Representation Style

As has surely become a monotonous (but, we hope, clarifying) pattern across the past three chapters, the line graph in Figure 6.3 displays the results, which are actually stronger than we had expected they would be. Citizens who perceive their representative to be an unequivocal trustee are roughly 18% more likely to be represented by a Republican, relative to those who have the clearest sense that their representative is a consistent instructed delegate.

## CONCLUSION

In this chapter, we have tried to provide additional empirical links in the theoretical chain foretelling a relationship between residing in parts of the country that are marked by cultural traditionalism having less democratic voice—stemming from the fact that large numbers of cultural traditionalists actually feel squeamish about the idea of people having a whole lot of democratic voice. Specifically, we have shown that Republican citizens are inclined to punish their representatives for "sticking their fingers in the wind" to determine constituent opinion and following those winds, but are not inclined to punish representatives who cover their ears and sing "la la la" to avoid hearing the clamoring from their districts. What is more, that pattern appears to be true even when citizens do actually frown upon such "drowning out" behavior by legislators in the abstract. And on the other side of things, Democrats and independents seem ready to throw the bums out when legislators don't listen to them as much as they would like, but are willing to put up with them not demonstrating very much independent leadership.

This pattern means that while legislators representing progressive or even moderate congressional districts have a strong incentive to pander to constituents in the traditional way (by tracking changes in constituent opinion and modifying their legislative behavior accordingly), legislators representing heavily traditionalistic districts are motivated to pander in a different way altogether (by respecting constituent wishes to not be pandered to in the traditional way!).

Furthermore, if legislators really do respond to mass representation preferences in the ways we have suggested, it only stands to reason that some constituents would recognize such responses. Accordingly, because Republicans usually represent traditionalistic areas, we predicted that more citizens would be able to recognize trustee-style representation coming from Republican legislators than they do from Democratic legislators. This prediction was also borne out by our data. So while citizens' perceptions might not necessarily correspond to reality, they do give us more indirect and suggestive evidence in support of our main theoretical argument. After all, as the old adage goes, politics is all about perception.

Hence, the stage has now been fully set to examine directly how lawmakers differ in terms of their representation styles. So it is on to Chapter 7 we go.

## CHAPTER 7

# Red Representation, Blue Representation

> Politics and government demand compromise. But these Christians believe they are acting in the name of God, so they can't and won't compromise. I know; I've tried to deal with them.
>
> *Barry Goldwater, 1994*
> *(as quoted by Dean, 2006)*

To this point, we have been able to demonstrate quite a few things in this book. First, in Chapter 2, we showed that individual preferences regarding styles of political representation vary in meaningful ways. Then, in Chapter 3, we provided a detailed theory to explain the variation in those preferences, which we grounded in the basic premise that instructed delegate-style representation is a manifestation of liberal popular democratic ideals such as humanism and basic egalitarianism. We argued that cultural traditionalists tend to feel less enthusiasm toward those particular democratic values than do cultural progressives, which predisposes the traditionalists toward the trustee style of representation, relatively speaking. And by extension, because such traditionalism has become so associated with Republican Party identification over the course of the past generation, we argued that GOP'ers tend to trust trustees more than Democrats do, all things being equal. In Chapter 4, we put these ideas to empirical test, finding considerable empirical support for each. In Chapter 5 we took the next step: we demonstrated that preferences for one representation style or another also help explain vote choices, even after the effect of party identification has been taken into account. Finally, in Chapter 6, we showed that people who are represented by Republican legislators are more likely to believe that what they are getting is trustee-style representation out of those legislators, but that they differ in terms of how they feel about that. Democratic and independent citizens tend to express disapproval toward members of Congress (MCs) whom they see as behaving too stubbornly (trustee style), but not toward MCs whom they see as following public opinion too intently. Republicans, on the other hand, tend not to mind so much when their representatives shirk public opinion—even excessively so (according to the citizens' own previously stated preferences)—but they express disapproval when they think their MCs are following public opinion too intently.

We consider these findings to be important in their own right. After all, increasing our knowledge of how citizens think about representation can help us gain insight into things like the mass citizenry's perceived political efficacy, trust in government, and general political psychology. Furthermore, knowing that such preferences affect voting behavior provides another tool with which political scientists can attempt to better understand electoral winners and losers. Finally, understanding how preferences about representation styles affect the working dialogue between citizens and lawmakers provides some much-needed Windex to help clarify our understanding of political representation as a concept more generally.

In another respect, though, one could say that everything we have done to this point has been a prelude to this chapter. That is, up until now, we have been trying to systematically build the case that the style of representation citizens want often translates into the style of representation citizens get. In other words, we have been setting the table to explain why, in some cases, it may actually be a bad idea for representatives to conduct opinion polls and to pay too much attention to those poll results. More precisely, we have argued that while lawmakers might be well served to pander to culturally progressive constituencies in the traditional way—by gauging constituents' policy preferences and adjusting their own policymaking behavior accordingly—lawmakers who serve more traditionalistic constituencies might pursue a quite different strategy: they might actually gain the respect and support of such constituencies by *not* responding too eagerly to their apparent policy demands.

In this chapter, we culminate this argument by considering legislative policymaking behavior directly. We hypothesize that if lawmakers try to appeal to progressive constituencies by governing as instructed delegates, but to traditionalistic constituencies by governing as trustees (regardless of whether they do it directly or indirectly, consciously or subconsciously, pre-election or post-election), we should observe weaker ideological congruence between constituent issue attitudes and legislative roll-call votes in "Redder" congressional districts than we do in "Bluer" congressional districts.

Some research by other scholars has hinted that such a pattern might be observable. For example, Francis and Kenny (1996) showed that when House members are gearing up for a Senate run, Democratic legislators are more likely than Republican ones to change their issue positions (to be more in line with constituent opinion at the state level). Moreover, Kousser et al. (2007) showed that following the 2003 California recall election, Democratic legislators moderated their voting behavior as a sign of ideological adaptation to their constituents, but there is no evidence of California Republican legislators behaving similarly. More broadly, focusing on legislative policy responsiveness to public opinion as it pertains to gay rights issues, Lax and Phillips (2009) observed that much less responsivenesss tends to occur when Republicans control the legislature than when Democrats control it.

While those studies provide support for our hypotheses that relate to partisanship, Hill and Matsubayashi's (2008) study provides direct support for our proposed Culture Wars mechanism, showing that local community leaders are in fact less responsive to citizen demands in areas containing large concentrations of evangelicals and other traditionalists, but more responsive in communities containing large numbers of mainline Protestants.

## DATA AND METHODOLOGY

To test our hypotheses, we begin by analyzing MCs' roll-call voting behavior from 1985 to 2010. The unit of analysis is MC (N ~ 435; larger in some years due to replacing retirees)[1] the two-year congressional number (N = 13), producing an overall sample of 5,723. Of course, in actuality, this is not a sample at all, but the entire universe of legislators for this time period. Thus, unlike the relationships described in previous chapters, the relationships we describe in this chapter are not estimates of some population—they are pinpoints of an entire population. However, if we want to draw inferences about behavior at other points in time, either in the future or the past, statistical tests of inference are still relevant. As such, when the time comes, we will discuss the results of such statistical tests (which are also be included in all regression tables).

### *Measuring Trustee-Style Behavior*

To measure our dependent variable, which is the variation in policy responsiveness of legislators to their district constituents, we needed a way to capture the degree to which the ideological character of a member's roll-call votes

[1] However, the working N in our estimated models wound up being somewhat smaller (see Tables 7.1–7.3). This is because our attempts at coding the religious identities of members of Congress (which we describe below) produced some uncodable cases, which we then treated as missing data.

corresponds to the ideological character of his or her district constituency. This necessitated a few steps. The first step was to identify the ideological character of an individual MC's roll-call voting behavior within a given session of Congress. To do so, we followed what has become standard practice among political scientists, which is to say that we used the first dimension of Keith Poole and Howard Rosenthal's "DW-Nominate scores" (e.g., 1997). Poole and Rosenthal derived their measure from a somewhat complicated statistical procedure of compiling all roll-call votes, coding them on a liberal/conservative dimension, and using scaling techniques to estimate overall relative scores of liberalism/conservatism (for details, see www.voteview.com). While the procedure is somewhat complex, the measure has been shown to capture legislator liberalism/conservatism remarkably consistently and efficiently, which is why it has been used to measure roll-call liberalism/conservatism in countless published articles and books by now (for an overview, see Thierault, Hickey, & Blass, 2011).[2]

The next step was to gain a measure of the liberalism/conservatism of a given legislative district in a given point in time. Importantly, we needed to measure such mass attitudes at points in time immediately prior to each period under which a given legislator's roll-call behavior was being observed. In other words, to calculate the degree to which legislators consider and follow their constituents' ideological preferences when deciding how to vote on pieces of legislation, we needed to include a slight temporal "lag" between the calculation of the constituent preferences and the roll-call voting behavior, because legislators need a little bit of time to observe constituent preferences and let them "sink in."

Temporal issues aside, to measure congressional district-level liberalism/conservatism, we again followed "market standards" by using the percentage of the district that voted for the Republican presidential candidate in the previous election as a proxy (which has been shown to correlate very highly with the ideological flavor of actual issue attitudes in districts). That is, if 52% of citizens living in district X voted for the Republican presidential candidate (whether George Bush in 1988 or John McCain in 2008), we can be

---

[2] Of course, other methods exist for measuring legislator liberalism/conservatism, including the many 0-to-100 scores that interest groups (most notably, the Americans for Democratic Action) have calculated. These measures tend to correlate quite highly with DW-Nominate scores. Not surprisingly, then, when we specify alternate statistical models in which we substitute some of these alternate measures for ours, we observe results that are consistent with those we report below.

confident that the citizens living in district X tend to hold moderate or disparate policy preferences, and thus that the district overall cannot be considered particularly Red or Blue—either culturally or politically speaking. On the other hand, if 74% of citizens living in district Y voted for the Republican presidential candidate, chances are that district is populated with a lot of cultural traditionalists, because really skewed votes in favor of Republican presidential candidates suggest culture warrior status on the part of district constituencies, overall.

The third step, then, was to create a measure that somehow calculates the degree of convergence between a MC's DW-Nominate score in a given Congress and the partisan vote share of her district in the previous presidential election. Unfortunately, creating a simple measure that would subtract one variable from the other, revealing variation in the gap between the two variables, is not a viable measurement strategy because the two variables are not measured on identical (or even particularly similar) scales. DW-Nominates typically range from –1 to 1, with some legislators occasionally receiving scores that fall outside that range. By contrast, partisan presidential vote share is obviously restricted to a possible range of 0 to 100, with the realistic range being somewhat "skinnier" than that (in our data, the observed range, over all years, is .04 to .83).

Thus, we again followed what has become standard practice (see a discussion by Hill & Hurley, 2010) by following a two-step process to create the variable. First, we estimated a regression equation that predicts a member's DW-Nominate score in a given year with the district presidential vote-share variable (this first-stage equation is included in the Appendix). We then saved the absolute values of the residuals of this regression equation (the distance between what the regression line predicts the value of the dependent variable to be for any particular observation in the data and the actual observed value of the dependent variable for that observation), which amount to 55% of the variance in MC ideology, as a new variable in our dataset. So the larger the value of this variable, the less well an individual MC's roll-call votes align ideologically with the views of her district constituents. The variable ranges from 0 to 1.34, with a mean of .25 and a standard deviation of .20. This new variable, which we call *Ideological Nonresponsiveness*, serves as the dependent variable for our analyses that follow.

Thus, while constituent ideology (as measured by presidential vote share in the previous election) explains much MC roll-call voting behavior, there is a considerable amount of variance in such behavior that is NOT explained, which suggests that there is a good deal of MC decision making going on that is based on considerations other than constituent ideology.

### *Constructing District Traditionalism*

Having constructed the dependent variable for our analysis, we needed to construct the main independent variable, which we have labeled *District Traditionalism*. This also turned out to be somewhat tricky. We wanted a way to measure the variation across districts in terms of their religious and cultural traditionalism, but in a way that would also capture a partisan dimension. Ideally, we would have percentages across districts in terms of the number of evangelical Christians, NRA members, and the like who live in those districts. Unfortunately, such data are not readily attainable. So we had to look for another proxy.

Conceptually speaking, partisan presidential vote share (described earlier) would seem to have served as a good proxy—it being known to correlate highly with the number of religious and cultural traditionalists in a district. However, methodologically speaking, this variable in its original constitution is problematic because it was included as part of the calculation of the dependent variable described above. Thus, to avoid modeling pitfalls attributable to artificially shared variance in the independent and dependent variables, we created an "instrumental variable" to stand in for partisan presidential vote share.

Creating this instrument again required estimating another first-stage regression equation—this time with partisan presidential vote share as the dependent variable in that equation. We wanted to generate predicted values of that vote-share variable from the regression equation, based on factors that fit our theory regarding the influence of evangelical religiosity and other aspects of cultural traditionalism. Thus, we included the following predictor variables in this first-stage regression equation: (1) MC partisan identity (1 = GOP), (2) the second dimension scores of Poole and Rosenthal's DW-Nominate scores (which have correlated with traditionalism in other studies), (3) whether the congressional district falls within a state that is culturally "Red" (i.e., if the state is Southern, rural, or known for cultural conservatism), (4) the religious identity of the particular MC representing that district (evangelical denominations and LDS = 1; others [seculars, mainline Protestants, Jews] = 0)[3]), and (5) dummy variables for

[3] Evangelical denominations include Southern Baptists and all other Baptists except the American Baptists, the Presbyterian Church in America (but not the Presbyterian Church of the USA), Wisconsin and Missouri Synod Lutherans (but not the Evangelical Lutheran Church), the Church of Christ (but not the United Church of Christ of the Disciples of Christ), the Church of the Nazarene, and Pentecostal/charismatic denominations such as the Assemblies of God and the various Churches of God. When MCs were identified as "Christian," or "nondenominational Christian," we had to search deeper, looking at speeches,

each Congress (100–111, with the 99th as the reference category), to make sure that any individual session does not disproportionately shape the estimate.[4] We then saved the predicted values of partisan presidential vote share generated by that equation. The resulting variable—our independent variable of primary theoretical interest—ranges from 11 to 83, with a mean of 50 and a standard deviation of 11.[5] Again, the results from the first-stage regression equation are available in the Appendix.

While recognizing that instrumental variables may be less desirable in some ways than directly measured concepts, we believe this measure achieves the best of all possible worlds. First, this measure is still an indicator of *mass* ideology. This distinction is important because the theory on which we have based this analysis, as established in the previous six chapters, is about the role played by mass preferences regarding representation styles—and representatives' incentives to placate to those style preferences (rather than listening exclusively to policy preferences). Thus, while it is true that we would envision the same dynamics that influence mass representation preferences also influencing such preferences among elites, if all we were to include in

endorsements, and other personal statements. If it was unequivocally clear that the member was an evangelical based on this search, we coded the member as an evangelical; if not, we coded the religious identification as "unknown," producing one source of random error in our data. Of course, this strategy of identifying MC religious traditionalism based on denominational affiliation is somewhat crude, based on the fact that many churches identified with the Protestant mainline function as evangelical churches and that even when they do not, many congregants within those churches are in fact evangelicals. This source of error biases the statistical analysis toward Type II errors of inference. In other words, this particular type of error made it somewhat harder for us to unearth relationships in the data. This is because, while many ostensibly mainline Protestants are in fact evangelical, the reverse is rarely true. Thus, by using this crude strategy to identify Christian traditionalism, we are surely leaving out considerable numbers of traditionalists from our measure, meaning that any relationships that we observe are likely to be stronger in reality, not weaker.

4 In this regression equation, as in all others described in this chapter, we clustered the standard errors of the estimated regression coefficients by the identification number of the MC, since within a given district, the same MC would represent that district for typically more than one session, creating shared variance across data points that needed to be controlled.

5 The extremely low predicted Republican vote shares are observed in districts drawn to be overwhelmingly African American. If such districts are removed from the analysis, the lowest value of the partisan presidential vote share variable is 28.

our statistical models were elite-level measures of district traditionalism, we would not be able to really put to the test the theoretical story on which these analyses are based. After all, any relationship that we might have observed under those modeling conditions could have just as easily been the byproduct of elites following their own preferred representation styles—perhaps based on the same factors we have described—but without any consideration (even subconsciously) of what their constituents want in that regard. That would have been useful information to know, to be sure, but it would have certainly been less than ideal for our purposes.

Second, the instrumental measure predicts 65% of the variance in actual partisan presidential vote share (which is somewhat unusually high, in our experience, for an instrumental measure), which demonstrates its validity as a measure of mass liberalism/conservatism across districts. What is more, we see the 35% of the variance in district partisan vote share that it does not explain as an added strength, not a weakness. That is, presidential candidates do better or worse in some districts depending on a variety of factors that have nothing to do with our theory—such as the candidate's "favorite son" status in a particular state or region, differences in campaign spending or tactics, differential economic interests and performance during the incumbent's administration, the slant of media coverage in particular markets, and so on. Thus, by creating a measure that is purged of these factors, which is what this instrumental approach has achieved, we are getting a purer operationalization of what we really want—district traditionalism.

Finally, the instrumental measure eliminates the potential statistical problems associated with using the original partisan presidential vote-share variable, as discussed earlier.

### Model Specification

Equipped, at this point, with useful measures of both *MC Ideological Nonresponsiveness* and *District Traditionalism*, we were (finally) able to specify and estimate our regression analysis model. Because the dependent variable is a continuous scale, Ordinary Least Squares (OLS) is an unbiased and efficient estimation technique.[6]

[6] However, the variable does display considerable positive skew. Alternate models estimated using Poisson and negative binomial regression estimators reveal statistically identical results. Similarly, when the variable is logged to generate more normality and models are re-estimated, our conclusions remain the same. We have decided to stick with the OLS results because they are more easily interpretable and are broadly robust.

We included a few other variables in our model. The first provides us with another way of testing our hypothesis. It is a trend variable (Congressional session: 99–111) that simply considers whether policy responsiveness grew or diminished over the period of time between 1985 and 2010. We know that during this period of time a few things occurred: (1) congressional polarization magnified (see Schnaffner, 2011, for an overview), (2) mass ideological constraint increased (e.g., Abramowitz & Saunders, 1998), (3) the numbers of religious traditionalists increased radically, within both the citizenry and the House of Representatives (*Congressional Quarterly* 1984–2010), which led to (4) greatly enhanced influence of religion over party identification and voting, at both the mass level and in the House of Representatives (see Smidt, Kellstedt, & Guth, 2009, for an overview). We reason that if traditionalism is associated with greater trustee-style representation, then as traditionalism grew over time in the House, so should have the overall amount of trustee-style representation in that institution (but not in secular or progressive districts). Furthermore, we expect that the relationship between *District Traditionalism* and *Ideological Nonresponsiveness* grew substantially between 1982 and 2008.

Second, we included a measure of whether the MC was an African American who identifies with an evangelical Christian denomination, because most African Americans identify as religious traditionalists but almost none of them vote for Republican presidential candidates (e.g., Fowler et al., 2010).[7] This variable provides yet another means of evaluating the extent to which traditionalism may predict ideological nonresponsiveness on the part of MCs (we will have more to say about this later).

Third, we controlled for the direction of the variation in the dependent variable. That is, while at this point we are trying to explain variation in the absolute gap between the ideological character of MCs' roll-call votes and their constituents' ideological predilections, regardless of whether MCs are behaving more conservatively than their constituents or more liberally than their constituents, it is important to control for that directionality, in case it is skewed in one direction or the other. If we had not controlled for

---

[7] We recognize, of course, that traditionally "black churches," while evangelical in many respects, differ from white evangelical churches in important ways, perhaps especially as it pertains to doctrine. Specifically, many (if not most) African American evangelical churches adhere to "liberation theology," which most white evangelical churches consider anathema. In most of the ways that matter to our hypotheses, though, black evangelical dogma resembles that of white evangelicals.

this directionality, the estimates of our hypothesized relationships could have been biased, in theory. For example, if, in general, MCs of most stripes tend to behave more conservatively than their district constituencies, the absolute measure of that ideological gap between representative and constituency would be biased toward finding stronger results among the most traditionalistic MCs. Thus, it was important that we rule out that alternate explanation.[8]

Fourth, we controlled for district ideological extremism, by creating a variable that subtracted the district's partisan presidential vote share from the mean (50). This was important because a certain amount of ideological noncongruence between districts and their representatives might result when districts are just overwhelmingly ideological. Because our main independent variable of interest, district partisan presidential vote share, will also capture extremism on one side of the ideological spectrum, we wanted to make sure that any relationship that we observe between GOP vote share and policy nonresponsiveness is not the simple byproduct of district extremism in general, rather than district cultural traditionalism, as we have hypothesized.

Fifth, we controlled for whether the MC was a newly elected freshman legislator, reasoning that such legislators are more electorally vulnerable than are legislators with more tenure—which might provide such legislators with greater incentives to follow public opinion.

Finally, we controlled for individual sessions of Congress with a series of dummy variables (omitting the 99th Congress as the reference category), to make sure that our findings were not being overly influenced by any particular year or set of years, which might have been exceptional.

Again, because each observation in the data is not independent—namely, individual MCs represent the same districts in multiple years—we calculated the standard errors of each slope coefficient using "robust" standard errors, clustered by the identification number of individual MCs. This procedure corrects for correlations that are a byproduct of this non-independence across observations (for a discussion, see Steffensmeier, Brady, & Collier, 2008).

It is important to note that we are taking a very cautious modeling approach by including so many statistical controls. Indeed, we are deliberately "overspecifying" our model, including many variables that are themselves correlated, for the purpose of making sure that we do not make type II

[8] However, when we remove this control from our models, the relationship between our dependent variable and independent variables of interest do not change.

statistical errors of inference. In other words, we are making our hypothesis work hard to achieve statistical significance.[9]

## RESULTS

The first results column of Table 7.1 displays the results. Focusing first on the relationship between *MC Ideological Nonresponsiveness* and *District Traditionalism*, if we multiply the regression coefficient associated with *District Traditionalism* ($b$ = .00447) by the full range of that variable (70 points), so as to obtain the difference in *Nonresponsiveness* between MCs representing the most and least traditionalistic districts (.00447*70 = .31), and then divide that by the range of the dependent variable (.31/1.34), we see that between 1985 and 2008, MCs representing the most traditionalistic districts tended to vote on legislation in ways that were 23% less consistent with the ideological predilections of their district constituencies, relative to MCs who represented the most progressive districts.[10]

---

9 It is also important to note that our results are very similar regardless of whether we (1) attempt to account for autocorrelation in the data (with a lagged AR-1 term), (2) employ "panel corrected standard errors" to account for contemporaneous (spatial) autocorrelation, (3) focus on modeling the within-unit over-time (fixed effects) variance (though those results are statistically suspect because of the small number of time points) or the between-unit cross-sectional variance, or both (which is what we report), or (4) use a "random coefficients model" to allow for unit heterogeneity (e.g., different MCs representing the same district over time). In light of this robustness, and in light of the large number of "panels" in our data (N), we have chosen to report the results from the simplest "pooled" OLS model (with Huber-White [robust] standard errors clustered by MC and dummy variables included for each Congress, as reported earlier) for each year.

10 This relationship is statistically significant when the sample is restricted to either Republican MCs only or Democratic MCs only. Also, in various alternate models, substituting the items used to create the partisan presidential vote-share instrument directly into the model (in place of the instrument), we observe statistically significant results for each of these items as well. This may reveal that traditionalism on the part of MCs themselves also affects their ideological responsiveness, which is also consistent with our theoretical argument. However, the substance of the relationships is always weaker, regardless of the variable used (party identification, Nominate score, MC religious identity), which suggests that mass traditionalism is ultimately more meaningful of a predictor of MC nonresponsiveness. Indeed, when we include both types of measures simultaneously in the model, the institution-level variables lose significant predictive power, but the mass-level measure does not lose nearly as much.

**TABLE 7.1** *REGRESSION (OLS) OF MC NONRESPONSIVENESS ON DISTRICT TRADITIONALISM AND CONTROLS, BY DISTRICT IDEOLOGY*

| | All Respondents, All Districts | Respondents in Conservative Districts | Respondents in Progressive Districts |
|---|---|---|---|
| District Traditionalism | 0.00447** | –0.000217 | 0.00781** |
| | (0.000585) | (0.000575) | (0.000945) |
| District Ideological Extremism | 0.0169** | 0.0163** | 0.0148** |
| | (0.000470) | (0.00174) | (0.00120) |
| Conservative Nonresponsiveness | –0.0453 | 0.108 | –0.248** |
| | (0.0243) | (0.0712) | (0.0489) |
| Black Evangelical MC | 0.151** | | 0.172** |
| | (0.0273) | | (0.0221) |
| First-Term MC | –0.00774 | –0.0102* | –0.000427 |
| | (0.00505) | (0.00482) | (0.00710) |
| Trend | 0.00810** | 0.0190** | –0.00895** |
| | (0.000917) | (0.00211) | (0.00143) |
| Constant | –0.245** | –0.0740* | –0.275** |
| | (0.0317) | (0.0374) | (0.0447) |
| Observations | 5,188 | 2,769 | 2,419 |
| R-squared | 0.606 | 0.693 | 0.794 |

Robust standard errors in parentheses. Congress dummies not shown in table.
** $p < .01$, * $p < .05$

Again, this relationship is almost certainly understated. The *Ideological Extremism* variable, in particular, shares a lot of variance with our dependent variable, *District Traditionalism*, which reduces the latter's predictive capacity. Given that, intuitively speaking, it is quite likely that the latter causes the former in many instances, it gives us strong reason to suspect that the "real" effect is greater than 23%. In fact, in alternative specifications in which we remove the ideological extremism control, the "effect" of interest jumps up to 34%. Now, as we discussed above, we had good reasons for including *Extremism* as a statistical control, so removing it from the model might wind up in an overstated impact for *District Traditionalism.* We prefer to err on the side of understating the relationships, so we consider it prudent to leave *Extremism* in the model. Having said that, we suspect that the "real" relationship between *District Traditionalism* and *Ideological Nonresponsiveness* falls somewhere between 23% and 34%.

### *A Simpler Test*

Still, there may be some readers who have the opposite worry. That is, they might be suspicious of these results—worrying that they are a byproduct of an awful lot of statistical "cooking" (using instrumental variables, residuals from earlier regression models, various statistical controls, clustered standard errors, etc.). To ease this concern, we also performed a much simpler analysis—one that just calculates the Pearson's correlation coefficient ($r$) between MCs' DW-Nominate scores and the lagged partisan presidential vote share in the district they represent, sorted according to whether the representative is a Republican or a Democrat.[11] Correlation coefficients are standardized, and range from –1 to 1. Variables that are perfectly correlated have scores of 1, whereas variables that have a perfect inverse relationship have scores of –1. Variables that are unrelated have scores of zero. By simply distinguishing between Democrats and Republicans, this is a very rough approximation of our theoretical mechanism, but it serves our purposes well in terms of simplicity.

The correlation between these two variables among Democratic representatives is a hearty .66, while that among Republican representatives is a mere .20. So according to this simple test, the relationship, or degree of policy responsiveness on the part of legislators, is more than three times as strong among Democratic legislators than Republican legislators during the time period under study.

### *African American Traditionalists*

Could the relationship we have discussed so far result from some other aspect of partisanship that does not have anything to do with religious or cultural traditionalism? To check out this possibility, we decided to take advantage of the congressional districts in our data that were represented by African Americans who identified with evangelical Protestant denominations.

---

[11] Pearson's correlation coefficients compare variables in terms of standard deviation units, making the fact that each variable is not measured on the same scale less problematic than when comparing the variables on their original, unstandardized metrics. These coefficients, however, do suffer from statistical problems relating to the fact that correlations can be larger or smaller based on the amount of variance that exists in each variable (e.g., King, 1986, but see Luskin, 1991), which is one reason why the previously discussed regression analysis provides a more sophisticated and reliable test of our hypothesis. Still, the fact that this simple test provides results that are so in keeping with those of the more sophisticated analysis provides a nice robustness check all the way around.

Given that African American Protestants tend to adhere to the same pieces of dogma that white evangelical Protestants do, tend to display high levels of religiosity relative to whites, and so on, it is reasonable to assume that many of the districts represented by African American Protestants are populated with large shares of cultural traditionalists, who also happen to be African American.

However, with very few exceptions, most African American districts are overwhelmingly Democratic in terms of their partisanship and presidential voting proclivities. Furthermore, Black evangelicals tend to be much more liberal than white evangelicals when it comes to economic and social welfare policy issues, for reasons that are not entirely explained by differences in socioeconomic status. This anomaly (similarity in terms of cultural traditionalism but differences in political partisanship and ideology) provides us with an opportunity to gain some greater insight into whether it is really cultural traditionalism that is leading to less policy responsiveness on the part of white MCs who represent more conservative districts, or if it is some other aspect of conservatism or Republicanism that is doing the lifting.

For this part of the analysis we simply examined the relationship between *MC Policy Responsiveness* and being represented by a *Black Evangelical*, which is shown in the same table above. Given that this variable is dichotomous, we do not have to multiply the regression coefficient by anything to obtain minimum-to-maximum effects. We do still have to divide the coefficient by the range of the dependent variable, though, to convert the effects to percentage changes. Doing that (.157/1.34 = .117), we see that African American evangelical MCs were around 12% less responsive to their constituents than were other MCs in the sample, on average. This somewhat unsophisticated test provides some suggestive evidence that traditionalism leads to less policy responsiveness, regardless of broader ideological moorings (i.e., whether the religious traditionalism reflects ideological liberalism or conservatism).

### *Trends*

What about trend effects? Was trustee-style representation more prevalent in more recent years? Or, stated in terms of our operationalization, did the ability of district ideological proclivities to predict MC roll-call votes increase over time, between 1982 and 2008, in conjunction with the religious and political changes identified earlier during this same period?

Looking at the *b* coefficient associated with the *Trend* variable in the first results column of the table (.01), again multiplying it by the range of the variable (.12), and again dividing by the range of the dependent variable (1.34), we see that in 2010, MCs tended to be about 9% less responsive to their constituents than were MCs in 1985. Of course, this number jumped around a bit from year to year, but the overall trend is toward less responsiveness over time. This supports our expectation that as the numbers of traditionalists grew over time in both the citizenry and in Congress, and as their political relevance also grew, so did trustee-style representation.

Does the trend effect change according to whether we are looking at progressive districts or traditionalistic ones? Our theory suggests that the trend should be pretty much restricted to the traditionalistic districts. As the second and third columns of Table 7.1 show, when we split the sample according to whether the partisan presidential vote-share instrument is either less than 50 or more than 50, we see that among the more progressive districts, MCs actually became 8% *more* responsive, from 1982 to 2008. However, within those districts that were more inclined to vote for Republicans, MCs became roughly 16% less responsive during this same period of time, on average.

After having seen how the effect of time differs according to *District Traditionalism*, the next step is to see how the effect of *District Traditionalism* may have changed over time. As we mentioned earlier, given the increased degree to which politics came to reflect religious differences over the course of the past generation, we also hypothesized that the relationship between district traditionalism and MC policy nonresponsiveness should have also grown substantially. To test this, we created an interaction term that multiplied *District Traditionalism* by the congressional session (recoded so that we gave the 99th Congress a score of 0 and the 111th Congress a score of 12) and added this variable to our model.

As Table 7.2 shows, the data support our hypothesis overwhelmingly. Because of the interaction term, the *District Traditionalism* variable now measures the effect *when the trend variable = 0* (i.e., for the 99th Congress). So, multiplying that coefficient (–.005) times the full range of the variable and then dividing it by the range of the dependent variable, as we did before, we see that during the 99th Congress, MCs representing the most traditionalistic districts were actually 28% *more* responsive to public opinion than were MCs representing the most progressive districts.

To see how the relationship changed over time, we must first multiply the interaction term coefficient by whatever number corresponds to the year we want to observe. So if we want to observe how things looked in 2010, we (1) multiply the interaction (.0016) times 12 (which represents the 111th Congress), which equals .02; (2) add it to the *District Traditionalism* coefficient (–.005 + .02 = .0145); (3) multiply that sum times the range of *District Traditionalism* (.0145*70 = 1.01), and (4) divide that product by the range of the dependent variable (1.01/1.34 = .75). Thus, we see that the relationship reversed and

**TABLE 7.2** *REGRESSION (OLS) OF MC NONRESPONSIVENESS ON DISTRICT TRADITIONALISM AND (DISTRICT TRADITIONALISM)*(CONGRESS NUMBER) WITH CONTROLS*

| | |
|---|---|
| District Traditionalism | –0.00600** |
| | (0.000640) |
| District Traditionalism*Trend | 0.00178** |
| | (7.07e–05) |
| District Ideological Extremism | 0.0178** |
| | (0.000380) |
| Conservative Nonresponsiveness | –0.0735** |
| | (0.0204) |
| Black Evangelical MC | 0.170** |
| | (0.0175) |
| First-Term MC | –0.0115** |
| | (0.00441) |
| Trend | –0.0843** |
| | (0.00398) |
| Constant | 0.283** |
| | (0.0354) |
| Observations | 5,188 |
| R-squared | 0.716 |

Robust standard errors in parentheses. Congress dummies not shown in table.
** $p < .01$, * $p < .05$

spiked over time. In 2009–10, the MCs representing the most traditionalistic districts were 75% less responsive than those representing the most progressive districts.

### *Trustee-Style Representation: Independently Liberal, Conservative, Extreme, or Moderate?*

So, to this point, it seems safe to conclude that, according to these data we have collected representing these particular 25 years, as cultural traditionalism takes greater root—either in a particular district or in the Congress as a whole, and whether manifested within primarily black constituencies or white ones—instructed delegate-style representation diminishes.

The next thing to consider, then, is the ideological character of the apparent relative lack of policy responsiveness on the part of many MCs who represent more traditionalistic districts. There are four possibilities. First, these MCs could tend toward consistently greater ideological conservatism than their constituents—even in the really conservative constituencies at the top of the scale. Second, the MCs could systematically tend to vote more liberally than their constituents would prefer (regardless of whether that liberalism reflects extremism or moderation). Third, they could tend toward ideological extremism in either direction, which is to say that they could tend toward disproportionate conservatism when they are Republicans (or when they represent districts that skew Republican) or toward disproportionate liberalism when they are Democrats (or represent districts that skew Democratic). Finally, they could tend toward disproportionate moderation from their constituents, whether those constituents tend to be liberal or conservative.

Theoretically, the third option would seem to make the most sense to us. In general, after all, Congress has become famously more polarized than the mass public, so we would expect gaps in responsiveness to reflect this polarization. Furthermore, the way we envision it and have discussed it in previous chapters, trustee-style representation equates to "sticking to one's ideological guns"—the guns that got one elected in the first place. That would mean *not* moderating one's behavior in the face of potential changes in the political landscape that produce changes in the distribution of district public opinion on some issue(s). Hacker and Pierson (2005) have argued that this is precisely what happens.

A perfect example to illustrate what we mean would be the dynamics of public opinion regarding the U.S. military conflict in Iraq between 2002 and 2009, which we referenced in the very first paragraph of this book. In 2002 and 2003, most Americans supported the invasion and subsequent attempt at nation-building there. By 2004, opinion had become more mixed, and was starting to polarize. By 2006–7, opinion had turned decidedly against the conflict, with most Americans (including many Republicans) clamoring for withdrawal (remember the exchange we quoted at the beginning of this book, between Vice President Cheney and ABC News correspondent Martha Raddatz). In that situation, if a Republican MC who had supported the war all along were to behave as an instructed delegate, we would expect that MC to modify her support for the conflict, in light of softening hawkishness in the constituency and the nation as a whole (think Sen. Richard Lugar [R-IN], in June 2007). A trustee, on the other hand, would find such moderation in response to changes in public opinion morally repugnant, and would double-down his support (think Sen. John McCain [R-AZ], during the same time period). We have been arguing throughout this book that there are more John McCains representing traditionalistic constituencies and more Richard Lugars representing progressive constituencies.

Another example, on the other side of the ideological spectrum, would be the health care reform debate of 2009–10. Public support for some version of national health insurance reform along the lines of what eventually became law in March 2010 was quite high in 2008 and early 2009. But as the debate dragged on and the Tea Party movement gained strength, support began to wane, even among Democrats. We would expect an instructed delegate to weaken or even abandon his or her support for reform if it became clear that the constituents no longer supported it (think Jason Altmire [D-PA-4], who made his change of heart on health care reform the centerpiece of his reelection bid in 2010). A trustee, however, would maintain his or her support in the face of changes in the constituency. Again, our contention is that there are more Jason Altmires in the progressive (or progressive-leaning) ranks than there are in the more traditionalistic ranks.

If the relative district nonresponsiveness we discussed above among those representing more traditionalistic constituencies is of a different character—that is, if it tends to take the shape of roll-call voting that is more moderate than the constituency would appear, then our theory would have to be called into question somewhat. In fact, by our measures, such a step toward moderation might even capture the opposite of what we want. That is, it could reflect instructed delegate-style behavior (since we do not have fine-grained measures of changes in constituency opinion that take place over the course of months rather than years).

Thus, identifying the ideological character associated with the policy nonresponsiveness we have observed is a very important piece in the puzzle we are trying to solve. To capture it, we pursued the following strategy. We created two variables. The first, *Ideologically Extreme Nonresponsiveness*, captures only MC nonresponsiveness that reflects more ideological extremism by the MC than can be observed in the district (regardless of whether that extremism is of a liberal or conservative ideological character). The second, *Ideologically Moderate Nonresponsiveness*, captures the opposite—only MC nonresponsiveness that reflects MC ideological moderation, relative to the district.[12]

---

[12] To do this, we took the raw policy nonresponsiveness variable described earlier (derived from the residuals of the first-stage regression equation predicting the MC DW-Nominate scores from the district's partisan vote share in the previous presidential election) *before* transforming it to its absolute value (recall that we had used the absolute version as the dependent variable in the earlier models). In this variable, negative values correspond to nonresponsiveness that is of a disproportionately liberal nature, and positive values correspond to nonresponsiveness that is of a more conservative nature. But our job did not end there, because depending on the nature of the district, that disproportionate liberalism (or conservatism) can be either moderate or extreme. So the next step, in creating the *Ideologically Extreme Nonresponsiveness* variable, was to restrict it

The *Ideologically Extreme Nonresponsiveness* variable ranges from 0 to 1.34 (mean = .24; standard deviation = .22), while *Ideologically Moderate Nonresponsiveness* ranges only from 0 to .26 (mean = .02; standard deviation = .05). So right off the bat, we see that there is a lot more ideologically extreme nonresponsiveness going on than there is moderate nonresponsiveness—as we expected.

For the data to support our hypotheses, we would expect *District Traditionalism* to significantly predict *Ideologically Extreme Nonresponsiveness* but not *Ideologically Moderate Nonresponsiveness*. We again turned to regression models (OLS estimation, in this case) to estimate these relationships (controlling for the same things as before, except for the district extremism variable).

Table 7.3 displays the relationship between *District Traditionalism* and *Ideologically Extreme Nonresponsiveness*. The MCs representing the most traditionalistic districts tended to have *Ideological Extreme Nonresponsiveness* scores that were roughly 55 points higher than those observed for the MCs representing the most progressive districts—a 41% difference (again, the full results can be seen in the Appendix).[13]

Though we have not graphed this relationship, we observed similar ideological extremism among African American evangelical MCs, though not in the same magnitude. African American evangelical MCs were about 10% more likely than other MCs to vote in ways that revealed disproportionate ideological extremism. Furthermore, also as expected, recent Congresses revealed greater ideologically extreme nonresponsiveness than did Congresses in the 1980s—but the difference amounts to only about 8%.

By contrast, the regression equation estimating *Ideologically Moderate Nonresponsiveness* showed revealed *District Traditionalism* to be a slight *negative* predictor. That is, MCs representing the most traditionalistic districts

---

such that it only included values when the nonresponsiveness was greater than zero (i.e., disproportionately conservative) *and* the district partisan vote share was greater than 50 (reflecting an aggregate vote favoring the Republican candidate), or when the nonresponsiveness was less than zero (i.e., disproportionately liberal) *and* the district partisan vote share was less than 50 (i.e., favoring the Democratic candidate). To create the *Ideologically Moderate Nonresponsiveness* variable, we did the same thing, but in reverse (restricted it so that the positive values on the MC nonresponsiveness variable were combined with values less than 50 on the district partisan vote-share variable, and negative values on the MC nonresponsiveness variable were combined with values greater than 50 on the district partisan vote-share variable).

13 This relationship is also stronger in more recent years, as expected.

**TABLE 7.3** *REGRESSION (OLS) OF REPRESENTATION GAP (IS–OUGHT) ON DISTRICT TRADITIONALISM AND CONTROLS FOR IDEOLOGICALLY EXTREME AND MODERATE MCS*

| | **Ideologically Extreme MCs** | **Ideologically Moderate MCs** |
|---|---|---|
| District Traditionalism | 0.00777** | –0.000283 |
| | (0.00106) | (0.000166) |
| Conservative Nonresponsiveness | –0.229** | –0.00277 |
| | (0.0571) | (0.00475) |
| Black Evangelical MC | 0.438** | –0.0244** |
| | (0.0486) | (0.00349) |
| First-Term MC | –0.0252** | 0.00352* |
| | (0.00736) | (0.00176) |
| Trend | 0.0105** | –0.00246** |
| | (0.00121) | (0.000330) |
| Constant | –0.256** | 0.0571** |
| | (0.0548) | (0.00997) |
| Observations | 5,188 | 5,188 |
| R-squared | 0.231 | 0.111 |

Robust standard errors in parentheses. Congress dummies not shown in table.
** $p < .01$, * $p < .05$

were about 7%, on average, *less* likely to behave in ways that were more ideologically moderate than their constituencies. However, this relationship just misses the standard threshold for statistical significance ($p = .127$), and is not substantively very large, so we do not feel comfortable making any more out of it (which is why we are not bothering to put it in a figure). Either *District Traditionalism* is not related to *Moderate Nonresponsiveness*, or it is negatively related. Either way, these findings provide support for our hypotheses.

When it comes to African American evangelical MCs, they were also about 7% less likely to reveal ideologically moderate nonresponsiveness—and in this case, the relationship does pass statistical muster ($p < .001$). Similarly, recent Congresses were about 11% less likely to display moderate nonresponsiveness ($p < .001$).

The real take-away points from this examination of extremist nonresponsiveness versus moderate nonresponsiveness, both of which conform to our expectations, are that (1) when MCs act like trustees, they tend to do so by voting in ways that reflect ideological extremism, not moderation, and (2) MCs representing traditionalistic districts (or who are themselves traditionalists) vote in ideologically extreme ways much more frequently than MCs representing progressive districts do.

## DISCUSSION

In this chapter, we have produced evidence that culminates the argument we have been putting forward in this book. Using data spanning 1985 to 2010 on MC roll-call voting behavior and the ideological tenor of the districts those lawmakers represent, we have shown that mass-level indicators can account for only around half of the ideological variance in how MCs vote on pieces of legislation. Moreover, we have shown that when MCs do not follow the ideological wishes of their constituents, they tend to do so by voting in ways that exhibit more ideological extremism, not moderation. Taken together, these findings suggest that it is not unusual for MCs to make policy without much regard to what the median voter in their districts might want, ideologically speaking. In other words, it would seem that while instructed delegate-style representation is alive and well, there are plenty of American citizens being represented by trustees as well.

More importantly for our argument, the variance in degree to which a MC "fits her district," ideologically speaking, is not distributed randomly; nonrepresentative polarizing behavior is observed disproportionately among MCs who represent district constituencies that can be characterized as culturally and religiously traditionalistic (i.e., "Red"). By contrast, MC–district ideological congruence is observed more often among MCs who represent the most culturally progressive districts.

What is more, we have also observed that such policy nonresponsiveness on the part of MCs has grown exponentially over time, as the number of traditionalistic MCs has grown—but only among those MCs who represent more traditionalistic districts.

So, at first blush, it would seem that those in traditionalistic districts are not getting represented very well. But maybe that is the wrong way to think about it: maybe they are, according to their preferred style of representation. In truth, that is probably not quite right either: very traditionalistic constituents in those districts are both getting the policy representation they want and the style of representation they want. Their more moderate neighbors, though, who may not make up the majority, would seem to be getting their democratic voices muzzled.

We will further contemplate these matters, and others, in the next chapter, which concludes this book. But first, we should mention a couple of limitations associated with our findings from this chapter and the conclusions we have drawn.

First, based on the fact that our measure of the variance in constituent opinion was nothing more than electoral returns across districts, we were forced to make the modeling assumption that such opinion is relatively static *in between* elections—something that we do not actually believe is always true (see our discussion in Chapter 3).

By then labeling gaps between the partisan vote share of a particular district in a previous election and the ideological character of that district's MC to be examples of policy nonresponsiveness on the part of the MC (i.e., trustee-style behavior), we also had to make the assumption that political representation is supposed to be what Mansbridge calls "promissory" (based on what a representative promised during the previous campaign) rather than "anticipatory" (based on what a representative anticipates is going to be valued by voters in the next election)—which we also do not necessarily think is an accurate assumption. To be sure, it is possible that when such gaps exist between the partisan vote share of a particular district in the previous election (used as a measure of aggregate constituent ideology) and the ideological character of that district's MC's roll-call votes the following year, those gaps could reflect changes on the part of the MC in response to changes in the district that we simply have not observed. To rule out this possibility, we would need much more frequent and fine-grained measures of issue attitudes at the district level, to see whether changes in public opinion preceded the seemingly discrepant roll-call voting behavior.

Additionally, the fact that district-level mass ideology is measured as the mean score across *many individuals from a single vote*, whereas MC ideology is measured as an aggregated score of *a single individual across many votes*, poses an analytical problem, depending again on which philosophical vision of representation one assumes. Even if we ignore the fact that ideology is not nearly a fine-grained enough measure of opinion (either among legislators or citizens) to really capture the degree to which representatives are listening to constituents, the bigger problem is that representatives are allowed to vote only "yay" or "nay" on bills. So if we imagine a district in which the majority opinion on every issue is just slightly right of the ideological center, the classic instructed delegate would have to cast a conservative vote on every bill that came her way. That would give her an extremely conservative DW-Nominate score, which would show up in our data as producing a big ideological gap between her and her constituents—even though she would have been broadly following the direction of their lead. The only way for her to appear as though she closely follows district opinion would be for her to vote liberally one out of three times or so, which doesn't make any sense.

The only real way around this challenge would be to change our legislative institutional voting rules. We can imagine a situation in which legislators would get to express support or opposition to a bill on a 0-to-100 scale, rather than a simple up-or-down vote. Unfortunately, we don't envision that happening any time soon, which means we will be left with our analytical challenge for some time. Truth be told, though, we do not think this weakness in measurement has posed too big of a problem in our analyses. Realistically, districts that vote for a Republican presidential candidate by a margin of 53–47 or so (making them appear slightly conservative in our data) are rarely, if ever, made up of a majority that is just a little right of center on virtually every issue (in the hypothetical way described above). Typically, such areas are "swing districts," made up of a diverse and cross-pressured set of constituents. As such, working majorities are typically liberal on some issues and conservative on other issues. Accordingly, if a representative is going to behave as an instructed delegate, she too will have to vote conservatively on some bills and liberally on others. Thus, the representative with the perfectly conservative DW-Nominate score really will be ignoring public opinion a large percentage of the time.

In Chapter 8, our concluding chapter, we discuss additional ways that the conclusions of this book are necessarily limited, after highlighting the various points that we believe readers should be taking away.

CHAPTER 8

# Quieting the Stable, Polarizing the Ranch

The very notion of someone "representing" someone else is a tricky one to really get one's head fully around. As over a century of Hollywood Westerns and TV shows has taught us, sheriffs need deputies to stand in for them sometimes. But it isn't always clear what the deputy is really authorized to do (Andy Taylor didn't allow Barney Fife to carry even a single bullet, remember?). So if you have been effectively deputized as someone's representative—whether as a Mayberry law-enforcement officer, public policymaker, dispute litigator, field sergeant, or even a high-school quarterback, figuring out how to best execute your appointed task is not going to be the easiest thing you have ever done.

Just imagine yourself as that quarterback for another minute. As you leave the huddle and look over at the alignment of the opposing defense, you realize that the play your coach just called probably isn't going to work. By contrast, you're pretty sure that a 15-yard out pattern would be wide open. What to do? Do you follow your coach's orders (execute the play called), or do you do what you think would be best for the team (and thus for the coach as well)? Complicating matters is the fact that Coach is not your only constituency here. The boosters, faculty, and local sports editor (not to mention your mom) have been objecting to his play-calling all year. You know what they would choose…but then again, they aren't the ones who can sit you on the bench next week. Hmmm.

As it turns out, this perplexed teen has a lot in common with the typical member of Congress (MC). She, the MC, has her own ideas about what would best benefit her constituents (and the country) or she wouldn't have gotten into politics in the first place. But her district constituents have ideas, too, which don't always jibe with hers. Worse yet, as coaches, those constituents don't exactly inspire a great deal of confidence: they bicker among themselves, change their mind every time she turns around, and don't really know what they're talking about a lot of the time anyway. Of course, none of that stops those constituents from filling her inbox with rather pointed e-mails every day. And then there are the others—the party leadership, the big donors, AARP, Gallup's weekly tracking poll, Jon Stewart... Ay yuhy yuhy.

But there is another factor in this equation that might simplify things a bit for our young athlete, and for our congresswoman. As we know, some coaches want complete control over what happens on the field, but others actually encourage some improvised playmaking. In this book, we have shown that constituents, who have the power to bench their representatives for fumbling the ball and such things, vary in much the same way that those coaches do. Some constituents want their representatives to routinely execute the plays called from the sideline, while others prefer representatives who exercise independent judgment. So if the quarterback (or representative) knows that the coach would be disappointed if he *didn't* follow his own instincts sometimes, his dilemma has gotten a lot easier to resolve. He can go ahead and throw that out pattern (or vote according to conscience)—knowing that failing to do what he thinks is right can land him on the bench just as quickly as failing to follow orders can.

Earlier studies of American political representation have largely failed to take such constituent "coaching preferences" into account. While researchers may instinctively understand that some constituents prefer to see some principled leadership out of their representatives (rather than strict following of public opinion), few have tried to figure out exactly who those particular constituents are, and no one has tried previously to incorporate that information into analyses of representative behavior. After chewing over those matters in this book, we think we've learned a few interesting things.

## WHAT WE'VE LEARNED

First, it has occurred to us that if a representative knows she is actually pleasing constituents by exercising leadership of her own, such behavior might not really count as leadership at all. It strikes us as being more like one of those chocolate/vanilla twist cones from Dairy Queen, with the chocolate leadership being swirled together with vanilla pandering—albeit pandering of a different sort. That is, appearing to stand on principle in the face of public outcries is one manifestation of what we have labeled "Pandering 2.0": attempting to mollify the most tuned-in constituents by making a big display out of ignoring the majority—and thereby giving the first group the *style* of governance they want. Identifying this alternative type of pandering does not only teach us new things about the nature of the constituent–lawmaker relationship; it also reminds us that public opinion relating to *political processes* can be just as important to representative government as is public opinion that pertains to public policy (e.g., Hibbing & Theiss-Morse, 2002).

It also seems that this type of pandering may make the most sense in societies like the United States, which are characterized by politically inattentive masses but ideologically polarized activists. Put another way, hearkening back to a metaphor we used in Chapter 1, perhaps the best way to saddle up a drunken mule may be to bait it with one of those pandering/leadership twist cones. After all, trying to satisfy constituents in the traditional way, by appeasing the public's policy preferences, is probably not the most fruitful strategy when the public is preoccupied with the flies swarming around their heads (e.g., "What if I lose the Johnson account?"; "Can you take Jr. to Little League practice tonight?"; "Is that the brakes squealing again?").

Such a traditional pandering strategy makes even less sense if the activist community—who *is* paying attention—starts flaring their nostrils at the mere whiff of ideological "flip-flopping" on the part of their representative. So, to reiterate, in the face of widespread constituent indifference coupled with ideological intransigence by activists, the art of pandering may have evolved into one that is more about appeasing constituents' representation-*style* preferences than their policy preferences.

Of course, there are a lot of communities in which the mules do actually want to take the lead. In such areas, pandering 2.0 turns out to be the same thing as old-fashioned policy pandering. In other words, in those communities, the leader/pander twist cones can be left in the freezer. One of the goals of this book has been to distinguish the communities in which politicians should hire a pollster from those in which they would be better off exclaiming their individual principles.

From what we have been able to tell, the folks who seem to enjoy those leader/pander twist cones the most tend to live in culturally traditionalistic Red America. That is, as we showed in Chapter 5, cultural traditionalists—and by extension, Republicans—are more inclined than are cultural progressives (a.k.a. liberal Democrats) to vote for representatives who appear to "stand on principle." They are also, as our Chapter 6 results revealed, more likely to hold it against representatives when those representatives cave in to changing constituent demands.

Importantly, it would also appear that the traditionalistic tendency to prefer trustee-style representation does not go unnoticed by representatives. In Chapter 7 we observed that those who represent traditionalistic communities are substantially less likely to vote on bills in ways that match up, ideologically speaking, with their constituents. Extrapolating things out, it would seem that people tend to have less political power if they happen to live in one of those traditionalistic communities, because their representatives have fewer incentives to listen to them. Or, to put it another way, one might say that Red American mules tend to wear thicker muzzles than do Blue American mules.

Indulging ourselves at this point to speak in more grandiose terms, we conclude from all this that representative government tends to mean something different in traditionalistic America than it does in progressive America. The traditionalistic cultures are more likely to function politically as institutionalized *republics*, whereas the progressive cultures tend to more closely approximate *liberal popular democracies*. Normatively speaking, these differences are not necessarily that big of a deal, in and of themselves. We certainly do not take a position on the desirability of republics versus popular democracies, in the abstract. The normative problem we see has more to do with differences in democratic voice across citizens. If some American citizens have less political power than others, based only on where they happen to live, then policy agendas and outcomes (and therefore material costs and benefits) become disproportionately and unfairly skewed.

Such differences across individuals, in terms of their political power, are all the more troublesome if the voices getting drowned out sing disproportionately in the same key. As we have shown, most of the silencing seems to be going on in traditionalistic communities. Accordingly, readers might be tempted to assume that the skewed policy outcomes to which we have just alluded tend to favor those with progressive values and interests. But that isn't actually the way it works out. Rather, as our analyses in Chapter 7 revealed, it is usually the ideologically moderate points of view that are getting ignored.

That is, if we compare the nature of representation across the country according to ideological "types," we would observe that very liberal districts (like those in Berkeley, CA, or Austin, TX) tend to receive very liberal representation, and that very conservative districts (like those in Folsom, CA, or Sugarland, TX) tend to get very conservative representation—as things should be. Moderate districts, however (especially those that are culturally traditionalistic but perhaps more left-leaning when it comes to economic policy—like those in western Pennsylvania) are getting disproportionately conservative representation a lot of the time (especially when it comes to economic policy), because they often elect trustee-style conservatives who are loath to do anything that could be construed as compromising a principle. This pattern helps to explain findings from earlier research, which had shown congressional policy nonresponsiveness growing considerably in recent decades, coinciding with the growth of ideological conservatism in that body (Jacobs & Shapiro, 2000).

Along the same lines, our findings also help to explain the increasingly polarized ranch that is the U.S. Congress. While polarization can be attributed to a number of factors, including redistricting (e.g., Carson et al., 2007), partisan sorting (Levendusky, 2009), and institutional changes in the House and Senate (for an excellent, integrated approach, see Theriault, 2008), one mostly overlooked mechanism has been the growing numbers of evangelicals in Congress, especially within the Republican Party, and the growing gap in traditionalistic religiosity between Republican and Democratic lawmakers. Our findings suggest that, whether measured as an MC's ideological distance from the mean, her willingness to compromise with lawmakers from the other side, or her willingness to moderate her position in response to public outcries, the much-ballyhooed rise in polarization appears to be disproportionately one-sided—attributable more to intransigence on the part of the ideological Right than the ideological Left (for more on this point, also see Hetherington & Weiler, 2009).[1]

These conclusions also speak to the scholarship surrounding the so-called Culture Wars in American politics and, more broadly, the role that higher-order values play in defining political cleavages. By showing that cultural traditionalism influences the style in which citizens want to be represented (and by extension the style in which they are represented), our findings strengthen and deepen the Culture Wars perspective on American politics considerably, revealing that cultural differences in fact underlie more than policy debates or even electoral outcomes; they also affect the fundamental essence of American democratic governance.

Of course, we can't talk about politics, values, and culture in the United States without talking about religion as well. Religious differences were

[1] We do not view this explanation as inconsistent with others. We suggest that ideologically based redistricting, partisan sorting, and even some other institutional mechanisms have also been disproportionately one-sided, and that they have been byproducts, to some extent, of the growing influence of religious traditionalists. We also do not view our observations as being competitive with those of McCarty, Poole, and Rosenthal (2008), who show that polarization has mirrored class inequality. In other words, we do not consider class-based and culture-based explanations of partisan sorting as mutually exclusive. Rather, we consider them complementary: religious-cultural cleavages facilitate ideological constraint, which manifests itself in heightened class cleavages (and inequality). Furthermore, gains in inequality are partially a byproduct of conservative ideological ascension in Congress and the executive branch over the past generation. And that ascension was due, in part, to the mobilization of traditionalistic Christians into the Republican ranks.

ignored for a long time by political researchers but are now widely appreciated as absolutely critical to understanding American differences in ideology, issue attitudes, partisanship, and vote choices (for excellent overviews, see Smidt, Kellstedt, & Guth, 2009). While we disagree with some observers who have argued that differences between traditionalistic Christians and everyone else are the end-all be-all of political-cultural conflict (racial attitudes are pretty important too, after all), our theoretical argument (which we developed fully in Chapter 3) has Christian traditionalism—and even particular Christian doctrines—occupying a central role.

In this regard, in Chapter 4 we found that those who value "faith over reason" are more likely to prefer trustee-style representation, as are those who (1) attend church regularly, (2) call themselves "born-again" Christians, (3) view the Bible as inerrant, (4) see human beings as inherently and utterly depraved, and (5) consider Jesus Christ the "only way to salvation." Thus, in this book we have been able to learn more about the role religion plays in contemporary American public life, by providing more depth and breadth to the subject. That is, we have not only provided more precise explanations of exactly how religion influences political phenomena than are typically observed, but we have also expanded the range of political phenomena that are understood to be influenced by religious variables.

But perhaps the religious-based findings are a byproduct of underlying psychological or personality-based predispositions—namely authoritarianism and (especially) dogmatism. Evangelical Christian religiosity correlates highly with the tendencies to crave certainty and strong leadership, and to loathe nuance; perhaps such religious traditionalism is partly an outgrowth of those deep-seated orientations. Regardless of "what causes what," the psychology associated with authoritarianism and especially dogmatism is at least as important to our theory as is the explicitly religious stuff. We see preferences for trustee-style representation as essentially manifesting distaste for the idea that "leaders" would compromise fundamental principles by chasing public opinion. And again, the empirical tests bear this out. These findings speak to the growing recognition among political scientists that dogmatism and authoritarianism play vital roles in drawing the lines of American political conflict.

Taken together, in this book we have argued that political representation doesn't just happen, and that differences in the way representatives do their jobs are neither random nor accidental. The manner in which politicians represent their constituents involves a delicate dance between representatives and the represented, which involves different steps depending on whether or not the represented want to take the lead. And those differences across citizens are in part an outgrowth of their worldviews, religious beliefs, and other cultural dispositions. Representatives must size up their dance partners with regard to these things and respond strategically—and they had better not step on any toes. In other words, there is a psychology of political representation, which we have begun to understand a little bit.

## LIMITATIONS AND REMAINING QUESTIONS

Although we certainly think the empirical findings (Chapters 4–7) take our theoretical argument (Chapter 3) well beyond the realm of speculation or conjecture, there remain several factors that keep us from drawing definitive conclusions. There are a good many limitations to our findings, and questions left to consider, before a step-by-step manual entitled "how to saddle a drunken mule" can be included in campaigning workshops or swag-bags for newly elected representatives. In this final section, we discuss some of those limitations and remaining questions.

First, it is certainly possible that some of the relationships we have uncovered are time-bound. After all, our public opinion data, on which we perform all the data analyses described in Chapters 2 and 4 through 6, are restricted for the most part to four years (with most of the analyses coming from 2006–2009, and some from even smaller subsets of those years).[2] We are comforted to some degree by the fact that the data we use to analyze representative behavior (Chapter 7) stretch back to 1985, but we still have no way of knowing whether the evidence supports a *general* theory of the psychology of representation, or one that is restricted to the past 30 years or so.

Importantly, though, we never expected that the *partisan* aspects of our story to hold prior to the early 1980s or so. Our contention that Republican districts are more likely to be represented by trustees is entirely an extension of the fact that religious and cultural traditionalism has begotten Republicans for the past 30 to 35 years. Prior to that, the most traditionalistic Americans tended to be Southern Democrats, and religious differences didn't influence politics very much at that time anyway. By the same token, looking ahead,

[2] However, as we also noted in Chapter 4, two survey data sources from the late 1970s (the 1977 Obey Commission data and the 1978 American National Election Study) revealed patterns in keeping with our findings from the late 2000s. Specifically, Republicans, Southerners, and especially Southern Democrats appear more likely to prefer trustees than do Northerners or especially Northern Democrats (Carman, 2007). This is exactly what we would expect; the South was, after all, categorized as the "traditionalistic" culture by Daniel Elazar (1966).

we expect trustee-style representation to coincide with wearing an elephant on your hat only for as long as the Culture Wars stay hot.[3]

Second, and somewhat relatedly, we do not claim to have identified the only, or even the most important, determinants of mass preferences regarding representation styles. We don't even think we have accounted for most of the variance in whether representatives act as either trustees or instructed delegates. In our view, while this book may represent the first word in a long time about some of these things, it should by no means be the last one. For one thing, as we have mentioned over and over in this book (including in the very first paragraph), we know political and material *interests* are undoubtedly very important shapers of representation preferences. We imagine that people who see themselves as part of the majority are more likely to prefer instructed delegates as representatives, because there is presumably more in it for them. Likewise, if one's preferred political "team" controls the corridors of power, one should be more likely to prefer trustee-style representation, particularly if majority opinion has come to reflect the opposite point of view.

Another way of putting this is to emphasize that we do not imagine very many citizens are out there who wish their representatives would stop listening to *them*. The difference between those who favor instructed delegates versus those who favor trustees is the degree to which people are willing to continue supporting politicians who stop listening to them—even though they may not like it—in favor of the district majority. Our evidence suggests that those people are more likely to be seculars and progressives—who also happen to be Democrats.

[3] Moreover, as we mentioned in earlier chapters, it is possible that the Culture Wars could progress in certain ways that could undermine some of the patterns that we have observed. Even now, if the stereotypes are true about Blue Americans being over-educated effete snobs who look down their noses (over the rims of their lattes) at common folks, and Red Americans being a bunch of rednecks who don't read, then the egalitarianism aspect of our findings could be reversing itself. At this point, we do not think this poses a problem for our theory, because we simply find no evidence to suggest that any of those stereotypes are accurate. That is, while there may be a segment of the secular, liberal, and Democratic population that is too snobby for its own good, and maybe even a segment of the traditionalistically religious, conservative, and Republican population that is proudly anti-intellectual and populist, in general we observe (both in our data and in other surveys of the mass public, such as the National Election Study surveys) that egalitarian sentiment, as well as support for measures of popular sovereignty, tends to correlate rather strongly with seeing the political world through Blue lenses.

For example, consider how liberals must have felt in 2009–10, at which time the Democrats controlled everything in Washington but a majority of the public had turned against the Obama health insurance reform bill. Under those conditions, even though progressives may be less inclined on average than traditionalists to appreciate trustee-style representation, we remember many liberals clamoring rather loudly for President Obama and the Democrats in Congress to act as trustees and stick to their ideological principles—not only because they wanted national health insurance to become law, but also because they were eager to see "their guys" actually win a policy battle for a change. We argue, however, that liberal Democratic clamoring in cases such as these tends to be quieter than is conservative Republican clamoring (e.g., the Tea Party activists) when the roles are reversed.

What remains to be seen is how such interest-based motivations may interact with values-based dispositions toward one or the other representation style. We suspect that, on average, immediate political and policy interests usually overpower the deep-seated and even subconscious inclinations we have spent most of our time discussing in this book. So in particular situations like the one we just mentioned in 2009–10, we would not be surprised to see Democrats, not Republicans, showing up in surveys of public opinion as the ones who tend to prefer trustees. However, when interest-based motivations and values-based motivations *complement* rather than contradict each other, we would expect the magnitude and consistency of preferences for one particular style of representation to spike. A perfect example could be found in 2011, when Republicans controlled the House of Representatives and were engaged in high-profile battles with Democrats (who controlled the White House and the Senate) over issues of taxes and spending. Even though surveys revealed that majorities clearly favored the Democratic approach, "Tea Party" conservatives made it very clear to their House representatives that they had better not cave to those majorities or there would be electoral hell to pay. But this is speculation of course. These interactions need to be examined systematically across multiple points in time and different partisan power-sharing scenarios.

Other interest-based motivators worth exploring would be those relating to descriptive representation (or what Mansbridge calls "surrogate" representation)—the degree to which representatives should mirror their constituents in terms of demographic characteristics such as race, ethnicity, gender, religious preference, and so on. If a constituent is a woman, let's say, does her preference for either trustees or instructed delegates depend on whether her representative is also a woman? How do such things interact with the values-based motivators on which we have focused? Given that many demographic characteristics are highly predictive of partisanship and of Culture War battle lines (e.g., race, ethnicity, religion, gender), understanding these interactions seems particularly relevant. One of us has contemplated such matters to some extent, finding that African Americans' preferences for representation style tended to be contingent on the race of their representative (Carman, 2007), but there is much more to be done.

Another limitation of this book is that, although we talked at some length in Chapters 2, 4, and 5 about the style in which people want to be represented by their president, governor, and senators, our exclusive focus when examining actual representative behavior (in Chapter 7) was on the House of Representatives.

Because in Chapter 2 we observed greater variation in representation-style preferences when people are asked to consider executive branch representation rather than legislative representation, we suspect that the empirical patterns we observed in Chapter 7 would be heightened if we were to analyze representative styles by presidents, governors, and even senators. After all, institutionally speaking, the House is the one that was designed, conceptually, to provide constituents with the most "say." From the beginning, senators and especially executives were presumed to exercise greater independent judgment when making policy—almost as a counterweight to the "voice of the people" that the House was expected to reflect. While such expectations regarding the different branches have surely evolved over time, the distributions of opinion revealed in Chapter 2 suggest that people still expect different things out of the different branches. From this, it is reasonable to suspect that presidents, governors, and (to a lesser extent) senators recognize that they could suffer politically if they look like they aren't strong enough leaders—especially with the types of constituents who really value such things.

Accordingly, we would expect, for example, that as the power of religious and cultural traditionalists has grown over time, presidents (especially Republican presidents) have become less responsive to national public opinion polls. Druckman and Jacobs' recent work (2011) speaks to that indirectly, as they find evidence that the Reagan administration was more responsive to indicators measuring religiously conservative constituent demands than to public opinion polling more generally.

In the same way that we do not really know how far our findings travel back in time, or how they may vary across different institutions, we also do not know how far they travel geographically. We developed the theory for this book with the United States in mind. We have no idea whether it would fit in nations with less religious variance (e.g., Latin America) or intensity (e.g., Europe), or with different institutional frameworks (e.g., proportional representation, unitary executive–legislative branches, open-list voting systems, multiparty arrangements, and so on). That isn't to say that the topic is irrelevant outside the American context. In more recent years there has certainly been an uptick in scholarly interest pertaining to representation preferences outside the United States (e.g., Bengtsson & Wass, 2010; Carman, 2006; Esaiasson & Holmberg, 1996; Mendez-Lago & Martinez, 2002). To this point, though, anything resembling our theory has not been tested (or even considered) in any of those settings. We think it should.

Another thing worth comparing is how the dynamics we have observed might differ according to differences in issue salience. Perhaps representatives who represent traditionalistic communities are not terribly responsive to public opinion, overall, but maybe they are more responsive when it comes to the issues that their constituents find most salient. At this point, we just don't know the answer (although some of the comparisons we make in Chapter 2, when we consider differences in representation-style preferences according to differences in issues, speak to this point a little bit). For more on considerations of representation as they pertain to salience (broadly defined), and how different institutions can affect those dynamics, see Soroka and Wlezien (2010).

An additional task we are leaving for other ambitious scholars to take on is how mass preferences for either instructed delegates or trustees might affect aspects of representative behavior other than how lawmakers vote on legislation. There are many other aspects to doing a representative's job besides roll-call voting, such as sponsoring bills, setting the agenda, adding amendments, making public statements, and scrapping for pork, just to name a few (Arnold, 1992). All of these would be relevant objects of study to more fully put our theory to the test. Some have already started. In one of the studies that gave us confidence in our own hypotheses, Hill and Matsubayashi found that (all the way back in the 1960s) local community leaders were more responsive to public demands about what issues should be on the policy agenda when they represented areas containing large concentrations of religious liberals than were their counterparts who represented large numbers of Christian traditionalists. More studies like that by Hill and Matsubayashi would also lend credence to our Chapter 7 findings.

One more way that this book could be expanded would be to consider differences across representatives in terms of the constituency to which they see themselves in service. We have spent most of our time considering "dyadic" representation, which is to say that we have focused on the relationship between a representative and the particular group of citizens who have an institutionalized say over whether she gets to keep her job. When, in Chapter 7, we observed gaps between the ideological character of a representative's roll-call voting behavior in a given year, overall, and that of her local electoral constituency, we chalked that up to trustee-style representation. However, such gaps would also be consistent with a representative who is acting as an instructed delegate but in service to a different constituency.

Such considerations about exactly whom the representative thinks she should be representing, rather than the particular manner in which she represents her constituents (whomever they may be), are typically referred to as matters of representation *focus*. And whereas studies incorporating citizen preferences regarding representation style have been few and far between, such studies regarding representation focus have been even scarcer (but see Doherty, 2010).

There are two alternate constituencies that a representative could be serving, as an instructed delegate, that could be mistaken for trustee-style representation. The first, and perhaps most obvious, is national public opinion. A representative's district constituency might favor a particular policy outcome that is out of step with the perspective of the nation as a whole, which the representative might consider more important to represent. Such nationally focused delegate-style representation, or what Mansbridge has termed "surrogate" representation (in her 2003 rumination on the subject), would look like trustee-style representation. We cannot rule out that possibility, because our legislative behavior data (analyzed in Chapter 7) was measured only dyadically. That is, we only considered the degree to which House members' behavior corresponded to preferences within their local districts.

However, we should say that we do not consider this alternate hypothesis all that plausible. The reason is that attitudes toward representation focus (local vs. national constituency) and those toward representation style (instructed delegate vs. trustee) are not orthogonal. In 2006, we asked our respondents to offer their preferences regarding representation focus, finding that those who prefer trustees are the same people who tend to believe that the representative should focus on her *local* constituency at the expense of national opinion. We also observed that such preferences for a local focus are predictable according to authoritarianism, anti-humanism, anti-egalitarianism, Christian traditionalism, and political conservatism, in the same way (and to just about the same degree) that trustee-style preferences are. And this stands to reason: local majorities are more likely to share the values of the local representative than are national majorities. So if one says she prefers a local representative focus, it could very well be another way of saying that one wants to the representative to listen to her values—*our values*—rather than the fluctuating whims of the masses. Of course, more analysis over the course of more years needs to be done, but at this point, it seems unlikely that when representatives buck local opinion they do so because they are trying to behave like instructed delegates to a national constituency.

The second alternate constituency to which the representative might appeal is what might be called the *electoral constituency* (i.e., the activist community) within her local district—that is, the subset of constituents who elected her in the first place, based on her promises and demonstrable traits at the time, and who also have the power to reelect her (or not!). Such constituents tend to be disproportionately ideological. So, even if the overall ideological makeup of a district is Center Right, the activists in the district (who donate money, attend rallies, and vote at higher levels) may be disproportionately right-wing, and if the representative can capture all the support of that community, she can rest at night knowing that her reelection is probably safe—even if she doesn't get a single vote from anyone even slightly Left of Center, ideologically speaking. So what may appear to be trustee-style representation might really capture legislators following the opinions of this alternate, more restrictive, constituency. This type of representation focus is akin to what Mansbridge termed "promissory" representation, and some recent scholarship has unearthed evidence that Republican legislators are more likely than Democrats to do precisely that (Clinton, 2006).

Upon further reflection, though, we are not convinced that this kind of appealing to the ideologues within a constituency is not really the same thing as trustee-style representation—or at least that both types of behavior manifest the same underlying motivations and orientations. To elaborate, if those ideologues are the ones who got the representative elected in the first place, it is probably because they recognized a kindred spirit, either ideologically or in terms of representation style. Naturally, then, a conservative voting pattern would ensue. The representative would vote in ways that would make it look like she was following those constituents' ideological lead, but it would really just reflect the fact that the representative and the constituents instinctively march to the same ideological beat. And indeed, as was the case with distinctions in preferences for local versus national constituencies, in 2006 we asked respondents whether they thought a representative's responsibility was to everyone in the district or to just those who had voted for her. We observed that preferences for the latter were predictable according to the exact same set of variables that predict trustee-style preferences (e.g., authoritarianism, anti-humanism, anti-egalitarianism, Christian traditionalism, Republican party identification).

On a somewhat related subject, we wonder if the *direction* of MC nonresponsiveness should affect our understanding of representation styles and policy (non)responsiveness on the part of representatives. In other words, does it matter whether the ideological gaps we observe between representatives and constituents reflect disproportionate extremism or moderation on the part of the representative? To elaborate, if one representative is a lot more ideologically conservative (or liberal) than her constituents, and another representative is a lot more moderate than the constituents, do both equally manifest the same trustee style of representation? Our theory presupposes that trustee-style representation is typically of the disproportionate extremism variety, and our empirics (in Chapter 7) support that presupposition. That is, from what we have observed, when representatives and constituents disagree on policy, constituents tend to be the more moderate than their representatives, not the other way around.

So it would appear that our intuitions about how trustee-style representation typically looks have been borne out, which lends some additional credence to our larger theory. However, it is surely the case that some trustee-style behavior on the part of representatives takes on the opposite character—moderate voting when the constituency prefers ideological purity. It may be the case that such trustee-style behavior, and mass preferences for it, are attributable to an entirely different set of variables than the ones we have identified, or perhaps that the direction of the relationships we have observed would need to be reversed.

Or perhaps what we have captured in this book is not really about representation styles after all. The extremist brand of trustee-style representation (but not the moderate brand) may be an observable manifestation of a different underlying dynamic, which is really about resistance toward bargaining and compromise. We discussed such dogmatism in Chapter 3 as part of our argument for why religious and cultural traditionalism should predict trustee-style representation, but perhaps that is the whole story. Perhaps all the other things we identified as antecedents of preferences for either instructed delegates or trustees—the degree to which one holds egalitarian, humanistic, or authoritarian sentiments (i.e., the degree to which one embraces liberal popular democracy vs. republicanism), and by extension the degree to which one identifies as a religious-cultural traditionalist (and a Republican)—are in fact just correlates of dogmatism. And perhaps that dogmatism leads representatives to resist compromise, leading to ideological extremism—which looks like trustee-style representation. On the flipside, perhaps the lack of dogmatism (i.e., ideological contextualism/flexibility) does not necessarily predict instructed delegate-style representation as much as it predicts moderation—which could in some cases lead to trustee-style representation of a different flavor.

Moreover, perhaps some representatives, constituents, and even interest groups (e.g., Grover Norquist's Americans for Tax Reform) view rigid ideological extremism as being a proper instructed delegate. For example, members of the conservative Tea Party movement in the United States were originally infuriated over what they viewed as the Republican Party's abandonment of principle during the Bush years—caving in to broader trends in public opinion. That sounds like a preference for trustee-style representation. But their calls for more principled leadership (as they saw it) didn't mean that they wanted their representatives to ignore *them*. It meant that they wanted their representatives to ignore *others—majority or not*—who were pressuring the representatives to change their mind. Indeed, the Tea Partiers organized rallies and letter-writing campaigns all over the country to make sure representatives knew just how angry they were about having been sold out. So that sounds a lot like a preference for instructed delegate-style representation. They also successfully extracted pledges from many campaigning representatives, who promised to never raise taxes under any circumstances. Those pledges nearly led the United States to default on its debt in the summer of 2011, because conservatives would not compromise during deficit-reduction negotiations tied to increases in the debt limit (which had always been noncontroversial and nearly automatic on the dozens of other occasions it had been raised since the early 1980s). During that near debt crisis, polls showed that clear majorities of citizens wanted the conservatives to compromise. But the Tea Partiers who had extracted those pledges sure did not.

So was the intransigence on the part of these conservative lawmakers indicative of trustee-style representation, or instructed delegate-style representation? We have made the case in this book that it reflects the trustee style, but that it is also an example of placating Tea Party constituents who have made it clear that they prefer trustees. But it isn't crystal clear, is it? And what about President Obama and some of the other Democrats, who behaved the opposite way—making it clear during the negotiations that while they did not want to cut entitlements, they would hold their noses and do it if that is what it would take to get a deal and avert financial crisis. Were they listening to constituent opinion, or were they ignoring it in favor of what they saw as doing the right thing for the country? Is that pandering or principled leadership? Or both? To answer these questions definitively, more work will need to be done. And that is our next project.

# Appendices

## APPENDIX CHAPTER 4: TABLES AND STATISTICAL OUTPUT

**TABLE A4.1** *MULTINOMIAL LOGITS OF REPRESENTATION PREFERENCES ON HUMANISM MEASURES*

| | Humanism 1 (Delegate, base category) (Results for Figure 4.1) | | Humanism 2 (Delegate, base category) (Results for Figure 4.2) | |
|---|---|---|---|---|
| | **Mixed** | **Trustee** | **Mixed** | **Trustee** |
| People not Capable | –0.0167 | 0.206* | | |
| | (0.0870) | (0.0917) | | |
| Faith over Reason | | | 0.615** | 0.619** |
| | | | (0.145) | (0.149) |
| Women | 0.0655 | 0.0161 | –0.150 | –0.296 |
| | (0.199) | (0.215) | (0.126) | (0.152) |
| Whites | –0.0832 | –0.847** | 0.124 | –0.0671 |
| | (0.167) | (0.236) | (0.107) | (0.153) |
| Education | 0.198** | 0.0182 | 0.104* | 0.118* |
| | (0.0559) | (0.0743) | (0.0409) | (0.0531) |
| Income | –0.0619 | –0.0140 | –0.0104 | –0.00591 |
| | (0.0349) | (0.0283) | (0.0180) | (0.0204) |
| Resides in South | 0.186 | –0.0523 | 0.0875 | –0.0199 |
| | (0.225) | (0.193) | (0.0970) | (0.110) |
| Married | –0.449 | –0.0807 | 0.101 | 0.0855 |
| | (0.254) | (0.202) | (0.103) | (0.135) |
| Birth Year | –0.00229 | 0.0145* | 0.00428 | 0.00791* |
| | (0.00411) | (0.00639) | (0.00356) | (0.00353) |
| Catholic | –0.227 | 0.0436 | 0.101 | 0.0735 |
| | (0.261) | (0.284) | (0.109) | (0.168) |

*(Continued)*

**TABLE A4.1** *(CONTINUED)*

| | Humanism 1 (Delegate, base category) (Results for Figure 4.1) | | Humanism 2 (Delegate, base category) (Results for Figure 4.2) | |
|---|---|---|---|---|
| | **Mixed** | **Trustee** | **Mixed** | **Trustee** |
| Constant | 3.696 | –28.83* | –9.673 | –16.58* |
| | (8.071) | (12.42) | (6.964) | (6.813) |
| Observations | 988 | 988 | 2,894 | 2,894 |

Robust standard errors in parentheses
** $p<0.01$, * $p<0.05$

**TABLE A4.2** *MULTINOMIAL LOGITS OF REPRESENTATION PREFERENCES ON DOGMATISM MEASURE*

| | Dogmatism (Delegate, base category) (Results for Figure 4.3) | |
|---|---|---|
| | **Mixed** | **Trustee** |
| Dogmatism | 0.326** | 0.407** |
| | (0.0637) | (0.0786) |
| Women | –0.325** | –0.562** |
| | (0.121) | (0.154) |
| Whites | 0.0143 | 0.0792 |
| | (0.140) | (0.153) |
| Education | 0.0763 | 0.244** |
| | (0.0461) | (0.0675) |
| Income | 0.0264 | 0.0122 |
| | (0.0251) | (0.0155) |
| Resides in South | 0.0537 | 0.0537 |
| | (0.144) | (0.150) |
| Married | 0.176 | –0.0221 |
| | (0.145) | (0.145) |
| Birth Year | 0.00468 | 0.00164 |
| | (0.00481) | (0.00487) |
| Catholic | 0.190 | 0.102 |
| | (0.155) | (0.204) |
| Constant | –10.38 | –4.828 |
| | (9.436) | (9.524) |
| Observations | 1,943 | 1,943 |

Robust standard errors in parentheses
** $p<0.01$, * $p<0.05$

**TABLE A4.3** *MULTINOMIAL LOGISTIC REGRESSION ANALYSES OF REPRESENTATION PREFERENCES ON EGALITARIANISM MEASURES*

| | Egalitarianism 1 (Delegate, base category) (Results for Figure 4.4) | | Egalitarianism 2 (Delegate, base category) (Results for Figure 4.5) | |
|---|---|---|---|---|
| | **Mixed** | **Trustee** | **Mixed** | **Trustee** |
| Equal Rights | –0.113* | –0.0807 | | |
| | (0.0441) | (0.0443) | | |
| Eliminate Elec. Coll. | | | –0.442** | –0.723** |
| | | | (0.105) | (0.0912) |
| Women | –0.115 | –0.314 | –0.458 | –0.529** |
| | (0.150) | (0.206) | (0.239) | (0.202) |
| Whites | 0.0607 | 0.288 | –0.241 | –0.0545 |
| | (0.153) | (0.149) | (0.210) | (0.199) |
| Education | 0.0846 | 0.180** | 0.0884 | 0.186* |
| | (0.0447) | (0.0567) | (0.0606) | (0.0929) |
| Income | –0.00466 | –0.00144 | 0.0527 | 0.0219 |
| | (0.0204) | (0.0273) | (0.0317) | (0.0290) |
| Resides in South | 0.119 | 0.120 | 0.143 | 0.0833 |
| | (0.169) | (0.169) | (0.204) | (0.126) |
| Married | 0.333** | 0.238 | 0.182 | –0.190 |
| | (0.126) | (0.163) | (0.208) | (0.199) |
| Birth Year | 0.00637 | 0.00347 | –0.00345 | –0.00517 |
| | (0.00508) | (0.00507) | (0.00914) | (0.00660) |
| Catholic | 0.171 | 0.152 | 0.0776 | –0.0845 |
| | (0.157) | (0.188) | (0.127) | (0.253) |
| Constant | –13.09 | –7.870 | 6.586 | 10.37 |
| | (9.947) | (9.963) | (17.92) | (12.89) |
| Observations | 1,909 | 1,909 | 937 | 937 |

Robust standard errors in parentheses
** $p < .01$, * $p < .05$

**TABLE A4.4** *MULTINOMIAL LOGISTIC REGRESSION ANALYSES OF REPRESENTATION PREFERENCES ON AUTHORITARIANISM*

| | **Authoritarianism (Delegate, base category) (Results for Figure 4.6)** | |
|---|---|---|
| | **Mixed** | **Trustee** |
| Authoritarianism | 0.279 | 0.567** |
| | (0.143) | (0.157) |
| Women | –0.127 | –0.170 |
| | (0.223) | (0.163) |
| Whites | 0.105 | 0.689** |
| | (0.238) | (0.261) |
| Education | 0.0326 | 0.215** |
| | (0.0763) | (0.0753) |
| Income | 0.0259 | –0.00684 |
| | (0.0286) | (0.0466) |
| Resides in South | 0.193 | 0.291 |
| | (0.285) | (0.248) |
| Married | 0.346* | 0.0934 |
| | (0.174) | (0.245) |
| Birth Year | 0.00851 | 0.0104 |
| | (0.00734) | (0.00743) |
| Catholic | –0.137 | –0.111 |
| | (0.224) | (0.289) |
| Constant | –18.06 | –22.22 |
| | (14.45) | (14.58) |
| Observations | 756 | 756 |

Robust standard errors in parentheses
** $p < .01$, * $p < .05$

**TABLE A4.5** *MULTINOMIAL LOGISTIC REGRESSION ANALYSES OF REPRESENTATION PREFERENCES ON TRADITIONAL CHRISTIAN RELIGIOSITY AND PARTY IDENTIFICATION MEASURES*

| | Traditional Christian Religiosity (Delegate, Base Category) (Results for Figure 4.7) | | Party ID (Delegate, Base Category) (Results for Figure 4.8) | | Traditional Christian & Party ID (Delegate, Base Category) | |
|---|---|---|---|---|---|---|
| | **Mixed** | **Trustee** | **Mixed** | **Trustee** | **Mixed** | **Trustee** |
| Trad. Christian Index | 0.367** | 0.354** | | | 0.310** | 0.310** |
| | (0.0531) | (0.0612) | | | (0.0685) | (0.0722) |
| Party ID (GOP high) | | | 0.731** | 0.708** | 0.535** | 0.388* |
| | | | (0.107) | (0.151) | (0.131) | (0.171) |
| Women | –0.216 | –0.310* | –0.0674 | –0.235* | –0.108 | –0.251 |
| | (0.119) | (0.136) | (0.114) | (0.118) | (0.125) | (0.132) |
| Whites | 0.0133 | –0.110 | –0.140 | –0.243 | –0.0985 | –0.238 |
| | (0.110) | (0.117) | (0.0974) | (0.124) | (0.111) | (0.128) |
| Education | 0.0836* | 0.114* | 0.0545 | 0.124** | 0.0779* | 0.127* |
| | (0.0396) | (0.0506) | (0.0328) | (0.0476) | (0.0343) | (0.0518) |
| Income | 0.00832 | 0.00310 | –0.000378 | –0.00451 | 0.00489 | 0.00251 |
| | (0.0193) | (0.0151) | (0.0200) | (0.0179) | (0.0206) | (0.0175) |
| Resides in South | 0.0499 | –0.0231 | 0.150 | –0.0258 | 0.0830 | –0.0892 |
| | (0.106) | (0.105) | (0.103) | (0.103) | (0.116) | (0.112) |
| Married | –0.0105 | –0.0642 | 0.0529 | 0.0929 | –0.0833 | –0.0505 |
| | (0.109) | (0.125) | (0.0908) | (0.132) | (0.110) | (0.136) |
| Birth Year | 0.00214 | 0.00817* | 0.00310 | 0.00575 | 0.00138 | 0.00695 |
| | (0.00327) | (0.00351) | (0.00336) | (0.00341) | (0.00340) | (0.00371) |
| Catholic | 0.147 | 0.0504 | 0.0454 | –0.0772 | 0.104 | –0.0503 |
| | (0.102) | (0.160) | (0.0985) | (0.162) | (0.0974) | (0.153) |
| Constant | –5.054 | –16.73* | –7.203 | –12.35 | –3.728 | –14.46* |
| | (6.391) | (6.758) | (6.596) | (6.549) | (6.657) | (7.102) |
| Observations | 3,328 | 3,328 | 3,632 | 3,632 | 3,109 | 3,109 |

Robust standard errors in parentheses
** $p < .01$, * $p < .05$

# APPENDIX CHAPTER 5: TABLES AND STATISTICAL OUTPUT

**TABLE A5.1** *PROBIT ANALYSIS OF 2008 PRESIDENTIAL VOTE ON REPRESENTATION PREFERENCES AND CONTROLS, AMONG INDEPENDENTS*

| | McCain Vote 2008 (Results for Figure 5.1) |
|---|---|
| Executive Representation Preferences | 0.581* |
| | (0.271) |
| Women | 0.0735 |
| | (0.248) |
| Whites | 0.579 |
| | (0.319) |
| Education | 0.0103 |
| | (0.0877) |
| Income | 0.125** |
| | (0.0454) |
| Resides in South | 0.883** |
| | (0.272) |
| Married | −0.0334 |
| | (0.295) |
| Birth Year | −0.0125 |
| | (0.00892) |
| Catholics | 0.655 |
| | (0.335) |
| Constant | 22.28 |
| | (17.54) |
| Observations | 167 |

Robust standard errors in parentheses
** $p < .01$, * $p < .05$

**TABLE A5.2** *MULTINOMIAL LOGISTIC REGRESSION ANALYSIS OF HOUSE VOTING (2006 & 2008) ON CONGRESSIONAL REPRESENTATION PREFERENCES AND CONTROLS*

| | House Vote 2006 & 2008 (Base Category, Dem. vote in 2006 & 2008) (Results for Figure 5.2) | |
|---|---|---|
| | **Mixed Vote** | **GOP 2006 & 2008** |
| MC Rep. Prefs. | 0.661* | 0.557* |
| | (0.287) | (0.277) |
| Women | 0.150 | –0.412 |
| | (0.267) | (0.264) |
| Whites | –0.228 | 0.599 |
| | (0.312) | (0.346) |
| Education | –0.307** | –0.0825 |
| | (0.109) | (0.0898) |
| Income | –0.0741 | 0.0177 |
| | (0.0380) | (0.0361) |
| Resides in South | –0.407 | –0.272 |
| | (0.321) | (0.281) |
| Married | 0.413 | 0.885** |
| | (0.295) | (0.283) |
| Birth Year | 0.0183 | 0.00133 |
| | (0.00998) | (0.00920) |
| Catholic | 0.457 | 0.0103 |
| | (0.319) | (0.324) |
| Constant | –35.03 | –3.832 |
| | (19.64) | (18.13) |
| Observations | 493 | 493 |

Robust standard errors in parentheses
** $p < .01$, * $p < .05$

**TABLE A5.3** *MULTINOMIAL LOGISTIC REGRESSION ANALYSIS OF SENATE VOTING (2006 & 2008) ON GENERALIZED REPRESENTATION PREFERENCES AND CONTROLS*

| | **Senate Vote 2006 & 2008 (Base Category, Dem. vote in 2006 & 2008) (Results for Figure 5.3)** | |
|---|---|---|
| | **Mixed Vote** | **GOP 2006 & 2008** |
| Generalised Rep. Prefs. | 0.509* | 0.704** |
| | (0.232) | (0.205) |
| Women | –0.0718 | –0.768* |
| | (0.383) | (0.330) |
| Whites | –0.0935 | –0.0476 |
| | (0.588) | (0.393) |
| Education | –0.636** | –0.332** |
| | (0.153) | (0.118) |
| Income | –0.0334 | –0.0241 |
| | (0.0609) | (0.0421) |
| Resides in South | 0.613 | 0.268 |
| | (0.404) | (0.339) |
| Married | 0.445 | 0.976** |
| | (0.442) | (0.357) |
| Birth Year | 0.0148 | 0.00887 |
| | (0.0144) | (0.0127) |
| Catholic | 0.543 | 1.309** |
| | (0.487) | (0.395) |
| Constant | –29.11 | –17.86 |
| | (28.09) | (24.97) |
| Observations | 319 | 319 |

Robust standard errors in parentheses
** $p < .01$, * $p < .05$

**TABLE A5.4** *MULTINOMIAL LOGISTIC REGRESSION ANALYSIS OF GUBERNATORIAL VOTING (2006 & 2008) ON EXECUTIVE REPRESENTATION PREFERENCES AND CONTROLS*

| | Governor Vote 2006 & 2008 (Base Category, Dem. vote 2006 & 2008) (Results for Figure 5.4) | |
|---|---|---|
| | **Mixed** | **GOP 2006 & 2008** |
| Executive Rep. Prefs. | 1.789** | 2.359** |
| | (0.485) | (0.359) |
| Women | 0.720 | 0.107 |
| | (0.489) | (0.350) |
| Whites | –0.553 | 0.373 |
| | (0.525) | (0.503) |
| Education | –0.345 | –0.232 |
| | (0.183) | (0.132) |
| Income | –0.0652 | –0.00419 |
| | (0.0647) | (0.0454) |
| Resides in South | –0.884 | –0.127 |
| | (0.625) | (0.450) |
| Married | 0.424 | 0.532 |
| | (0.539) | (0.374) |
| Birth Year | –0.00327 | –0.0123 |
| | (0.0162) | (0.0122) |
| Catholic | –0.0942 | 0.146 |
| | (0.586) | (0.405) |
| Constant | 6.266 | 23.03 |
| | (31.86) | (23.93) |
| Observations | 266 | 266 |

Robust standard errors in parentheses
** $p < .01$, * $p < .05$

**TABLE A5.5** *OLS REGRESSION OF RESPONDENTS' PRIORITIZATION OF TRAITS VS. POLICIES WHEN EVALUATING CANDIDATES, ON REPRESENTATION PREFERENCES AND CONTROLS*

| | |
|---|---|
| Representation Prefs. (Trustee high) | –0.0156* |
| | (0.00749) |
| African American | 0.0775* |
| | (0.0304) |
| Resides in South | –0.0293* |
| | (0.0141) |
| Women | –0.0119 |
| | (0.0148) |
| Married | –0.00890 |
| | (0.00837) |
| Age (in years) | –3.27e–05 |
| | (0.000510) |
| Education | 0.00302 |
| | (0.00563) |
| Income | 0.00381 |
| | (0.00297) |
| Constant | 0.688 |
| | (1.005) |
| Observations | 3,429 |

Robust standard errors in parentheses
** $p < .01$, * $p < .05$

**TABLE A5.6** *OLS REGRESSION OF EXPERIMENTAL SUBJECTS' EVALUATION OF HYPOTHETICAL CONGRESSIONAL CANDIDATE, ACCORDING TO DIFFERENCES IN CHRISTIAN TRADITIONALISM*

| | Delegate Treatment | Trustee Treatment | Control |
|---|---|---|---|
| Christian Traditionalism | .03 (.02) | .09 (.02)** | .02 (.02) |
| Constant | .64 (.02)** | .65 (.01)** | .66 (.02)** |
| N | 251 | 208 | 238 |

Robust standard errors in parentheses
** $p < .01$, * $p < .05$

**TABLE A5.7** *OLS REGRESSION OF EXPERIMENTAL SUBJECTS' EVALUATION OF HYPOTHETICAL CONGRESSIONAL CANDIDATE, ACCORDING TO DIFFERENCES IN PARTISAN ORIENTATION*

| | Delegate Treatment | Trustee Treatment | Control |
|---|---|---|---|
| Partisan Orientation (GOP) | .00 (.02) | .07 (.01)** | .00 (.02) |
| Constant | .63 (.01)** | .64 (.01)** | .66 (.01)** |
| N | 322 | 286 | 334 |

Robust standard errors in parentheses
** $p < .01$, * $p < .05$

**TABLE A5.8** *SUPPLEMENTARY ANALYSIS: OLS REGRESSION OF EXPERIMENTAL SUBJECTS' EVALUATION OF HYPOTHETICAL CONGRESSIONAL CANDIDATE, ACCORDING TO DIFFERENCES IN EGALITARIANISM*

| | Delegate Treatment | Trustee Treatment | Control |
|---|---|---|---|
| Egalitarianism | .03 (.04) | –.12 (.04)** | .05 (.04) |
| Constant | .61 (.03)** | .70 (.02)** | .63 (.03)** |
| N | 344 | 298 | 338 |

Robust standard errors in parentheses
** $p < .01$, * $p < .05$

**TABLE A5.9** *SUPPLEMENTARY ANALYSIS: OLS REGRESSION OF EXPERIMENTAL SUBJECTS' EVALUATION OF HYPOTHETICAL CONGRESSIONAL CANDIDATE, ACCORDING TO DIFFERENCES IN HUMANISM*

| | Delegate Treatment | Trustee Treatment | Control |
|---|---|---|---|
| Humanism | .02 (.04) | –.14 (.04)** | .01 (.04) |
| Constant | .62 (.02)** | .59 (.02)** | .66 (.02)** |
| N | 343 | 297 | 344 |

Robust standard errors in parentheses
** $p < .01$, * $p < .05$

# APPENDIX CHAPTER 6: TABLES AND STATISTICAL OUTPUT

**TABLE A6.1** *ORDERED LOGISTIC REGRESSION ANALYSES OF MC DISAPPROVAL ON PERCEIVED MC REPRESENTATION STYLE, BY PARTY IDENTIFICATION (RESULTS FOR FIGURES 6.1 AND 6.2)*

| | Democrats & Independents | Republicans |
|---|---|---|
| MC Representation Eval. (Trustee high) | 0.353** | –0.258* |
| | (0.0656) | (0.150) |
| Birth Year | 0.0149** | 0.0112* |
| | (0.00353) | (0.00536) |
| Income | 0.0140 | –0.00976 |
| | (0.0135) | (0.0191) |
| Education | –0.00563 | 0.0528 |
| | (0.0411) | (0.0608) |
| Whites | –0.0373 | –0.224 |
| | (0.0951) | (0.254) |
| Women | 0.00504 | 0.246 |
| | (0.143) | (0.163) |
| Catholic | –0.0801 | –0.101 |
| | (0.119) | (0.149) |
| Married | –0.0577 | –0.317 |
| | (0.156) | (0.180) |
| cut1 | | |
| Constant | 29.30** | 21.93* |
| | (6.839) | (10.51) |
| cut2 | | |
| Constant | 30.00** | 22.59* |
| | (6.844) | (10.52) |
| Observations | 1,880 | 805 |

Robust standard errors in parentheses
** $p < .01$, * $p < .05$

**TABLE A6.2** *PROBIT ANALYSIS OF MC PARTY IDENTIFICATION ON MC'S PERCEIVED REPRESENTATION STYLE*

| | |
|---|---|
| Rep. Evaluation ("Is"), Trustee high | 0.459** |
| | (0.146) |
| Party Identification (GOP high) | 0.250* |
| | (0.0982) |
| Birth Year | 0.000658 |
| | (0.00204) |
| Income | 0.00564 |
| | (0.00927) |
| Education | 0.000805 |
| | (0.0262) |
| Whites | 0.312** |
| | (0.109) |
| Women | –0.0211 |
| | (0.0572) |
| Catholic | –0.170 |
| | (0.104) |
| Married | 0.188 |
| | (0.0991) |
| Constant | –1.848 |
| | (4.037) |
| Observations | 1,782 |

Robust standard errors in parentheses
** $p < .01$, * $p < .05$

# APPENDIX CHAPTER 7: TABLES AND STATISTICAL OUTPUT

**TABLE A7.1** *OLS REGRESSION ANALYSIS OF MC NONRESPONSIVENESS ON DISTRICT TRADITIONALISM AND CONTROLS, BY DISTRICT IDEOLOGY (DISPLAYING CONGRESSIONAL SESSION DUMMIES)*

| | All Districts | Respondents in Conservative Districts | Respondents in Progressive Districts |
|---|---|---|---|
| District Traditionalism | 0.00447** | –0.000217 | 0.00781** |
| | (0.000585) | (0.000575) | (0.000945) |
| District Ideological Extremism | 0.0169** | 0.0163** | 0.0148** |
| | (0.000470) | (0.00174) | (0.00120) |
| Conservative Nonresponsiveness | –0.0453 | 0.108 | –0.248** |
| | (0.0243) | (0.0712) | (0.0489) |
| Black Evangelical MC | 0.151** | | 0.172** |
| | (0.0273) | | (0.0221) |
| First-Term MC | –0.00774 | –0.0102* | –0.000427 |
| | (0.00505) | (0.00482) | (0.00710) |
| Trend | 0.00810** | 0.0190** | –0.00895** |
| | (0.000917) | (0.00211) | (0.00143) |
| Congress: 100 | –0.0419** | 0.00723 | 0.0589** |
| | (0.00575) | (0.00912) | (0.0175) |
| Congress: 101 | 0.0318** | 0.0424** | 0.0215** |
| | (0.00606) | (0.00674) | (0.00794) |
| Congress: 102 | 0.0216** | 0.0224** | 0.0350** |
| | (0.00675) | (0.00703) | (0.00901) |
| Congress: 103 | 0.0582** | 0.0727** | 0.0174 |
| | (0.00746) | (0.0117) | (0.00973) |
| Congress: 104 | 0.0754** | 0.132** | 0.0231 |
| | (0.00922) | (0.0183) | (0.0128) |
| Congress: 105 | 0.0751** | 0.149** | 0.0414** |
| | (0.00984) | (0.0209) | (0.0137) |
| Congress: 106 | 0.0645** | 0.131** | 0.0404** |
| | (0.00917) | (0.0186) | (0.0129) |
| Congress: 107 | 0.0618** | 0.0732** | 0.0442** |
| | (0.00604) | (0.0105) | (0.00881) |
| Congress: 108 | 0.0550** | 0.0671** | 0.0323** |
| | (0.00598) | (0.00999) | (0.00860) |

(*continued*)

**TABLE A7.1** *(CONTINUED)*

| | All Districts | Respondents in Conservative Districts | Respondents in Progressive Districts |
|---|---|---|---|
| Congress: 109 | 0.0465** | 0.0419** | 0.0362** |
| | (0.00496) | (0.00722) | (0.00709) |
| Congress: 110 | 0.0240** | –0.0104* | 0.0592** |
| | (0.00435) | (0.00480) | (0.00609) |
| Constant | –0.245** | –0.0740* | –0.275** |
| | (0.0317) | (0.0374) | (0.0447) |
| Observations | 5,188 | 2,769 | 2,419 |
| R-squared | 0.606 | 0.693 | 0.794 |

Robust standard errors in parentheses
** $p < .01$, * $p < .05$

**TABLE A7.2** *OLS REGRESSION ANALYSIS OF MC NONRESPONSIVENESS ON DISTRICT TRADITIONALISM OVER TIME (DISPLAYING CONGRESSIONAL SESSION DUMMIES)*

| | |
|---|---|
| District Traditionalism | –0.00600** |
| | (0.000640) |
| District Traditionalism*Trend | 0.00178** |
| | (7.07e–05) |
| District Ideological Extremism | 0.0178** |
| | (0.000380) |
| Conservative Nonresponsiveness | –0.0735** |
| | (0.0204) |
| Black Evangelical MC | 0.170** |
| | (0.0175) |
| First-Term MC | –0.0115** |
| | (0.00441) |
| Trend | –0.0843** |
| | (0.00398) |
| Congress: 100 | 0.0184** |
| | (0.00563) |
| Congress: 101 | 0.0434** |
| | (0.00488) |
| Congress: 102 | 0.0321** |
| | (0.00536) |
| Congress: 103 | 0.0472** |
| | (0.00677) |

(*continued*)

**TABLE A7.2** *(CONTINUED)*

| | |
|---|---|
| Congress: 104 | 0.0728** |
| | (0.00903) |
| Congress: 105 | 0.0827** |
| | (0.00976) |
| Congress: 106 | 0.0856** |
| | (0.00896) |
| Congress: 107 | 0.0794** |
| | (0.00563) |
| Congress: 108 | 0.0770** |
| | (0.00570) |
| Congress: 109 | 0.0631** |
| | (0.00476) |
| Congress: 110 | 0.0421** |
| | (0.00436) |
| Constant | 0.283** |
| | (0.0354) |
| Observations | 5,188 |
| R-squared | 0.716 |

Robust standard errors in parentheses
** $p < .01$, * $p < .05$

**TABLE A7.3** *OLS REGRESSION ANALYSIS OF REPRESENTATION GAP (IS–OUGHT) ON DISTRICT TRADITIONALISM, FOR FOR IDEOLOGICALLY EXTREME AND MODERATE MCS (DISPLAYING CONGRESSIONAL SESSION DUMMIES)*

| | **Ideologically Extreme MCs** | **Ideologically Moderate MCs** |
|---|---|---|
| District Traditionalism | 0.00777** | –0.000283 |
| | (0.00106) | (0.000166) |
| Conservative Nonresponsiveness | –0.229** | –0.00277 |
| | (0.0571) | (0.00475) |
| Black Evangelical MC | 0.438** | –0.0244** |
| | (0.0486) | (0.00349) |
| First-Term MC | –0.0252** | 0.00352* |
| | (0.00736) | (0.00176) |
| Trend | 0.0105** | –0.00246** |
| | (0.00121) | (0.000330) |
| Congress: 100 | –0.0737** | 0.00533* |
| | (0.00871) | (0.00223) |

(*continued*)

**TABLE A7.3** *(CONTINUED)*

| | | |
|---|---|---|
| Congress: 101 | 0.000451 | –0.0249** |
| | (0.00711) | (0.00323) |
| Congress: 102 | –0.0195* | –0.0204** |
| | (0.00819) | (0.00308) |
| Congress: 103 | 0.0427** | –0.0316** |
| | (0.0111) | (0.00270) |
| Congress: 104 | 0.0655** | –0.0104** |
| | (0.0145) | (0.00338) |
| Congress: 105 | 0.0742** | 0.00416 |
| | (0.0161) | (0.00407) |
| Congress: 106 | 0.0566** | 0.00539 |
| | (0.0155) | (0.00385) |
| Congress: 107 | 0.0763** | –0.0139** |
| | (0.0118) | (0.00207) |
| Congress: 108 | 0.0750** | –0.0125** |
| | (0.0120) | (0.00212) |
| Congress: 109 | 0.0674** | –0.0124** |
| | (0.0104) | (0.00181) |
| Congress: 110 | 0.0389** | –0.0128** |
| | (0.00777) | (0.00165) |
| Constant | –0.256** | 0.0571** |
| | (0.0548) | (0.00997) |
| Observations | 5,188 | 5,188 |
| R-squared | 0.231 | 0.111 |

Robust standard errors in parentheses
** $p < .01$, * $p < .05$

**TABLE A7.4** *INSTRUMENTAL VARIABLE CREATION OF MC IDEOLOGICAL RESPONSIVENESS TO DISTRICT: OLS REGRESSION ANALYSIS OF DW-NOMINATE (FIRST DIMENSION) SCORES ON REPUBLICAN PRESIDENTIAL VOTE (PREVIOUS ELECTION) AND CONGRESSIONAL SESSIONS*

| | |
|---|---|
| District Republican Presidential Vote | 0.0239** |
| | (0.000679) |
| Congress: 100th | –0.00134 |
| | (0.00646) |
| Congress: 101st | 0.133** |
| | (0.00977) |
| Congress: 102nd | 0.124** |
| | (0.0121) |
| Congress: 103rd | 0.311** |
| | (0.0176) |
| Congress: 104th | 0.421** |
| | (0.0191) |
| Congress: 105th | 0.470** |
| | (0.0203) |
| Congress: 106th | 0.469** |
| | (0.0208) |
| Congress: 107th | 0.384** |
| | (0.0200) |
| Congress: 108th | 0.394** |
| | (0.0199) |
| Congress: 109th | 0.379** |
| | (0.0195) |
| Congress: 110th | 0.335** |
| | (0.0201) |
| Congress: 111th | 0.425** |
| | (0.0227) |
| Constant | –1.461** |
| | (0.0430) |
| Observations | 5,708 |
| R-squared | 0.551 |

Robust standard errors in parentheses
** $p < .01$, * $p < .05$

**TABLE A7.5** *INSTRUMENTAL VARIABLE CREATION OF DISTRICT TRADITIONALISM: OLS REGRESSION ANALYSIS OF REPUBLICAN PRESIDENTIAL VOTE (PREVIOUS ELECTION) ON DISTRICT AND MC CHARACTERISTICS*

| | |
|---|---|
| District in Red State | 2.641** |
| | (0.627) |
| DW-Nominate 2nd Dimension | 12.15** |
| | (0.885) |
| Representative Republican | 18.03** |
| | (0.678) |
| MC: Evangelical | 2.494** |
| | (0.908) |
| MC: Mormon | 6.576** |
| | (1.376) |
| MC: Jewish | 2.091 |
| | (1.179) |
| MC: Catholic | 0.156 |
| | (0.841) |
| MC: Methodist | 3.321** |
| | (0.890) |
| MC: Presbyterian | 3.104** |
| | (0.866) |
| Congress: 100th | 0.164 |
| | (0.234) |
| Congress: 101st | –5.338** |
| | (0.324) |
| Congress: 102nd | –5.085** |
| | (0.404) |
| Congress: 103rd | –12.23** |
| | (0.538) |
| Congress: 104th | –14.39** |
| | (0.548) |
| Congress: 105th | –16.15** |
| | (0.579) |
| Congress: 106th | –15.97** |
| | (0.580) |
| Congress: 107th | –11.95** |
| | (0.608) |
| Congress: 108th | –11.61** |
| | (0.573) |
| Congress: 109th | –10.62** |
| | (0.575) |

(*continued*)

**TABLE A7.5** *(CONTINUED)*

| | |
|---|---|
| Congress: 110th | –10.03** |
| | (0.584) |
| Congress: 111th | –14.35** |
| | (0.614) |
| Constant | 49.31** |
| | (0.883) |
| Observations | 5,704 |
| R-squared | 0.611 |

Robust standard errors in parentheses
** $p < .01$, * $p < .05$

# References


Abramowitz, Alan I., and Kyle L. Saunders. 1998. "Ideological Realignment in the US Electorate." *Journal of Politics* 60: 634–652.

Adler, Bill. 2004. *The Quotable George W. Bush: A Portrait in his Own Words*. Kansas City, MO: Andrews McMeel.

Adorno, Theodor W., Else Frenkel-Brunswick, and Daniel J. Levinson. 1950. *The Authoritarian Personality*. New York: WW Norton.

Alford, John R., Carolyn L. Funk, and John R. Hibbing. 2005. "Are Political Orientations Genetically Transmitted?" *American Political Science Review* 99(2): 153–167.

Altemeyer, Robert. 1996. *The Authoritarian Specter.* Cambridge: Harvard University Press.

American Humanist Association. 1933. "Humanist Manifesto I." *The New Humanist*.

Ansolabehere, Stephen. 2009. "Guide to the 2008 Cooperative Congressional Election Survey." Available online at ftp://voteview.com/CCES_Guide_2008_Rough_Draft_v2.pdf.

Ansolabehere, Stephen. 2010. "Dyadic Representation." In Schickler, Eric, and Frances E. Lee (eds.), *The Oxford Handbook of the American Congress*. New York: Oxford University Press.

Arnold, Douglas. 1992. *The Logic of Congressional Action.* New Haven: Yale University Press.

Bafumi, Joseph, and Robert Y. Shapiro. 2009. "A New Partisan Voter." *Journal of Politics* 71(1): 1–24.

Barber, Benjamin. 1985. *Strong Democracy*. Berkeley: University of California Press.

Barker, David C., and Christopher Jan Carman. 2009. "Political Geography, Church Attendance, and Mass Preferences Regarding Representation." *Journal of Elections, Public Opinion, and Parties* 19: 125–145.

Barker, David C., and Christopher Jan Carman. 2010. "Yes We Can or Yes He Can? Citizen Preferences regarding Styles of Representation and Presidential Voting Behavior." *Presidential Studies Quarterly* 40: 431–448.

Barker, David C., and James L. Tinnick. 2006. "Competing Visions of Parental Roles and Ideological Constraint." *American Political Science Review* 100: 249–263.

Bartels, Larry M. 2006. "What's the Matter with *What's the Matter with Kansas?*" *Quarterly Journal of Political Science* 1: 201–226.

Bengtsson, Åsa, and Hanna Wass. 2010. "Styles of Political Representation: What Do Voters Expect?" *Journal of Elections, Public Opinion and Parties* 20(1): 55–81.

Bianco, William T. 1994. *Trust: Representatives and Constituents.* Ann Arbor: University of Michigan Press.

Bowler, Shaun, Donovan, Todd, and Jeffrey A. Karp. 2007. "Enraged or Engaged? Preferences for Direct Citizen Participation in Affluent Democracies." *Political Research Quarterly* 60: 351–362.

Box-Steffensmeier, Janet M., Henry E. Brady, and David Collier. 2008. *The Oxford Handbook of Political Methodology*. New York: Oxford University Press.

Brock, David, and Paul Waldman. 2008. *Free Ride: John McCain and the Media.* Norwell, MA: Anchor Press.

Burke, Edmund. 1774 (Nov. 3). "Speech to the Electors of Bristol."

Campbell, Angus, Philip E. Converse, Warren E. Miller, and Donald E. Stokes. 1960. *The American Voter*. New York: Wiley and Sons.

Canes-Wrone, Brandice. 2006. *Who Leads Whom: Presidents, Policy, and the Public.* Chicago, IL: University of Chicago Press.

Canovan, Margaret. 1981. *Populism*. New York: Harcourt Brace Jovanovich.

Cantril, Hadley, and Mildred Strunk. 1951. *Public Opinion: 1936–1946*. Princeton, NJ: Princeton University Press.

Carman, Christopher Jan. 2006. "Public Preferences for Parliamentary Representation in the UK: An Overlooked Link?" *Political Studies* 54: 103–122.

Carman, Christopher Jan. 2007. "Assessing Preferences for Political Representation in the US." *Journal of Elections, Public Opinion and Parties* 17: 1–20.

Carmines, Edward G., and James A. Stimson. 1980. "Two Faces of Issue Voting." *American Political Science Review* 74(1): 78–91.

Carson, Jamie L., Michale H. Crespin, Charles J. Finocchiaro, and David W. Rohde. 2007. "Redistricting and Party Polarization in the US House of Representatives." *American Politics Research* 35:878–904

Chang, Lin Chiat, and Jon Krosnick. 2009. "National Surveys Via RDD Telephone Interviewing Versus the Internet: Comparing Sample Representativeness and Response Quality." *Public Opinion Quarterly* 73(4): 641–678.

Clement, Scott, and John C. Green. 2011. "The Tea Party, Religion and Social Issues." *Pew Forum on Religion and Public Life,* February 23.

Clinton, Joshua D. 2006. "Representation in Congress: Constituents and Roll Calls in the 106th House." *Journal of Politics* 68(2): 397–409.

Cooper, Joseph. 1999. *Congress and the Decline of Public Trust.* Boulder, CO: Westview Press.

Cooperative Congressional Election Study (CES). 2006–2009. Barker, David C. and Christopher Jan Carman, University of Pittsburgh/University of Strathclyde Team Content. Available at: http://projects.iq.harvard.edu/cces/data.

Crossan, John Dominic. 1994. *Jesus: A Revolutionary Biography*. New York: Harper Collins.

Dahl, Robert A. 1989. *Democracy and Its Critics*. New Haven, CT: Yale University Press.

Davidson, Roger. 1969. *The Role of the Congressman*. New York: Pegasus.

Davidson, Roger. 1970. "Public Prescriptions for the Job of Congressman." *Midwest Journal of Political Science* 14: 648–666.

Dean, John. 2006. *Conservatives without Conscience*. New York: Viking.

Delli Carpini, Michael X., and Scott Keeter. 1996. *What Americans Know about Politics and Why it Matters*. New Haven, CT: Yale University Press.

Dixon, A.C. (ed.). 1910–1915. *The Fundamentals: A Testimony to the Truth*. Grand Rapids, MI: Baker Books.

Djupe, Paul A., and Christopher P. Gilbert. 2009. *The Political Influence of Churches*. New York: Cambridge University Press.

Doherty, David. 2010. "Who Do People Think Representatives Should Respond To: Their Constituents or the Country?" Working paper: http://orion.luc.edu/~ddoherty/documents/Representation.pdf (accessed August 2, 2011).

Druckman, James N., and Lawrence R. Jacobs. 2011. "Segmented Representation: The Reagan White House and Disproportionate Responsiveness." In Enns, Peter K., and Christopher Wlezien (eds.), *Who Gets Represented?* New York: Russell Sage Foundation.

Elazar, Daniel J. (1966) *American Federalism: A View from the States*. New York: Crowell.

Erikson, Robert S., and Gerald C. Wright. 2000. "Representation of Constituency Ideology in Congress." In David Brady, John Cogan, and Morris Fiorina (eds.), *Continuity and Change in House Elections*. Stanford: Stanford University Press.

Erikson, Robert S., Gerald C. Wright, and John P. Mciver. 1993. *Statehouse Democracy: Public Opinion and Policy in the American States*. New York: Cambridge University Press.

Esaiasson, Peter, and Sören Holmberg. 1996. *Representation from Above. Members of Parliament and Representative Democracy in Sweden*. Dartmouth: Aldershot Press.

Etzioni, Amitai. 1968. *The Active Society*. London: Collier-MacMillan.

Eulau, Heinz, and Paul D. Karps. 1977. "The Puzzle of Representation: Specifying Components of Responsiveness." *Legislative Studies Quarterly* 2: 233–254.

Eulau, Heinz, John C. Wahlke, William Buchanan, and Leroy C. Ferguson. 1959. "The Role of the Representative: Some Empirical Observations on the Theory of Edmund Burke." *American Political Science Review* 553: 742–756.

Feldman, Stanley. 2003a. "Values, Ideology, and the Structure of Political Attitudes." In Sears, David O., Leonie Huddy, and Robert Jervis (eds.), *The Oxford Handbook of Political Psychology*. New York: Oxford University Press.

Feldman, Stanley. 2003b. "Enforcing Social Conformity. A Theory of Authoritarianism." *Political Psychology* 24(1): 41–74.

Fenno, Richard F. 1978. *Homestyle: House Members in Their Districts*. Boston: Little, Brown.

Fiorina, Morris. 1989. *Congress: Keystone of the Washington Establishment* (2nd ed.). New Haven, CT: Yale University Press.

Fiorina, Morris, Samuel J. Abrams, and Jeremy C. Pope. 2005. *Culture War? The Myth of a Polarized America*. New York: Pearson-Longman.

Fishkin, James S. 1995. *The Voice of the People*. New Haven, CT: Yale University Press.

Fowler, Robert Booth, Allan D. Hertzke, Laura R. Olson, and Kevin R. den Dulk. 2010. *Religion and Politics in America*. Boulder, CO: Westview.

Fox, Justin, and Kenneth Shotts. 2009. "Delegates or Trustees? A Theory of Political Accountability." *Journal of Politics* 71(4): 1225–1237.

Francis, Wayne L., and Lawrence W. Kenny. 1996. "Position Shifting in Pursuit of Higher Office." *American Journal of Political Science* 40(3): 768–786.

Geer, John G. 1996. *From Tea Leaves to Opinion Polls*. New York: Columbia University Press.

Gelman, Andrew, David Park, Boris Shor, Joseph Bafumi, and Jeronimo Cortina. 2008. *Red State, Blue State, Rich State, Poor State: Why Americans Vote The Way They Do*. Princeton, NJ: Princeton University Press.

Gerber, Alan S., Gregory A. Huber, David Doherty, Conor M. Dowling, and Shang E. Ha. 2010."Personality and Political Attitudes: Relationships across Issue Domains and Political Contexts." *American Political Science Review* 104(1): 111.

Goodhart, Michael. 2005. *Democracy as Human Rights: Freedom and Equality in the Age of Globalization*. New York: Routledge.

Grill, Christopher J. 2007. *The Public Side of Representation: A Study of Citizens' Views of Representation and the Representative Process*. Albany: SUNY Press.

Hacker, Jacob S., and Paul Pierson. 2005. *Off Center: The Republican Revolution and the Erosion of American Democracy*. New Haven: Yale University Press.

Haidt, Jonathan. 2012. *The Righteous Mind: Why Good People are Divided by Politics and Religion*. New York: Pantheon Books.

Held, David. 1996. *Models of Democracy* (2nd ed.). Stanford, CA: Stanford University Press.

Hetherington, Marc J., and Jonathan D. Weiler. 2009. *Authoritarianism and Polarization in American Politics*. New York: Cambridge University Press.

Hibbing, John R., and Elizabeth Theiss-Morse. 2001. "Process Preferences and American Politics: What the People Want Government to Be." *American Political Science Review* 95: 145–153.

Hibbing, John R., and Elizabeth Theiss-Morse. 2002. *Stealth Democracy: American's Beliefs About How Government Should Work*. Cambridge: Cambridge University Press.

Hill, Kim Quaile, and Tetsuya Matsubayshi. 2008. "Church Engagement, Religious Values and Mass-Elite Policy Agenda Agreement." *American Journal of Political Science* 52: 570–584.

Hobbes, Thomas. 1651. *Leviathan*. Available online at: http://www.gutenberg.org/files/3207/3207-h/3207-h.htm (accessed August 10, 2011).

Howe, Ben. 2011. "Again, No Compromise." RedState.com. Available at: http://www.redstate.com/aglanon/2011/07/25/again-no-compromise/ (accessed August 2, 2011).

Hunter, James Davison. 1991. *Culture Wars: The Struggle to Define America*. New York: Basic Books.

Hurley, Patricia, and Kim Quaille Hill. 2010. "In Search of Representation Theory." In Leighley, Jan E. (ed.), *The Oxford Handbook of American Elections and Political Behavior*. New York: Oxford University Press.

Hurwitz, Jon, and Mark Peffley. 1987. "How Are Foreign Policy Attitudes Structured? A Hierarchical Model." *American Political Science Review* 89: 1099–1120.

Ignatius, David. 2004 (June 8). "Protean Leader." *The Washington Post*.

Isserman, Maurice, and Michael Kazin. 1999. *America Divided: The Civil War of the 1960s*. New York: Oxford University Press.

Jacobs, Lawrence R., and Robert Y. Shapiro. 2000. *Politicians Don't Pander: Political Manipulation and the Loss of Democratic Responsiveness*. Chicago: University of Chicago Press.

Jacoby, William. 2006. "Value Choices and American Public Opinion," *American Journal of Political Science* 50: 706–723.

Jacoby, William. 2010. "The American Voter." In Leighley, Jan E. (ed.), *The Oxford Handbook of American Elections and Political Behavior.* New York: Oxford University Press.

Jewell, Malcolm E. 1985. "Legislators and Constituents in the Representative Process." In Loewenberg, Gerhard, Samuel C. Patterson, and Malcolm E. Jewell (eds.), *The Handbook of Legislative Research*. Cambridge, MA: Harvard University Press.

Johnston, Richard. 2008. "Survey Methodology." In Box-Steffensmeier, Janet, Henry E. Brady, and David Collier (eds.), *The Oxford Handbook of Political Methodology*. Oxford: Oxford University Press.

Jost, John T., Jack Glaser, Arie W. Kruglanski, and Frank L. Sulloway. 2003. "Political Conservatism as Motivated Social Cognition." *Psychological Bulletin* 129(3): 39–75.

Judge, David. 1999. *Representation: Theory and Practice in Britain*. London: Routledge.

Keith, Bruce E., David B, Magleby, Candice J. Nelson, Elizabeth Orr, and Mark C. Westlye. 1992. *The Myth of the Independent Voter*. Berkeley: University of California Press.

Kennedy, Peter. 2003. *A Guide to Econometrics* (5th ed.). Cambridge: MIT Press.

Kernell, Samuel. 1997. *Going Public: New Strategies of Presidential Leadership*. Washington, DC: CQ Press.

Kessebir, Selin, and Jonathan Haidt. 2010. "Morality." In Fiske, Susan T., Daniel Todd Gilbert, and Gardner Lindzey (eds.), *Handbook of Social Psychology*. Hoboken, NJ: John Wiley.

Kim, Jae-On, and Charles W. Mueller. 1978. *Factor Analysis: Statistical Methods and Practical Issues*. Beverly Hills, CA: Sage.

King, Gary. 1986. "How Not to Lie with Statistics: Avoiding Common Problems in Quantitative Political Science." *American Journal of Political Science* 30: 666–687.

King, Anthony. 1997. *Running Scared*. New York: Free Press.

Kousser, Thad, Jeffrey B. Lewis, and Seth E. Masket. 2007. "Ideological Adaptation? The Survival Instinct of Threatened Legislators." *Journal of Politics* 69(3): 828–843.

Krosnick, Jon A. 1999. "Survey Research." *Annual Review of Psychology* 50: 537–567.

Kuklinski, James H., and Gary M. Segura. 1995. "Engogeneity, Exogeneity, Time and Space in Political Representation: A Review Article." *Legislative Studies Quarterly* 20: 3–21.

Kurland, Philip B., and Ralph Lerner. 1987. *The Founder's Constitution*, vol. 1. Indianapolis: Liberty Fund.

Lakoff, George. 2006. *Thinking Points: Communicating Our American Values and Vision*. New York: Farrar, Straus and Giroux.

Lamont, Corliss. 1997. *The Philosophy of Humanism*. Washington D.C.: The Humanist Press.

Lax, Jeffrey R., and Justin H. Phillips. 2009. "Gay Rights in the States: Public Opinion and Policy Responsiveness." *American Political Science Review* 103: 367–386.

Layman, Geoffrey. 2001. *The Great Divide*. New York: Columbia University Press.

Layman, Geoffrey C., and John C. Green. 2006. "Wars and Rumours of Wars: The Contexts of Cultural Conflict in American Political Behaviour." *British Journal of Political Science* 36: 61–89.

Lee, Frances E., and Bruce I. Oppenheimer. 1999. *Sizing up the Senate: The Unequal Consequences of Equal Representation*. Chicago: University of Chicago Press.

Leege, David C., and Lyman A. Kellstedt. 1993. *Rediscovering the Religious Factor in American Politics*. New York: ME Sharpe.

Leege, David C., Kenneth D. Wald, Brian S. Krueger, and Paul D. Mueller. 2001. *The Politics of Cultural Differences: Social Change and Voter Mobilization Strategies in the Post New-Deal Period*. Princeton, NJ: Princeton University Press.

Lehrer, Eli. 1998 (Oct. 12). "For GOP Pundit Fitzpatrick, Principles Outweigh Polls." *Insight on the News*.

Levendusky, Matthew. 2009. *The Partisan Sort: How Liberals Became Democrats and Conservatives Became Republicans*. Chicago: University of Chicago Press.

Lipinski, Daniel. 2002. "Rhetoric on Representation: What Members of Congress tell Constituents about Representational Roles." Paper presented at the Southern Political Science Association Annual Meeting, Nov. 7–9, Savannah, GA.

Locke, John. 1689. *The Two Treatises of Government*. Available online at: http://www.gutenberg.org/files/7370/7370-h/7370-h.htm (accessed August 10, 2011).

Long, J. Scott, & Jeremy Freese. 2006. *Regression Models for Categorical Dependent Variables Using Stata* (2nd ed.). College Station, TX: Stata Press.

Luntz, Frank. 1994. "Voices of Victory, Parts I and II." Available online at: http://www.pollingreport.com/focus.htm (accessed May 30, 2011).

Luskin, Robert C. 1991. "Abusus Non Tollit Usum: Standardized Coefficients, and $R^2$'s." *American Journal of Political Science* 35(4): 1032–1046.

Madison, James. 1787. *Notes on the Constitutional Convention of 1787*. Available online at: http://www.archive.org/details/jamesmadisonsnot00scot (accessed January 10, 2012).

Main, Jackson Turner. 2004. *The Anti-Federalists: Critics of the Constitution, 1781–1788*. Chapel Hill: University of North Carolina Press.

Manin, Bernard, Adam Przeworski, and Susan Stokes. 1999. "Elections and Representation." In Przeworski, Adam, Susan Stokes, and Bernard Manin (eds.), *Democracy, Accountability and Representation*. Cambridge: Cambridge University Press.

Mansbridge, Jane. 2003. "Rethinking Representation." *American Political Science Review* 97: 515–528.

Marietta, Morgan. 2008. "From My Cold, Dead Hands: Democratic Consequences of Sacred Rhetoric." *Journal of Politics* 70:767–779.

Marsden, George M. 2006. *Fundamentalism and American Culture*. New York: Oxford University Press.

May, J.D. 1978. "Defining Democracy." *Political Studies* 26:1–14.

McCarty, Nolan, Keith T. Poole, and Howard Rosenthal. 2008. *Polarized America: The Dance of Ideology and Unequal Riches*. Boston, MA: MIT Press

McMurray, Carl D., and Malcolm B. Parsons. 1965. "Public Attitudes Toward the Representational Roles of Legislators and Judges." *Midwest Journal of Political Science* 9: 167–185.

Mendez-Lago, M., and Martinez, A. 2002. "Political Representation in Spain: An Empirical Analysis of the Perception of Citizens and MPs." *Journal of Legislative Studies* 8: 63–90.

Mill, John Stuart. 1861. *Representative Government*. Available online at: http://www.gutenberg.org/ebooks/5669 (accessed January 17, 2012).

Miller, Joshua I. 1991. "Direct Democracy and the Puritan Theory of Membership." *Journal of Politics* 53(1): 57–74.

Miller, Warren E., and Donald E. Stokes. 1963. "Constituency Influence in Congress." *American Political Science Review* 57: 45–56.

Miroff, Bruce, Raymond Seidelman, Todd Swanstrom, and Tom DeLuca. 2009. *The Democratic Debate: American Politics in an Age of Change*. Boston: Wadsworth Publishing.

Mitchell, Joshua M. 1992. "Protestant Thought and Republican Spirit: How Luther Enchanted the World." *American Political Science Review* 86(3): 688–695.

Mlodinow, Leonard. 2008. *The Drunkard's Walk: How Randomness Rules Our Lives*. New York: Vintage Books.

Parker, Glenn R. 1974. *Political Beliefs about the Structure of Government: Congress and the Presidency*. Beverly Hills: Sage.

Patterson, Samuel C., Ronald D. Hedlund, and G. Robert Boynton. 1975. *Representatives and the Represented: Bases of Support for the American Legislatures*. New York: Wiley.

Pew Forum on Religion and Public Life. 2008. "2008 Religious Landscape Survey." Available online at: http://religions.pewforum.org/ (accessed August 1, 2011).

Pitkin, Hanna Fenichel. 1967. *The Concept of Representation*. Berkeley: University of California Press.

Poole, Keith T., and Howard Rosenthal. 1997. *Congress: A Political-Economic History of Roll Call Voting*. New York: Oxford University Press.

Putnam, Robert D. 2000. *Bowling Alone: The Collapse and Revival of American Community*. New York: Simon and Schuster.

Ray, John J. 1992. "Defining Authoritarianism." *South African Journal of Psychology* 22: 178–179.

Rehfeld, Andrew. 2009. "Representation Rethought: on Trustees, Delegates and Gyroscopes in the Study of Political Representation in Democracy." *American Political Science Review* 103: 214–230.

Reynolds, David S. 2008. *Waking Giant: America in the Age of Jackson*. New York: Harper Collins.

Rivers, Douglas. 2009. "Douglas Rivers: Second Thoughts about Internet Surveys." Pollster.com. Available online: http://www.pollster.com/blogs/doug_rivers.php.

Rokeach, M. 1954. "The Nature and Meaning of Dogmatism." *Psychological Review* 61: 194–204.

Rokeach, M. 1973. *The Nature of Human Values*. New York: Free Press.

Rosenthal, Alan. 1998. *The Decline of Representative Democracy*. Washington, DC: CQ Press.

Rousseau, Jean Jacques. 1762. *The Social Contract*. Available online at: http://www.constitution.org/jjr/socon.htm (accessed January 17, 2012).

Sabine, G.H. 1952. "The Two Democratic Traditions." *The Philosophical Review* 61(4): 451–474.

Schnaffner, Brian F. 2011. "Party Polarization." In Schickler, Eric and Frances E. Lee (eds.), *The Oxford Handbook of the American Congress*. New York: Oxford University Press.

Shadish, William R., Thomas D. Cook, and Donald T. Campbell. 2001. *Experimental and Quasi-experimental Designs for Generalized Causal Inference* (2nd ed.). Boston: Wadsworth Publishing.

Sidanius, Jim, and Felicia Pratto. 2001. *Social Dominance: An Intergroup Theory of Social Hierarchy and Oppression*. New York: Cambridge University Press.

Sigelman, Lee, Carol K. Sigelman, and Barbara J. Walkocz. 1992. "The Public and the Paradox of Leadership: An Experimental Analysis." *American Journal of Political Science* 36: 366–385.

Smidt, Corwin E., Lyman A. Kellstedt, and James L. Guth. 2009. *The Oxford Handbook of Religion and American Politics*. New York: Oxford University Press.

Soroka, Stuart, and Christopher Wlezien. 2010. *Degrees of Democracy: Politics, Public Opinion and Policy*. Cambridge: Cambridge University Press.

Stark, Rodney. 1996. *The Rise of Christianity*. Princeton, NJ: Princeton University Press.

Stenner, Karen. 2005. *The Authoritarian Dynamic*. Cambridge: Cambridge University Press.

Stimson, James A., Michael B. Mackuen, and Robert S. Erikson. 1995. "Dynamic Representation." *American Political Science Review* 89: 543–565.

Tetlock, Philip E. 1986. "A Value Pluralism Model of Political Reasoning." *Journal of Personality and Social Psychology: Personality Processes and Individual Differences* 50: 819–827.

Theriault, Sean M. 2008. *Party Polarization in Congress*. New York: Cambridge University Press.

Theriault, Sean, Patrick Hickey, and Abby Blass. 2011. "Roll Call Votes." In Schickler, Eric, and Frances E. Lee (eds.), *The Oxford Handbook of the American Congress*. New York: Oxford University Press.

Wald, Kenneth. 2003. *Religion and Politics in the United States*. New York: Rowman and Littlefield.

Weßels, Bernhard. 2007. "Political Representation and Democracy." In: *The Oxford Handbook of Political Behavior*. New York: Oxford University Press.

Williams, Peter W. 2008. *America's Religions: From their Origins to the 21st Century*. Urbana-Champaign, IL: University of Illinois Press.

Wlezien, Christopher. 1995. "The Public as Thermostat: Dynamics of Preferences for Spending." *American Journal of Political Science* 39: 981–1000.

Wlezien, Christopher and Stuart Soroka. 2007. "The Relationship between Public Opinion and Policy." In Dalton, Russell, and Han-Dieter Klingemann (eds.), *The Oxford Handbook of Political Behavior*. New York: Oxford University Press.

Wood, B. Dan. 2009. *Myth of Presidential Representation*. Cambridge: Cambridge University Press.

Wuthnow, Robert. 1999. *Growing Up Religious: Christians and Jews and their Journeys of Faith*. Boston: Beacon Press.

Zaller, John R. 1992. *The Nature and Origins of Mass Opinion*. New York: Cambridge University Press.

# INDEX